# FROM SAIL TO STEAM

## STUDIES IN THE NINETEENTH-CENTURY HISTORY
## OF THE CHANNEL ISLANDS

# FROM SAIL TO STEAM

## STUDIES IN THE NINETEENTH-CENTURY HISTORY OF THE CHANNEL ISLANDS

CAROLINE WILLIAMS

Phillimore

2000

Published by
PHILLIMORE & CO. LTD.,
Shopwyke Manor Barn, Chichester, West Sussex

ISBN 1 86077 159 9

*For my mother,*
*Mary Patricia Hansen,*
*and in memory of my father,*
*Erik David Hansen*

Printed and bound in Great Britain by
THE CROMWELL PRESS
Trowbridge, Wiltshire

# CONTENTS

*Part 1*

## THE CHANNEL ISLANDS
## AND MARITIME TRADE, 1815–1865

PAGE 1

*Part 2*

## THE DECLINE OF CHANNEL ISLAND
## SHIPPING, 1865–1900

PAGE 21

*Part 3*

## POPULATION, EMPLOYMENT AND MARITIME TRADE
## JERSEY AND GUERNSEY, 1821–1881

PAGE 65

# LIST OF ILLUSTRATIONS

# LIST OF TABLES

# Acknowledgements

Many people in Jersey, Guernsey, and England have helped me in the process of researching and writing these essays. In addition to the staff of the institutions where research was undertaken (the Public Record Office, the British Library, the Chambers of Commerce of Jersey and Guernsey, the Société Jersiaise, the Société Guernsiaise, and the Priaulx Library in St Peter Port), I would like to thank the members of the Channel Island Advisory Committee in the Department of History of University College London, for their help and advice when the project first began. I have also incurred many more personal debts of gratitude. In Guernsey, Mr. Barry Lovell and his family offered assistance and hospitality in the early stages of research, and I am especially indebted to the late Mr. John Sarre and Mrs. Isabel Sarre, for their kindness, friendship, and advice during my visits to St Peter Port. In Jersey, Sir Martin Le Quesne and Dr. John Kelleher similarly offered me hospitality as well as assistance when I first began work on this project, and both made helpful comments on an earlier version of the manuscript. Mrs. Marie-Louise Backhurst has not only been an enthusiastic supporter and reader but has recently taken responsibility for seeing the project through to publication, for which I am very grateful. Research in the Channel Islands was supported by a grant from the British Academy. To my father-in-law, Mr. Tim Williams, I am immensely grateful for his help in compiling the index.

For their particular support and friendship, however, I would like to thank Mr. Robin Craig, without whose extraordinary knowledge of maritime history and generosity of spirit in supporting young researchers this book would never have been completed; and Professor John North, Head of the History Department at University College London, for his unflinching and cheerful encouragement throughout the project. I also owe a great deal to my friends at UCL, most especially Dr. Nicola Miller, Dr. Christopher Abel, and Rachel Aucott, who at times must have thought that this book would never see the light of day. As ever, my greatest debt is to my husband, Dr. Richard Williams, for his loyalty and companionship.

CAROLINE WILLIAMS
UNIVERSITY OF BRISTOL
DECEMBER 2000

# PREFACE

In 1977 a group of enthusiasts, including Deputy Philip de Veulle, Sir Martin Le Quesne and Conseiller Barry Lovell, in Jersey and Guernsey, decided that an academic book on the maritime history of the Channel Islands should be researched and published. They commissioned Alan Jamieson of University College, London, as the editor, and the result was *A People of the Sea: A Maritime History of the Channel Islands* published in 1986. The fundraising for the book had been most successful and some funds remained which enabled further research to be carried out.

It was felt that there had been too little work done on the very important period of the 19th century, and so Dr. Caroline Williams, then of University College, London, and now of the University of Bristol, undertook to do some original research using many records which had barely been studied before.

This book is the result of that research and provides an original academic study of the economic and social history of a crucial period for both Jersey and Guernsey. So much of what happened then has shaped the economies of both islands throughout the 20th century.

Sir Martin Le Quesne has played a pivotal role in ensuring that this work was commissioned, written and published. Only very recently has ill health obliged him to pass the final details on to others. Sir Martin clearly recognised the importance of the granite quarrying industry as his own ancestors were involved in it, and was always deeply interested in Caroline's research. The title of the book was of his choosing as it aptly represented the transition from the great days of sail and the Newfoundland cod banks to the more difficult years when sail and wood were superseded by steam and iron, destroying the successful ship building industry yet opening up new opportunities.

These studies belong to a new generation of research into the history of the Channel Islands. For too long half truths were believed and trickled down to the level of popular story telling without the benefit of any in-depth research. Now the reality and interpretation of events and trends can be seen more clearly and perhaps some myths may even be dispelled. Dr. Williams' grasp of Channel Islands history is remarkable for its clarity and impartiality. I believe that the book will be a source of great interest and debate and will inspire others to research further into other neglected areas of Channel Islands history.

MARIE-LOUISE BACKHURST

# Introduction

The 19th century was a period of great change for the Channel Islands. For approximately half a century following the end of the Napoleonic Wars, both Guernsey and Jersey enjoyed a period of great prosperity, based on the rapid expansion of maritime trade, including, in the case of Jersey, the extension of its connections with the cod fisheries of British North America, and the development of successful local shipbuilding industries. This was accompanied by high rates of population growth, fed by immigration. None of these developments were new to the Channel Islands: the participation of the two largest islands in maritime trade dates back to the 16th century at least; and both Guernsey and Jersey experienced frequent waves of immigration long before the 1800s. But in their scale, these transformations were unprecedented.

The prosperity which more intensive involvement in maritime activities brought to the Islands was, however, short-lived. By the late 1860s, a variety of factors, of which a depression in world trade and important technological changes in British shipping are the most significant, brought about a steep decline in the Islands' participation in the foreign trades. The following years witnessed the gradual withdrawal of both Islands from overseas trade (including Jersey's bases in the cod fisheries), the collapse of their respective shipbuilding industries, and, over a relatively short space of time, the disintegration through loss, sale or transfer, of large local sailing fleets. Jersey felt the impact of decline first and more deeply; the resulting unemployment in sectors connected with merchant shipping led to rapid and substantial population decline.

The Islands nevertheless proved remarkably resilient in overcoming the severe difficulties which arose in their respective economies during the closing decades of the 19th century. From the mid-1870s, great efforts were made to further those economic activities in which the Islands already held a competitive edge, and to create new ones, so as to offset the losses made in shipping and related industries. Thus, towards the end of the century, both Guernsey and Jersey demonstrated a renewed interest in the export of agricultural products, such as vegetables and potatoes; efforts were also made to foster horticulture and glass-house agriculture, aimed at developing the export of tomatoes, grapes and flowers. The potential of a new branch of industry—namely, tourism—was also recognised, and received considerable encouragement. In Guernsey, the granite trade, which had been growing steadily since the mid-1840s, and the expansion of local ship-repairing facilities, were heavily promoted, and became of vital importance to the Island in a difficult period of transition.

The 19th century, then, is a key period in Channel Island history, and of central importance to understanding the bases upon which the Island economies rested by the beginning of the 20th century. The collection of essays presented in the following pages seeks to make a contribution to that history by explaining the rise and later decline of shipping and trade through this critical period, and the ways in which the Channel Islands responded to the crises of the late 19th century by re-focusing their activities on other, in the long-term more lucrative, ventures. Accordingly, Part I examines the phenomenal growth of sectors connected with merchant shipping in the decades to mid-century (which was especially manifest in Jersey), considers the contribution made by local shipbuilding yards to the expansion of the shipping fleets, compares the types of trades in which Island vessels were engaged during the years of expansion, and discusses briefly the early development of the granite trade in Guernsey. Part II covers the years of decline from 1865 to 1900, with particular reference to the causes of decline, and to the response of the commercial communities to the collapse of hitherto flourishing industries. It is in this context that the development of agriculture, horticulture, tourism and ship-repairing during the latter part of the century are discussed. This section also considers the role of the granite export trade in Guernsey in ameliorating the worst effects of this Island's diminishing participation in the carrying trades and shows how, by the late 1860s, all but a handful of the most prominent shipowners had come to depend on this trade to a greater or lesser extent. Part III applies a similar analysis to demographic trends: it traces population changes over the decades from 1820 to 1881, but with particular reference to the years 1851 to 1881, as it is in this period that the impact of the expansion and later contraction of shipping-related activities on employment, population movements within the Islands, and immigration are most marked.

No attempt has been made in this collection of essays, however, to provide a background history to the period under study, or a discussion of the Islands' constitutional relationship with the mainland, or to provide an analysis of Jersey's connections with the cod fisheries of British North America—all topics which have been covered amply elsewhere. Indeed, the publication of several important studies over the past 15 years—among which Alan Jamieson's *A People of the Sea: The Maritime History of the Channel Islands* (1986); Rosemary Ommer's *From Outpost to Outport: A Structural Analysis of the Jersey-Gaspé Cod Fishery* (1991); and John Kelleher's *The Triumph of the Country: The Rural Community in Nineteenth Century Jersey* (1995) are the most significant—have already contributed greatly to increasing our knowledge and understanding of these issues. A more recent study, by Gregory Stevens Cox, *St Peter Port 1680-1830: The History of an International Entrepôt* (1999), should also be added to this list.[1]

The purpose of the studies presented here is instead to approach the sources relating to this period of Channel Island history from a comparative perspective. Many 19th-century writers and visitors to the Islands assumed that Guernsey's development paralleled that of its larger neighbour, except that its efforts were on a smaller and less ambitious scale, and were thus less successful. There were, of course, many similarities between Guernsey and Jersey, but these essays seek to assess the extent to which the paths followed by the two largest islands diverged during the century, and the consequences of their differences for future developments. It is hoped that such an approach may lead to further research on some of the problems raised in these pages as well as on new ones: as Gregory Stevens Cox's study of St Peter Port suggests, a comparative approach to the 18th century should provide some fruitful avenues for new research on issues such as urban development and the growth of the merchant class.[2]

Many of the sources used in these studies are statistical, and most have only been sampled. They include the Shipping Lists published in the Annual Almanacs of Guernsey and Jersey, the *London Customs Bills of Entry*, Crew Lists and Agreements, Ship Registers, Census Reports and Occupational Tables published in *Parliamentary Papers*, and the manuscript returns of the census enumerators. These have been supplemented with the records of the Jersey Merchant Seamen's Benefit Society, the records of the Jersey and Guernsey Chambers of Commerce, and local newspapers, as well as journals, letter/log books, and other contemporary sources. With the exception of the records of the Jersey Merchant Seamen's Benefit Society, for which there was no exact counterpart in neighbouring Guernsey, only comparable sources have been analysed.

The sources upon which the following studies are based enable us to draw some important conclusions regarding such crucial questions as the way in which trade patterns varied between the Islands, the contribution made by shipping-related occupations to employment, the places of origin and age-structure of seafarers serving on Channel Island vessels during the 19th century, changes in the sources of immigration, the role of granite exports in easing the worst effects of decline in sailing ship employment, and so on. But the figures, instructive though they are, are less enlightening on other issues which are equally important, such as the living and working conditions of the thousands of men employed on Island sailing ships during this period; or the reasons why tens of thousands of immigrants, from England and Ireland especially, chose to settle here; or indeed the reception accorded immigrants after they arrived. Other documents will need to be consulted to answer such questions.

Many valuable and still largely unused records exist in British and Channel Island archives which should prove useful for the purpose of examining the working lives of seafarers during the 19th century, for example. After the passage of the Merchant Shipping Act of 1854, masters of British merchant ships employed in the foreign trade were required by law to keep an official log book in which every incident of importance on board the vessel while at sea was to be recorded: offences committed by members of the crew and the punishments inflicted, cases of illness or injury and the treatment administered, deaths and the causes thereof, all cases of desertion, and so on.[3] Though the log books do not lend themselves easily to quantification, and though not all log books survive for voyages made by Channel Island vessels after 1854, they survive in sufficient number to constitute, together with journals and newspaper reports, an excellent source for reconstructing a picture of life on board wooden sailing ships, and for gaining some insight into the quality of the working lives of Island seafarers during the 19th century. The most superficial examination of the log books corresponding to the year 1856, for instance, provides ample evidence of the incidence of severe discontent on the part of crew members on certain voyages— in some cases over relatively minor irritations; in others sufficiently serious to provoke large-scale desertion. Thus, the displeasure of the crew of the *Geffard* of Jersey, on a return voyage from Valparaiso to Liverpool, was provoked by the fact that, 'having found that there were not sufficient Pease on board for the passage to Liverpool the master ordered Rice soup to be issued this day as a substitute ...'.[4] No details were recorded of the causes of discontent among the crew of the *Atrevida* of Jersey, on a voyage to Veracruz. The log book does show, however, that five members of the crew deserted at the port in September 1856. When a sixth sailor, the boatswain James Harvell, appeared to be taking a similar course, a confrontation with the master of the vessel ensued:

> on being ordered to turn to his work answered that he should not work any more on board the Ship and asked for his discharge but would not give it to him and began to use abusive language and told me that I had no business to have slept on board during the night that I had not to fear that he should not run away and that I had my pistols with me during the night and told me that he had some as good as mine and to be sure to take a good aim if I should use mine for his pistols were very good and he should not miss me with his meaning to shoot me he also said that the ship's anchor should not be hove up from this port and that he would stop the ship and ruin her.[5]

The log books contain much useful information on the difficulties of life at sea— caused by discontent over the quantity and quality of victuals, by the desperation brought about by poor weather and slow progress, by illnesses which at times were the result of heavy drinking, but at other times resulted from working for long periods in wet conditions, or from infectious diseases which could wipe out a large proportion of a vessel's crew in a matter of days: such was the case of the *Laura* of Guernsey, which lost five men to 'fever' at Berbice.[6] To take one further example of the nature of the information contained in the documents, and of their potential as a source for a social history of this important sector of the Islands' working population, the log book of the *Byzantium*, also of Jersey, records the suicide in 1856 of Edward Frances, cook and steward, who threw himself overboard after having been repeatedly reprimanded by the master for incompetence. According to fellow seaman Frederick Whyte,

> while washing Decks, there was a pair of old trousers lying on deck belonging to the Cook, he told the Boy Jas to throw them overboard. He told the Cook to throw them overboard himself. I coming forward at the time to pass water so they were just under my feet so I asked him if I should throw them overboard, he said yes heave them, in about ten minutes after he hove to draw Bucket into the wash Deck Tub, he then jumped over the rail with his feet on the Covering board outside, and deliberately jumped overboard and was drowned.[7]

Another important area still to receive the attention of historians relates to the immigrant population. This and other studies, such as those of John Kelleher and G.C. Powell,[8] show just how large the immigrant presence in Jersey and Guernsey was by the middle of the 19th century. Yet we know little about the attitudes of Channel Islanders towards outsiders, about the kinds of jobs which immigrants did, or the lives they led once in the Islands. While in 1833 Henry Inglis commented on the relationship between Jerseymen and English immigrants that 'there is not a perfect cordial feeling between the natives and the residents',[9] Kelleher found that wealthy immigrants were not only welcomed but positively encouraged to settle: in Jersey the local elite, if not the rest of the population, sought to emulate the lifestyles of the wealthy English.[10] The evidence gleaned from newspaper reports in Jersey in the late 1840s and early 1850s as well as from other sources from Guernsey indicates, however, that attitudes towards poorer arrivals, especially the Irish, were far more negative, particularly when there was any suspicion that they might become a burden on the native population. An article entitled 'A Good Lesson', which was published in the *Jersey Times* in February 1848, for example, described how the '20 penniless Irishmen' who had come to St Helier from Plymouth on board the *Melita*, commanded by Captain Marshall, and proceeded to apply to the Authorities for relief as soon as they had landed, were consigned to the Hospital, there to be maintained at the expense of the owner of the vessel.[11] Three years later, in 1851, the *Jersey Times* again despairingly reported how 'Yesterday ... did the steamer *Sir Francis Drake*, coming for the second time this season, disembark on our quays a new load of some fifteen indigent Irish people, whose whole wardrobe consisted of the few rags in which they were clad.'[12]

By the mid-19th century, as the proportion of English and Irish immigrants reached a quarter of the total population, the Islands appear to have made serious efforts to rid themselves of immigrants whom the authorities believed were or might become a financial burden. In January 1848, for instance, the *Jersey Times* reported that the States had spent a total of £160 in sending poor people from that Island during the year 1847 alone.[13] It was not only poor Irish families who ran the risk of expulsion however, as the case of the Goff family from Alderney, expelled first from Jersey and then from Guernsey in the mid-1840s, shows. According to correspondence exchanged between the Islands' authorities, John Goff, 'having no means of obtaining his livelihood', and having for some time been maintained 'at the public expense' in Jersey, was ordered by the Royal Court to be returned to Alderney via Guernsey, there being no direct communications between Jersey and Alderney at this time. But instead of forwarding the Goffs to Alderney, the authorities in Guernsey, having had no prior warning of their arrival, paid their passage back to Jersey, whereupon the Goffs asked to be admitted to the General Hospital. In April 1845, the Bailiff of Guernsey finally agreed to allow the Goff family to return to the Island, from where 'they shall be passed on to Alderney by the first vessel'. At the same time he requested, in no uncertain terms, that Jersey should not take this case as a precedent for sending people on to Guernsey without means for their maintenance whilst in transit: 'the

Court wish this case not to be regarded as establishing a precedent', the Bailiff informed his counterpart in Jersey, 'no notice on the part of the authorities of St Helier to those of St Peter Port, of their intention to forward Goff and his family through Guernsey having been given, nor any means provided for their maintenance during the journey or for their passage to Alderney'.[14]

While the potential cost to Island taxpayers may have been the principal reason for the authorities wishing to rid themselves of 'imported pauperism'—the result, as Kelleher explains in Jersey's case, of a cheap cost of living combined with the perception that there was employment to be had in the Islands[15]—such hostility towards outsiders may also have reflected fears of rising crime. Stevens Cox found evidence, for example, that in Guernsey street disorder was commonly blamed on migrants.[16] This is also the suggestion contained in a report presented by a committee of the Royal Court on the state of the prison in November 1850:

> the population of the island has … considerably increased within the last forty years; and with it there has been a corresponding increase of crime: the consequence is, that the number of prisoners is often so great that the Gaoler is obliged to confine two or more in the same cell … the clothes which offenders have on their backs, when apprehended, are often in rags … [17]

One response to the problem seems to have been the transportation of at least some of these problematic immigrants to penal colonies, for periods varying between seven years to life. Many immigrants in Guernsey shared this fate in the early 1850s: among these were George Hobbey, of Lymington, who was convicted of 'certain felonies'; William Croucher, of Ringwood, Hants., convicted of 'several larcenies committed by breaking into warehouses—and … receiving stolen Goods'; William Curran, of Dungarvon, Co.Kilkenny, convicted of manslaughter; and Henry Webb, of Nailsworth, Gloucestershire, convicted of passing off a forged Bank of England note.[18]

As the census figures show, however, thousands of immigrants were allowed to remain on the Islands, and settled here permanently. But what kind of working and living conditions did the families who did remain enjoy? In the early 1830s it was said that in Jersey the standard of living of immigrant families was well below that of even the poorest native families. Writing in 1833 on the cholera epidemic which struck the Island the previous year, George Symes Hooper, Secretary to the Jersey Central Board of Health, observed that poverty and misery

> do not, it is true, belong to the indigenous population of this island, the poor of which are liberally provided for … It is, in fact, almost exclusively chargeable to the constant influx of labouring men and disabled pensioners from England and Ireland … who, with their families, depend upon precarious support, which flows from scanty means, and insufficient employment …[19]

Hooper's report showed that the immigrant population, especially of St Helier, where seven-eighths of all cases of cholera reported on the Island occurred, were more badly struck by the epidemic than other groups. In Gorey, too, immigrants were found to have been worst affected. Here, where 108 families shared 64 houses, 62 cases were reported, among a total population of 513—an average of one in eight. 'Most of these families', Hooper observed, 'are very numerous; the father is commonly not a native, and earns a scanty livelihood by fishing; so that poverty is very general among them. Drunkenness is here also a very prevalent vice.'[20] English and Irish immigrants who came to Jersey in the early 1830s were therefore, according to this report, more likely than Jerseymen to be under-employed, and to maintain their families on what Hooper recognised to be inadequate incomes. In Guernsey, although the mortality rate from cholera was lower than in Jersey, it was also the immigrants, in this case the English who resided in the poorer parts of St Peter Port, especially by the harbour, who were worst affected by the epidemic.[21]

As Part III of this study shows, immigrants travelled principally to the towns, where employment opportunities were most likely to be concentrated. On the whole, they came to take jobs in expanding economic sectors which were generally based in St Helier and St Peter Port—except, that is, for the granite quarrying industry of Guernsey, which was based in St Sampson and Vale. A cursory examination of the census returns for the districts sampled in this study suggests, however, that by the early 1850s the greatest differences lay between the Irish on the one hand and the English and Jersey-born on the other. Comparison of data on employment indicate that whilst English immigrants were marginally more likely than their native-born counterparts to be employed in unskilled occupations, the Irish-born were much more likely than either of the other two groups to find employment in unskilled occupations—generally as labourers in the principal industrial sectors.

The importance of the 19th century lies not only, therefore, in that this is the period covering the phenomenal expansion and later collapse of trade, shipping, and related industries, and the development of new sectors which are still of crucial importance to the Island economies. This was also a period which witnessed the arrival of thousands of English and Irish families who, in settling here, contributed to changing the make-up of the Channel Islands. Many aspects of the history of the Islands still remains to be explored, and it is hoped that the findings presented in the following pages will encourage local historians to consider filling in the gaps which so clearly remain to be filled.

# Part 1

# THE CHANNEL ISLANDS
# AND MARITIME TRADE, 1815–1865

## -I-

The end of the Napoleonic Wars appeared, at least at first, to spell disaster for the Channel Islands, whose economies had been buttressed, during the war years, both by privateering activities and by the presence in the Islands of garrison troops, naval squadrons and exiled French. In Jersey, the expansion of the local market during the war period and high market prices for local produce actually brought prosperity for some, particularly in the agricultural sector.[1] Guernsey also profited from the years of war. 'This was', Ferdinand Brock Tupper wrote, '… a time of high excitement, as the tide of wealth was constantly on the flow.'[2] The return of peace, however, and the consequent departure of the troops and French refugees, deprived many Islanders of employment. In addressing the States of Jersey in 1819, in an attempt to obtain a ban on the importation of French cider to protect local producers, the Rector of the parish of St Ouen, the Reverend Ricard, observed that the countryside was in a state of depression: farmers were facing low prices, a shortage of outlets for their exports, and a contraction of the Island market. But the situation was said to be particularly critical in St Helier, where mass unemployment and low wages for those fortunate enough to be employed were sources of particular concern.[3] Guernsey suffered similar problems. According to Tupper, the end of the wars 'at first affected so deeply the interests of all classes, dependent on trade for a subsistence, that many gloomy forebodings were entertained for the future, not only as to the commercial, but as to the general prospects of the island'. Here, the withdrawal of the garrison— except for one regiment—and the naval squadron—except for one cutter—resulted also in rising unemployment,[4] which, combined with bad harvests and high prices for food, forced many Islanders to emigrate.[5] In 1817, the Chamber of Commerce expressed dismay at the numbers leaving Guernsey. In a petition to the Lieutenant Governor Major Bayly, the Chamber explained

> That the recent emigration of upwards of 125 persons in one vessel, which took place but a few days since, from this once flourishing island, and who are only part of a much greater number who would have accompanied them, had they had it in their power, must alone have convinced Your Excellency of the distressed state to which it is now reduced.[6]

Yet despite the concerns voiced in many quarters about the future prospects of the Channel Islands, by the 1820s both Guernsey and Jersey had entered a period of steady growth that was sustained until the mid-1860s. And, while some emigration from Jersey and especially from Guernsey continued throughout these decades, neither Island suffered a large-scale exodus of the kind predicted by the Guernsey Chamber of Commerce in 1817.[7] In fact, over the three decades between 1821 and 1851, the situation was reversed, as many migrants, principally but not exclusively from England and Ireland, moved to and settled in the Channel Islands, attracted by the prospect of work, better conditions, and a lower cost of living.[8] Between 1821 and 1851, Jersey's population almost doubled—from 28,600 to 57,020—and that of Guernsey grew by 50 per cent, from 20,227 (approximately), to 29,733.[9] By the middle of the 19th century the English and Irish alone constituted nearly one-quarter of the total population of the Channel Islands.[10]

The economic success which enabled the two largest of the Islands to absorb thousands of immigrants and their families, despite their restricted size and limited domestic resources, was based largely on the great expansion of trade worldwide in which both participated fully. In the case of Jersey, participation in the world-wide carrying trade grew out of and was connected with its involvement in the cod fisheries of British North America. As Rosemary Ommer explained in the case of that island—but it is an observation which might equally well apply to Guernsey—it would not have been possible for Jersey, given its size and small resource base, either to develop great wealth or sustain an expanding population on the basis of its domestic economy alone. Without its external connections, Jersey would most probably have been condemned to a permanent cycle of population growth and emigration.[11] Instead, far from suffering large-scale emigration as a result of overburdened economic resources, the Channel Islands were to experience great prosperity and rapid population growth for almost half a century after 1820.

It was the steady increase in the volume of trade and consequent rise in demand for maritime transport during this period which provided the Channel Islands with an opportunity to enter the worldwide carrying trades. Both Islands successfully exploited this opportunity, leading to the growth of locally registered shipping tonnage, and to the development of successful shipbuilding industries. The development of shipbuilding, in turn, made possible the construction of bigger and better ships and the expansion of activities to more distant regions.

Guernsey and Jersey already had important fishing industries by the beginning of the 19th century, and fishing boats, some of which were large enough to engage in fishing off the coasts of Devon and Cornwall, clearly had been built locally long before the period covered by this study. But the building of merchant vessels was a recent development. According to Alec Podger, the first large ship ever built in the Channel Islands was the *Elisha Tupper*—a 280-ton vessel built in 1789 in the parish of St Lawrence, Jersey, and named after the prominent Guernsey merchant. However, no long-lasting shipyard existed in either Island before 1815. But over the following decades, several shipyards were established in both Guernsey and Jersey—among others, those of Deslandes, Le Vesconte, Allen, Clarke, and Mauger in Jersey; and De La Mare, Thom, and Sebire in Guernsey.[12]

Despite the late development of shipbuilding in the Channel Islands, expansion was rapid and substantial, and its impact evident from the number of island-built vessels registered there in the decades after 1815. Between 1815 and 1890, the shipyards of Guernsey and Jersey supplied more than three quarters of all new built tonnage registered at both ports. 79.03% of the 329 new built vessels registered in Guernsey between 1817 and 1890—or 78.89% of a total tonnage of 46,634—were locally built. 80.45% of the 962 newly built vessels registered in Jersey—75.59% of a total tonnage of 104,279—were supplied by local shipbuilders. During the years of highest growth, 1830 to 1870, these proportions were slightly higher: Guernsey shipyards supplied 83.41% of all new built vessels (80.28% of tonnage) registered in the island; Jersey shipyards produced 82.18% of newly built vessels (77.11% of tonnage) registered there.[13]

| Year | Jersey | | Guernsey | |
|------|--------|---------|----------|---------|
| | Vessels | Tonnage | Vessels | Tonnage |
| 1815 | 69 | 7,519 | 61 | 6,662 |
| 1820 | 96 | 9,883 | 66 | 7,827 |
| 1825 | 142 | 13,756 | 79 | 7,298 |
| 1830 | 205 | 18,601 | 77 | 8,096 |
| 1835 | 243 | 23,221 | 78 | 9,186 |
| 1840 | 269 | 23,529 | 118 | 13,298 |
| 1845 | 311 | 27,690 | 120 | 12,898 |
| 1850 | 347 | 32,331 | 143 | 16,743 |
| 1865 | 422 | 48,628 | 133 | 24,698 |

Table 1: Channel Island Shipping, 1815-1865[14]

Between 1820 and 1870, then, an important shipbuilding industry was developed in both Guernsey and Jersey. In 1864, the peak year for Island shipbuilders, the shipyards of the Channel Islands produced 5.9% of the total tonnage of wooden sailing vessels built in the whole of the United Kingdom during that year, although this figure has to be read in the context of a national shipbuilding industry which by this period included a large component of iron-built steamships. By 1880, when Channel Island shipping was already in a state of serious and irreversible decline, the shipyards of Guernsey had built 300 vessels measuring a total of nearly 40,000 tons; more than 850, totalling almost 102,000 tons, had been built in Jersey. Most of the vessels produced in the Islands were built for Island shipowners, although some were also built for British shipowners—approximately 23,000 tons of shipping in total.[15]

Analysis of the Shipping Lists published in the Annual Almanacs of Guernsey and Jersey shows that, as the 19th century progressed, and until the sailing ship industry began its decline, the Islands also shared in the general changes taking place in shipbuilding nationally, specifically the production of ever-larger sailing ships.[16] At the end of 1844 the largest vessels registered in Jersey measured between 300 and 500 tons, and of these there were only five. Twenty years later,

1   Ship in course of construction, Jersey, *c.*1860. © Société Jersiaise.

there were 26 vessels measuring over 300 tons registered in the Island: of these, nine measured over 500 tons and two over 1,000 tons. These developments were less marked in Guernsey, but there, too, they are apparent. At the end of 1844 only ten vessels registered in Guernsey were in the 200-300 ton range, and these were the largest in the Island. By 1865, there were 38 vessels in this tonnage range—many of which were by this date deployed in the export of granite—and a further five measured between 300 and 700 tons.[17]

## –II–

All the indicators discussed in the preceding section show that it was in Jersey that the expansion of sectors connected with shipping and maritime trade was most marked—the result, above all, of its connections with the cod fisheries of British North America. As Table 1 above showed, whereas locally-registered tonnage in Guernsey increased from 6,662 tons (61 vessels) in 1815 to 24,698 tons (133 vessels) in 1865—a growth rate of 270%—Jersey's shipping fleet grew from 7,519 tons (69 vessels) to 48,628 tons (422 vessels) over the same period—a growth rate of 547%.[18]

The larger island's involvement in the fisheries of course long pre-dated the 19th century: the earliest intrusions of Jerseymen in the cod trade date back to the years before the reign of Elizabeth I; and permanent Jersey bases had been established in British North America by the 1670s.[19] The Island's commitment to the fisheries was sustained and long-lasting: it was not until 1886 that the last of the Jersey cod firms finally withdrew from the region. Through its cod connections, the Island acquired a resource, codfish, that it did not possess at home; [20] the need to market the fish and acquire supplies for the bases in turn provided Island shipowners with an entry into the general carrying trades. As a report published in the *Quebec Mercury* in November 1833 explained, Messrs Robin and Company 'have extensive commercial establishments in Brazil, Foreign Europe and other ports. They export fish in their own vessels and bring return cargoes to Hamburg and other ports in foreign Europe.'[21] It was this involvement that formed the basis of what Rosemary Ommer called 'the Jersey merchant triangle'—a term utilized to describe a trade which depended on the extraction of a staple (fish) in a location other than the 'metropole' (Jersey) and its disposal in a third location—the market.[22] The importance of cod to the Island, however, transcended the trade itself. For, as Ommer has shown, it was the cod trade merchants who provided much of the capital investment required for the development of local shipbuilding during the late 1810s to mid-1820s—years when Jersey-built shipping gradually began to supersede New World-built tonnage.[23]

Guernsey also had connections with the fisheries. During the late 16th century[24] and throughout most of the 17th century, Guernsey merchants and shipowners were deeply involved in the cod trade with Newfoundland, and although from the 1690s the Island concentrated more on its smuggling and privateering activities, the links with the fisheries were probably never completely broken: as John Sarre pointed out, some shipowners—such as Carteret Priaulx—combined smuggling and privateering with the cod trade.[25] Guernseymen again became more generally involved with the fisheries of the Gulf of St Lawrence after the defeat of the French in Canada in 1763, and from the end of the 18th century and through the years of the Napoleonic Wars, Guernsey and Jersey merchants co-operated in the trade: the Janvrins of Jersey, for example, co-operated with both Elisha Tupper and the Carteret Priaulx family in its exploitation.[26] But after the end of the Napoleonic Wars, when merchants and shipowners in Guernsey faced the urgent need to find new trades to replace smuggling and privateering, these were largely found in the fruit trade with Spain, Portugal and the Azores, for which their experience in the wine trade had undoubtedly prepared them; in developing their role in the carrying trades, especially with ports in South and Central America—then in the process of obtaining their independence—and in the coasting trade with Britain. Jersey merchants were left to exploit the fisheries undisturbed.

Many Jerseymen since the 19th century have remarked on the importance of the cod trade to the Island. In an 1837 article in the *Jersey and Guernsey Magazine*, for example, it was reported that the cod fisheries were 'the root of other indirect industry, and the means of supporting many families'.[27] In December 1841, in a letter to the President of the Board of Trade, Philip de Quetteville, President of the Chamber of Commerce, noted the contribution which the fisheries made not just to the Island's industry, but also to employment: 'There are employed ... as seamen, fishermen and landsmen about 4000 persons. There are in this Island many families engaged in the making of worsted hose and mitts, wearing apparel, boots and shoes for the use of the fisheries.'[28] And in the 1850s, Charles Le Quesne, President of the Jersey Chamber of Commerce, informed the Earl of Clarendon

> That the number of vessels employed in the fisheries by the merchants of this Island may be estimated at about 100, measuring upwards of 10,000 tons, giving employment to about 2,000 British seamen, and a still greater number of fishermen in the Colonies ... the fisheries are therefore of great value not only from the number of vessels and the Capital employed in them, but also as a nursery for seamen ...[29]

Other writers, in discussing Jersey's external trade, compared Guernsey unfavourably with its neighbour. Writing in the early 1830s, for instance, Henry Inglis observed that Guernsey's commerce 'was much less important' than that of Jersey, and that the smaller Island afforded 'fewer facilities for an extended commerce'. Furthermore, so little was there 'of produce or manufacture to export' that vessels commonly left the Island in ballast, 'for another country, there to begin their mercantile adventure'. The merchants of Guernsey, unlike those of Jersey,

> do not ... possess extensive establishments in North America, which afford markets for the export of foreign, British and colonial produce; or British, or island manufacture. Nor, although there is abundance of wealth in Guernsey, is that wealth so extensively embarked in ship ownership, and foreign trade.[30]

Writing for *The Guernsey and Jersey Magazine* in 1837, Guernseyman Ferdinand Brock Tupper also compared his native Island unfavourably with neighbouring Jersey. Despite the fact that the Islands were 'similarly situated in point of fertility, climate, harbours, resources, and fiscal laws', Guernsey's foreign trade he described as 'depressed and declining' and its commerce as 'listless and retrograding'. Jersey's foreign trade, on the other hand, 'is prosperous and annually augmenting'; its commerce, 'flourishing and progressive'.[31] Nearly twenty years later, in his *History of Guernsey*, Tupper returned to the same theme, censuring the merchants of the Island for what he perceived as their unwillingness or inability to match the success of Jersey. The commerce and shipping of the latter Island, he concluded, were 'superior to those of Guernsey'. Whereas Jersey was deeply involved not just in the cod fisheries but in the Honduras and African trades, Guernsey at that time 'had scarcely a vessel engaged in the carrying or freight trade of Brazil, the River Plate, and Havannah'. His comparison extended not just to the trade of the Islands, but to the relative success of their shipbuilding industries, too. In June 1854, Tupper wrote, there were 19 vessels on the stocks in Jersey, amounting to a combined tonnage of 5,853, and this included two large ships of 2,200 and 1,050 tons under construction at the shipyard of F.C. Clarke for sale at Liverpool; in Guernsey at that time there were but four, a total of 1,050 tons.[32]

There can be little doubt that the growth of registered tonnage, and the development of local shipbuilding were more rapid and impressive in Jersey than in Guernsey. And by the middle of the 19th century, the Islands' trade routes and networks—the regions to which Island vessels voyaged and the products which they carried—had also diverged in some important respects. While Jersey merchants and shipowners focused mainly on developing their trade with the cod fisheries of British North America, and on the carrying trade to which cod gave them an entry, Guernsey merchants and shipowners instead concentrated primarily on servicing the fruit trade with Spain, Portugal and the Azores, and on the coasting trade with Britain. These were, however, only the principal trades in which Guernsey vessels engaged. At least until the mid-19th century, Guernsey merchants also remained heavily involved in trade with South and Central America, and thereafter in the coffee trade with Costa Rica.

The contrast between the two largest of the Channel Islands was to have important implications for the development of their shipping later in the century. It was Guernsey's involvement in the coasting trade with the mainland—in particular the transportation of a domestic export, namely granite, which was generally combined with the coal trade from the ports of northern England—that was to be of greatest significance to this Island, for it was the stone trade that was to protect Guernsey from the worst effects of the combination of both the crisis in world trade from the end of the 1860s and competition from steam in the years after 1870. As this collection of essays shows, during the half century after 1815 the coasting trade with Britain appears to have been seen as a less attractive and profitable endeavour than those in which Jersey was involved—Henry Inglis, for instance, dedicated far less space to the trade of Guernsey, and just two sentences to its exports of stone[33]—but the coasting trade, especially since it involved the export of a product quarried in the Island and transported largely in locally-registered and locally-owned tonnage, proved in fact to be far more durable an enterprise than the cod and carrying trades, subject as these were not just to the fluctuations which characterised international trade, but also to political decisions over which the Island had no control.[34]

The impact of these differences on the trade, shipping, population, and employment patterns of the two largest of the Channel Islands is one of the main themes that will be developed in the remaining pages of this essay and through the two essays that follow. Accordingly, Sections III and IV below examine in detail the deployment of Guernsey and Jersey shipping during one year just prior to mid-century, 1845, for the purpose of both comparing the voyage patterns of vessels engaged in the foreign trades and the trades in which coasting vessels were engaged, and examining the early development of the granite export trade from Guernsey to the mainland. Our purpose is not so much to provide an exhaustive analysis of vessel deployment during the century but rather to illustrate through examination of voyages conducted in that year how the trade of the Islands had diverged by a mid-way point in the period of expansion of maritime trade, as an introduction to the discussions presented in Parts II and III.

## -III-

Two main sources have been used in this analysis: first, the Crew Lists and Agreements, which arose out of a system of registration of seamen introduced under the terms of the Merchant Shipping Act of 1835.[35] As they record details of vessels, voyages, and crew members engaged in both the foreign and domestic trades, the crew lists and agreements are an invaluable source for reconstructing the deployment of Channel Island vessels at mid-century and for the study of seafaring labour. This source has been supplemented by the *London Customs Bills of Entry*. Unlike the crew agreements, the *Customs Bills of Entry* are a comparatively little-used source.[36] The *London Bills*, which have been used exhaustively in these essays, record all arrivals of vessels—British and foreign—in the ports of London, Liverpool, Bristol and Hull, and for this reason they constitute an excellent source for the study of Britain's foreign trades. But they are especially useful for an examination of the domestic trades of the Channel Islands, including the development and expansion of Guernsey's granite trade: since the Islands fell outside the British Customs area, the *London Bills* recorded all arrivals of ships and their cargoes from Guernsey and Jersey to the ports covered by the *Bills*.

Despite the potential of the crew lists and agreements, several problems do nevertheless emerge in their analysis, which diminish their accuracy, and which should be borne in mind in this discussion of Island trading patterns. First, the voyage information supplied by masters should have included port of departure, final destination, and port of return, and in most cases it does. But masters did not always comply with the requirement to have their crew agreements endorsed by the consular authorities at all ports of call (in many ports with which Island vessels traded there were no consuls), and this means that we may be simplifying the complexity of the routes followed by Island vessels. Secondly, crew lists and agreements have not survived for all vessels registered at the ports of Jersey and Guernsey in the year chosen for analysis. According to shipping lists published in Guernsey, at the start of 1845 there were registered 117 vessels amounting to an aggregate tonnage of 13,268.[37] Crew lists and/or agreements have survived for voyages made by 81 vessels (69.2% of the total registered) totalling 8,700 tons (65.6% of registered tonnage in 1845).[38] In Jersey, shipping lists show a total of 267 vessels on the register at the beginning of 1845—amounting to a combined tonnage of 27,714.[39] Crew lists and/or agreements have been found for voyages made by 150 vessels (56.2% of the 1845 total)—an aggregate tonnage of 18,034 (65.1% of the total).[40] Of these, four vessels, employed exclusively as fishing boats, have been excluded from the analysis. Although it is quite likely that at least some of those vessels for which crew lists have not been found were laid up for all or part of the year—for repairs, lengthening, sale, etc.—it is also certain either that some crew lists have been lost, or that some merchant captains failed to complete and return these to the Registrar of Shipping. Thirdly, while the paragraphs that follow aim to show the ways in which the voyage patterns and trades of the two largest of the Channel Islands had diverged by mid-century, it should not of course be assumed that there were no similarities between them: the vagaries of

| Trade Route | No. of Voyages | % of Total | No. Vess. | Total Tonn. | Av. Tonn |
|---|---|---|---|---|---|
| *Total of Voyages* | *101* | *100* | | | |
| Africa | 1 | 0.99 | 1 | 134 | 134 |
| Azores | 33 | 32.67 | 18 | 1,089 | 60 |
| Azores-Spain/Portugal | 2 | 1.98 | 2 | 117 | 58 |
| Spain/Portugal-Azores | 1 | 0.99 | 1 | 54 | 54 |
| Baltic | 4 | 3.96 | 4 | 561 | 140 |
| Caribbean | 10 | 9.90 | 9 | 1,360 | 151 |
| South America-Caribbean | 1 | 0.99 | 1 | 168 | 168 |
| Central America/Mexico | 1 | 0.99 | 1 | 141 | 141 |
| Central America/Mexico-South America | 3 | 2.97 | 3 | 525 | 175 |
| Indian Ocean | 1 | 0.99 | 1 | 248 | 248 |
| Mediterranean-Indian Ocean | 1 | 0.99 | 1 | 162 | 162 |
| Mediterranean (1) | 12 | 11.88 | 12 | 1,406 | 117 |
| Spain/Portugal-Mediterranean | 1 | 0.99 | 1 | 115 | 115 |
| South America | 5 | 4.95 | 4 | 584 | 146 |
| Spain/Portugal-South America | 2 | 1.98 | 2 | 277 | 138 |
| South America-Mediterrean | 2 | 1.98 | 2 | 339 | 169 |
| Spain/Portugal | 21 | 20.79 | 18 | 1,192 | 66 |

**Table 2: Guernsey Foreign Trade Routes, Voyage by Voyage, 1845**[43]
(1) Excludes Spanish Mediterranean Ports

maritime trade in the 19th century were such that merchant sailing ships involved in the carrying trade moved freely around the world in competition for cargo and in search of the most favourable freights, and this required considerable flexibility on the part of owners, masters and crews. The arrival of several vessels at the same port, in the expectation of favourable freights, could immediately push these down, forcing masters to make immediate decisions about whether to take the available cargoes or move on in search of better freights elsewhere.[41] The letter/log book of Captain Philip de Gruchy, master of the *Fairlina* of Jersey in 1868-9, illustrates precisely the problems which could arise on a long trading voyage. As one letter despairingly written by De Gruchy to his employers in Jersey, Messrs Le Maistre & Co., explained,

> I am still in port, and hardly know what to write, there is no improvement in freights at all, and North it is equally as bad vessels are chartering at Pernambuco 3/8 to load at Maceio, Bahia 15 [shillings] to 1 £ sugar, the last charter here to America were 20 [shillings] New York, with a limited number of bags; and at present that can hardly be had, one vessel chartered yesterday 20 [shillings] Gibraltar for orders, I do not see any prospect in going North, and South it is equally as bad, really I hardly know what

| Trade Route | No. of Voyages | % of Total | No. Vess. | Total Tonn. | Av. Tonn |
|---|---|---|---|---|---|
| *Total of Voyages* | *169* | *100* | | | |
| | | | | | |
| Africa | 15 | 8.88 | 12 | 1,516 | 126 |
| Africa-Spain/Portugal | 1 | 0.59 | 1 | 135 | 135 |
| Azores | 7 | 4.14 | 5 | 298 | 60 |
| BNA Fisheries | 13 | 7.69 | 13 | 1,755 | 135 |
| BNA Fisheries-Spain/Portugal | 2 | 1.18 | 2 | 250 | 125 |
| Spain/Portugal-BNA Fisheries | 2 | 1.18 | 2 | 290 | 145 |
| Spain/Portugal-BNA Fisheries-Spain/Portugal | 2 | 1.18 | 2 | 246 | 123 |
| Spain/Portugal-BNA Fisheries-Mediterranean | 2 | 1.18 | 2 | 273 | 136 |
| BNA Fisheries-Spain/Portugal-Mediterranean | 1 | 0.59 | 1 | 139 | 139 |
| BNA Fisheries-Mediterranean | 7 | 4.14 | 7 | 1,020 | 146 |
| BNA Fisheries-South America | 1 | 0.59 | 1 | 163 | 163 |
| Caribbean-BNA Fisheries | 1 | 0.59 | 1 | 186 | 186 |
| Baltic | 3 | 1.78 | 2 | 329 | 164 |
| Caribbean | 7 | 4.14 | 6 | 1,132 | 189 |
| Caribbean-Mediterranean | 1 | 0.59 | 1 | 119 | 119 |
| Central America/Mexico | 8 | 4.73 | 7 | 1,411 | 202 |
| Central America/Mexico-Caribbean | 1 | 0.59 | 1 | 130 | 130 |
| South America-Central America/Mexico | 2 | 1.18 | 2 | 644 | 322 |
| Indian Ocean | 4 | 2.37 | 4 | 811 | 203 |
| Mediterranean (1) | 34 | 20.12 | 31 | 3,857 | 124 |
| Spain/Portugal-Mediterranean | 1 | 0.59 | 1 | 155 | 155 |
| South America | 16 | 9.47 | 15 | 2,314 | 178 |
| Spain/Portugal-South America | 4 | 2.37 | 4 | 792 | 198 |
| South America-Mediterranean | 2 | 1.18 | 2 | 443 | 221 |
| Spain/Portugal | 32 | 18.93 | 22 | 1,623 | 74 |

**Table 3: Jersey Foreign Trade Routes, Voyage by Voyage, 1845**
(1) Excludes Spanish Mediterranean Ports

to do, perhaps the rates may improve a little here for the States. Paranaguay there is nothing offering nor for the Cape ...[42]

The analysis presented in Tables 2 and 3 has been carried out on a voyage-by-voyage basis, which means that some vessels, completing two or more voyages over the course of the year, figure more than once in the tables.[43] In seeking to capture the diversity of trade routes and voyages conducted by Channel Island vessels, all the information provided in the crew lists and agreements has been utilised—including final destination, consular endorsements where available, place of employment, discharge or death of crew members, and so on—the purpose being not just to show final destinations, which can conceal as much as they reveal, but the variety of trade routes on which Island vessels embarked. Even with this aim in mind, the tables cannot really high-light the often quite sophisticated trading networks which could take a vessel on a voyage beginning in the Channel Islands and/or another British port and calling at ports in southern Europe, Canada, South America or the Caribbean and the Mediterranean before returning home. Nor do the tables illustrate those long trading voyages that could take a vessel from one region to another in search of cargoes and favourable freights. Vessels sailing out of the Islands on voyages such as these could set out with only the vaguest notion of their destination. The crew agreement of the 113-ton *Antelope* of Jersey, for example, stated that this vessel was to sail 'from London to Gibraltar and Malta from thence on a trading voyage wherever the ship may find employment and back to a port in Great Britain. Terms of service not to exceed two years.'[44] The crew of Captain Philip De Gruchy's *Fairlina* had a similarly vague idea of its destination when it set off, in 1869, on a voyage from 'Liverpool to Rio de Janeiro thence to any port or ports North and South Atlantic Indian or Pacific Oceans thence to a port for orders ...'.[45]

But not all voyages were complicated and involved—in 1845, the vast majority of vessels made straightforward out and back voyages to stated destinations to collect and deliver specific cargoes, and some vessels clearly specialized in particular trades and routes. The 150-ton *Crusader* and the 413-ton *St Croix*, both of Jersey, for example, made two voyages each from London to Honduras, returning with cargoes of mahogany, logwood, indigo and cochineal. The 145-ton *Navigator*, also of Jersey, made one voyage to Buenos Aires and another to Montevideo, returning from Buenos Aires (and undoubtedly from Montevideo) with cargoes of hides and tallow; and the 78-ton *Rowena* made three voyages in 1845 from London to Africa, returning with cargoes consisting principally of hides, beeswax and nuts.[46] Many Guernsey vessels also specialized in specific trades—this is especially true of the fast schooners, such as the 58-ton *Ace of Trumps*, dedicated to servicing the fruit trade between Britain, the Iberian Peninsula and the Azores.

Indeed, Table 2 shows that more than half the voyages conducted by Guernsey vessels in 1845 (54 of 101) were out and back voyages to Spain, Portugal and the Azores, carrying shipments of fruit (principally oranges) to British cities like London and Liverpool. A further 15 voyages were conducted to ports in the Caribbean and South America, where return cargoes included sugar, rum, hides, tallow and coffee. Twelve voyages were conducted to the Mediterranean. Since eight of these voyages began in Newcastle or Welsh ports, or involved stops at these ports on the outward journey, we may assume that most were in the coal or iron trade—an extension of the coal and stone trade between the Island and the ports of northern England. A further seven voyages also showed the same out and back pattern—to ports in Africa, the Baltic, the Indian Ocean and Central America. Only 13 of the 101 voyages for which we have details in 1845 showed ports of call at places other than the final destination. Voyages to South America with ports of call in Spain or Portugal most likely involved the shipment of salt,

**2**  St Peter Port Harbour, Guernsey, *c*.1860. © Priaulx Library, Guernsey.

or wines and other foodstuffs to the region; those from South America (both from Brazil) showing ports of call in the Mediterranean, no doubt involved the shipment of sugar, rum or coffee back to Europe. For 1845, no crew lists were found for Guernsey voyages in the cod trade, or showing ports of call at the fisheries.

Far more complex, in 1845, were the voyage patterns of Jersey vessels. First, the fisheries employed a significant proportion of the Island's shipping, and here we see evidence of numerous voyages in the 'triangular' trade incorporating the fisheries, Spain and Portugal, the Mediterranean, and the Caribbean and South America. Thirty-one of 169 voyages analysed (18%) are classified as cod trade voyages, and 18 of these showed ports of call where supplies would be collected or where fish would be sold. At least a proportion of the 34 voyages classified as Mediterranean voyages in the tables, moreover, may have been connected with the cod trade—the Mediterranean being the traditional market for this trade[47]—but certainly not all, since some vessels carried coal rather than cod: the *Ninus*, for example, sailed 'from St Helier to the North after coals for Marseilles and back …'.[48]

The trading patterns of Jersey vessels, then, were more complex than those of Guernsey, and were also more likely to be in the long-distance trades. Twenty out of 169 voyages, for example, were destined for Africa and the Indian Ocean, compared with only three for Guernsey. From Africa, vessels brought timber, beeswax, resin, nuts and nut oil, as well as guano. From the Indian Ocean came

| Port | Departures | Arrivals | Port | Departures | Arrivals |
|------|-----------:|---------:|------|-----------:|---------:|
| Jersey | 76 | 0 | Hull | 0 | 4 |
| Liverpool | 37 | 45 | Gloucester | 0 | 2 |
| London | 29 | 66 | Ipswich | 1 | 0 |
| Cork | 6 | 14 | Bristol | 0 | 2 |
| Dublin | 1 | 5 | Exeter | 0 | 3 |
| Belfast | 0 | 2 | St.Ives | 1 | 0 |
| Glasgow | 4 | 5 | Plymouth | 2 | 11 |
| Leith | 0 | 1 | Yarmouth | 0 | 1 |
| Wick | 2 | 2 | Southampton | 1 | 2 |
| Cardiff | 1 | 1 | Gaspé | 1 | 0 |
| Swansea | 1 | 1 | Labrador | 1 | 0 |
| Newport | 4 | 0 | Unspecified | 0 | 1 |
| Newcastle | 1 | 1 | *Total* | *169* | *169* |

**Table 4: Ports of Departure and Arrival, Jersey Vessels, 1845**

cargoes of sugar. Eleven of 169 voyages, compared with only four for Guernsey, were destined for Central America—from where logwood, mahogany, rosewood, indigo and cochineal were the principal exports transported back to Britain. Twenty-four voyages showed ports of call in South America—principally Colombia, Brazil and Chile, but also Callao on Peru's Pacific coast. From these regions came shipments of copper, wool, hides, tallow, hoofs and horns; rosewood; fustic; tobacco; coffee, cacao, tapioca, arrowroot, sugar and rum; and, from Peru, guano. Only twelve Guernsey voyages are shown for South America in 1845.[49] Conversely, while 56% of all Guernsey voyages in the foreign trade were straightforward out and back voyages to Spain, Portugal and the Azores, only 23% of Jersey voyages followed these routes.

The voyages conducted by Guernsey and Jersey vessels were not, of course, dedicated generally to servicing the trade of the Channel Islands. Island shipowners were participating in a carrying trade in which goods were collected at one foreign port for delivery at another, or were destined for delivery in mainland Britain. As Tables 4 and 5 show, although many of the voyages analysed in this chapter sailed out of Channel Island ports, none of the crew lists or agreements showed vessels returning to the Islands. Indeed, 66% of all voyages conducted by Channel Island vessels in 1845—the proportions were the same for both Islands—ended at either Liverpool or London. Some imports, though, did return to the Islands. In Jersey, for example, raw materials could be purchased directly with the produce of the fisheries or with goods exchanged for fish, and then processed further in the Island before sale back to the fisheries.[50]

The analysis offered in Tables 2 to 5 offers only a static picture of the deployment of Channel Island vessels at a half-way point in the period of growth of shipping and maritime trade. But clearly the trading patterns of the Islands

| Port | Departures | Arrivals | Port | Departures | Arrivals |
|------|-----------|----------|------|-----------|----------|
| Guernsey | 59 | 0 | Gloucester | 0 | 1 |
| Liverpool | 18 | 25 | Bristol | 4 | 4 |
| London | 7 | 42 | Exeter | 1 | 1 |
| Belfast | 0 | 1 | Bridport | 0 | 1 |
| Cork | 0 | 1 | Dartmouth | 1 | 0 |
| Glasgow | 5 | 6 | Plymouth | 0 | 2 |
| Leith | 2 | 4 | Portsmouth | 0 | 1 |
| Greenock | 0 | 1 | Southampton | 0 | 1 |
| Newport | 1 | 0 | Unspecified | 0 | 4 |
| Newcastle | 2 | 1 | | | |
| Hull | 1 | 5 | *Total* | *101* | *101* |

**Table 5: Ports of Departure and Arrival, Guernsey Vessels, 1845**

varied from year to year, depending on a wide variety of factors, some of which—the supply of shipping, the availability of cargoes, and freight rates—have been mentioned in the text. Voyage routes 'danced to the tune of trade', and any shift in the supply of or demand for shipping would lead to immediate changes in vessel deployment: within the space of just a few years vessels might be engaged on voyages to regions as distant as the Baltic and South America, in response to whatever opportunities arose for cargo. And, as Sarah Palmer observed, 'the life cycle of a vessel might take it through several existences, moving from distant to nearer trades as time and the sea took its toll on hull and rigging ...'[51] This, for instance, was the experience of the brigantine *Surprise* of Guernsey. Built in France in 1827 (as a ketch), this vessel was employed in the deep sea trades for many years before being relegated to the granite trade, where it was still in use in 1900.[52] Many Guernsey vessels made the transition from the foreign trades to the domestic trades over the course of the period under study. But this is not to say, however, that new ships were not deployed in the granite trade to the mainland. In 1837, for example, *The Star* of Guernsey reported that 'We understand that the brig now on the stocks in Mr. William Machon's yard, has been sold for £1,680, to Mr. R.W. Isemonger. She is no doubt destined for the coal and stone trade.'[53]

In the Channel Islands, furthermore, the development of shipbuilding which grew out of the general expansion of trade worldwide made possible the construction of bigger and better ships and with this the extension of activities to more distant regions. Alan Jamieson found, for example, that by 1855, Jersey's shipowners had successfully exploited the opportunity to participate in the carrying trade to the Indian Ocean and the Far East—the number of vessels arriving in London from these regions increasing from one to seven between 1840 and 1855. Guernsey, meanwhile, had become increasingly involved in trade with Central America, carrying cargoes of coffee from the Pacific ports of Costa Rica to

3    St Peter Port, Guernsey, with the town church in the background, *c.*1860.
© Priaulx Library, Guernsey.

Britain.[54] When the 636-ton *Golden Spur* was completed in Guernsey in 1864 for Messrs Carrington & Co., it was said that the vessel—the largest ever built in this Island—was intended specifically for the China trade:[55] this was not a trade in which Guernsey vessels had been involved in the mid-1840s.

On the whole, however, the voyage patterns identified in 1845 were those into which the Islands were to settle throughout their years of involvement in maritime trade. Jamieson's analysis of the *London Customs Bills of Entry* for 1840 and 1855 shows that whereas in 1840, 42 of the total 83 Channel Island vessels which arrived in that port from overseas were Guernsey vessels, by 1855, only 45 of 116 Island arrivals from overseas belonged to Guernsey. The remaining 75 were Jersey-registered, and many of these participated in trades which were taking them to ever more distant regions—China and Australia, for example. 'This was indicative', Jamieson concludes, 'of Jersey's greater success in seizing the opportunities of the expanding worldwide carrying trade.' His comparison of figures drawn from the customs bills also confirms that by 1855 Guernsey was far more involved in the Azores fruit trade than it had been in 1840.[56]

But, as explained earlier, any examination of the trade of the Channel Islands during the 19th century has to take account not just of the foreign trade but also of the coasting trade with British ports. As we shall see later in this study, the fact that Guernsey had an important bulk export product—granite—which Jersey did

| Tonnage Range | Guernsey Vessels | | Jersey Vessels | |
|---|---|---|---|---|
| | No. of Vessels | Total Tonnage | No. of Vessels | Total Tonnage |
| 15-50 | 9 | 306 | 19 | 601 |
| 50-100 | 8 | 611 | 9 | 587 |
| 100-200 | 15 | 2,187 | 1 | 105 |
| Total | 34 | 3,104 | 29 | 1,293 |

**Table 6: Number and Tonnage of Channel Island Vessels in the Coasting Trade, 1845**

not,[57] had important implications for the shipping of this Island in the years when sailing ship technology went into decline. The granite trade grew substantially during the 19th century, and over time the proportion of shipping dedicated to servicing granite exports increased proportionately. By mid-century, however, the greater importance for Guernsey shipowners of the coasting trade with Britain was already apparent.

Table 6 shows that almost 36% of Guernsey-registered tonnage for which crew lists survive for the year 1845 (3,104 of 8,700 tons) found some employment in trade with the mainland,[58] and that the granite trade—usually combined with the coal trade with the ports of northern England, especially Shields and Newcastle—formed an integral part of the Island's domestic trades is clear from the higher tonnage ranges employed on these routes. Conversely, as Table 7 below shows, only 7% of the tonnage registered at Jersey for which crew lists survive for the same years (1,293 of a total 18,034 tons) found employment as coasting vessels, the vast majority being exclusively engaged in the foreign trades.

The *London Customs Bills of Entry*, which record all entries of Channel Island vessels in the port of London and have therefore been used to supplement the crew lists which, as explained above, do not cover all voyages made by Island vessels in the year chosen for analysis, support the conclusion that the domestic trades were of far greater importance to Guernsey than to Jersey in 1845. They also show that figures shown in Table 6 actually conceal the true extent of the reliance of Guernsey shipowners on its trade with the mainland. Whereas only 1,343 tons of Jersey shipping (4.8% of the total registered) was involved in carrying goods from the Island to the port of London in 1845, the corresponding figure for Guernsey was 4,459 tons (33.6% of total shipping tonnage). This difference was based on the composition of the Islands' export trades. Jersey's exports to London, as shown in the *Bills*, consisted mainly of potatoes, as well as smaller quantities of apples, cider, wines, etc. Guernsey's export trade, on the other hand, consisted mainly of stone, though agricultural produce—potatoes and apples—as well as wines, brandy, and other goods, were also transported from this Island. In terms of bulk, however,

| | Guernsey Vessels | | Jersey Vessels | |
|---|---|---|---|---|
| *Tonnage Range* | *No. of Vessels* | *Total Tonnage* | *No. of Vessels* | *Total Tonnage* |
| 15-50 | 2 | 90 | 6 | 217 |
| 50-100 | 18 | 1,110 | 28 | 1,947 |
| 100-200 | 30 | 4,320 | 71 | 10,452 |
| 200-300 | 3 | 687 | 14 | 3,253 |
| 300-400 | - | - | 2 | 612 |
| 400-500 | - | - | 1 | 413 |
| **Total** | **53** | **6,207** | **122** | **16,894** |

**Table 7: Number and Tonnage of Channel Island Vessels
in the Foreign Trade, 1845**

granite was Guernsey's principal export. The impact of the stone trade on Island shipping is clear. Between 1 January and 31 December 1845, 41 Guernsey-registered vessels (4,459 tons of shipping) made a total of 138 voyages from the Island to London, carrying 27,548 tons of granite, and employing an average of 231 men. Conversely, 21 Jersey-registered vessels (a total of 1,119 tons) made a total of 28 voyages from this Island to London, carrying shipments of potatoes totalling 1,943 tons, and employing an average of 98 men.[59] The figures for Jersey may, however, underestimate slightly the proportion of the fleet normally dedicated to the coasting trade: this was a particularly bad year for Jersey exports because of the potato blight that struck the Island in June 1845, which by January 1846 had caused the loss of about one-third of the crop.[60]

### -IV-

Guernsey granite, as well as granite from Devon, had begun to be used for the paving of roads in London at least from the beginning of the 19th century, as an alternative to Aberdeen granite.[61] This appears to have been the principal use that was to be made of most of the granite exported from this Island for the rest of the century: in the mid-1890s, according to Ansted, it was utilised for paving purposes in London because of its extreme hardness and toughness, and because it did not become slippery with wear. Granite was therefore cut and sold in the shape of cubes and pitchers for paving and for kerbs, although smaller cuts and chippings were also sold, as were some more ornamental types of stone, utilised for architectural purposes.[62]

Export volumes were small during the early decades of the 19th century. The *Almanac* of Guernsey of 1830 listed granite among the Island's exports in 1829:

**4** St Peter Port, Guernsey, *c.*1860. © Priaulx Library, Guernsey.

**5** Town Church, St Peter Port, Guernsey, *c.*1860. © Priaulx Library, Guernsey.

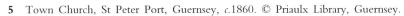

| Year | Exports (tons) |
|---|---|
| 1840 | 47,777 |
| 1841 | 37,551 |
| 1842 | 55,992 |
| 1843 | 56,320 |
| 1844 | 57,544 |
| 1845 | 60,259 |
| 1846 | 66,829 |
| 1847 | 83,338 |
| 1848 | 97,660 |
| 1849 | 90,473 |
| 1850 | 82,593 |
| 1851 | 108,176 |
| 1852 | 103,820 |
| 1853 | 119,508 |
| *Total (1840-53)* | *1,067,840* |

**Table 8: Exports of Granite from St Sampson's, 1840-1853**

13,547 tons for the construction of roads and a further 11,656 tons of paving stones.[63] By the mid-1830s, *The Star* of Guernsey was reporting 'increasing activity' in the trade and a growing demand for Island granite, while congratulating the merchants for the 'spirited manner in which the trade is conducted': more than twenty vessels at a time, the report observed, could often be seen at St Sampson's harbour, either loading or waiting to load.[64] Relatively modest in extent, granite was probably also of little importance to Island shipping at this stage. In 1840, according to Alan Jamieson, 39,502 tons of stone were transported from Guernsey to London in 264 shipments: of these, the vast majority—215, or 81%—were carried in non-Island vessels; only 44 (17%) were transported by Guernsey-registered vessels.[65] These were still the early stages of the granite trade, however. As the table above shows, exports began to expand at a phenomenal rate from 1840.[66] By 1845, exports of stone had increased by 26%—and by this date, Guernsey-registered vessels carried almost 46% of the total transported in that year. Indeed, by this time, Jersey shipowners may also have begun to recognise the importance of the granite trade: 9 Jersey-registered vessels (a total of 1,037 tons of shipping) carried between them in 1845 granite totalling 2,550 tons (4.2% of total granite exports from Guernsey).

Despite many similarities, and despite the general assumption, evident in the work of 19th-century writers and visitors to the Islands, that the trading activities of Guernsey merely mirrored those of its larger neighbour, but on a smaller scale, the two islands did not follow identical paths, as the analysis presented in the preceding sections clearly shows. Some important differences had emerged between Guernsey and Jersey by the middle of the 19th century, and it is to the impact of those differences on later developments that the following two essays now turn. Part II considers the effects on Channel Island shipping of the transformations which took place in the British shipbuilding industry as a consequence of the introduction of steam, the ways in which Guernsey and Jersey sought to overcome the difficulties which arose in their economies as a result, including the early development of the tourist industry, and the role of the granite trade in easing the worst effects of these changes on the shipowners of Guernsey. Part III, meanwhile, analyses the impact of the phenomenal expansion in shipping-related activities in the decades from 1820 to 1850 on the population of the Islands, and the role of these sectors in providing employment to their rapidly growing populations, before examining the effects of the later fall in demand for sailing tonnage on trade, shipbuilding, immigration and employment.

# Part 2
# THE DECLINE OF CHANNEL ISLAND
# SHIPPING, 1865–1900

## -I-

Over the half century following the end of the Napoleonic Wars, the Channel Islands experienced a period of rapid economic growth, based principally on the development of maritime trade and associated industries. Maritime trading activities were not new to the Channel Islands; the 19th century merely witnessed a great expansion of trade along routes and networks which were already well established in the 18th century, although some new trading regions had been added to these, such as the former Spanish colonies of South and Central America.[1] As the Jersey Chamber of Commerce put it in 1845, in describing its own Island's trading connections, 'now vessels from the Island frequent all parts of the Globe. You will find them in the South Seas at our Antipodes. They may be seen at New Holland and in the Indian Ocean.'[2]

As we saw in Part I, the development of the Islands' maritime trading activities led to a growth in demand for new vessels, which in turn resulted in a substantial increase in registered tonnage, and in the rapid expansion of shipbuilding in both Islands. However, despite many similarities, the Islands did not follow absolutely parallel paths of development. The expansion of the shipping and shipbuilding sectors, for example, was far more impressive in Jersey than in Guernsey. Whereas in Guernsey total registered tonnage increased from 6,662 to 24,698 (approximately) tons between 1815 and 1865, in Jersey, between 1815 and 1865, registered tonnage increased from 7,519 to 48,628 tons (approximately).[3] And, while some 40,000 tons of shipping were launched from the shipyards of Guernsey between 1815 and 1879, the corresponding figure for Jersey was more than two-and-a-half times larger—a total of 101,638 tons.[4]

The more rapid and substantial growth of Jersey's merchant shipping fleet—paralleled in its shipbuilding sector—can be attributed largely to this Island's greater participation in the international carrying trade, including, and partly resulting from, the cod trade with the fisheries of British North America. This is not to say that only Jersey had connections with the fisheries. During the late 16th century, and throughout most of the 17th, Guernsey merchants were deeply involved in the cod trade with Newfoundland. Furthermore, from the end of the eighteenth century and through the years of the Napoleonic Wars, Guernsey and Jersey merchants cooperated in the trade, not just in Newfoundland but also in Gaspé. After 1815, however, Guernsey's participation in the cod trade diminished; some of the Guernsey bases in Gaspé were actually taken over by the Jersey firm of Janvrin. Jersey merchants, on the other hand, steadily expanded their activities in the fisheries from the 16th century until their final withdrawal following the bank crash of January 1886.[5] Their interests in the fisheries gave them an edge and an incentive in exploiting opportunities in other trades. As Rosemary Ommer explains, 'it was in the nature of the cod trade to create an entry in the carrying trades, by virtue of the trading structures involved in marketing and supplying the staple trade'.[6]

The trading patterns of the Islands, then, diverged in at least one important respect after 1815. We have seen from the analysis of the crew agreements of 1845 presented in the previous section, that during the course of that year 31 Jersey vessels, representing more than 4,000 tons of shipping, were employed in the cod trade with the BNA fisheries.[7] Cod was not a component of Guernsey's trade, at least not in 1845: of the vessels for which crew lists survive for that year, none conducted voyages to the fisheries of British North America.[8] The Islands' trading patterns diverged in other respects as well. For example, although Guernsey vessels did make voyages far afield, to the Mediterranean, Caribbean, South America, Africa, and the Indian Ocean, much like Jersey vessels did, this Island's most important trading activities took place far closer to home: more voyages were made to the Azores and the Iberian Peninsula than to any other foreign destination. On these routes, Guernsey vessels plied the fruit trade with the United Kingdom. Indeed, the fruit trade was of enough importance for Island shipbuilders to specialise in the construction of fast schooners specifically for the purpose of carrying this produce to Britain.[9] Finally, one other crucial difference emerged between the Islands—trade with the mainland, in particular the stone trade, was of far greater importance to shipowners in Guernsey than to those in Jersey, and this was to have profound implications for the survival of the smaller Island's shipping fleet in the latter decades of the 19th century.

Channel Island involvement in maritime trade peaked in the mid-1860s. It was also at this time that the finest vessels ever built in the Islands were launched. In 1864, for example, the largest ship ever built in Guernsey was completed—this was the *Golden Spur*, of 636 tons, built for Messrs Carrington & Co. by Peter Ogier at St Sampson, intended for the China trade and said to be 'a credit to the island, to their builders, and to their owners'.[10] Before the end of the decade, however, the participation of the Channel Islands in the foreign trades began a steep decline from which neither would recover. The immediate cause, in the 1860s, was a depression in world trade, which was accompanied by a fall in freight rates, leading in turn to a reduction in profits. This was compounded, after 1873, by a general drop in prices which continued until the end of the century. As Ommer observed, in explaining the causes of decline in Jersey, this 'Great Depression was in fact a series of booms and slumps … Sugar, petroleum, cotton, tea, silk, wheat, iron and steel particularly suffered from falling prices; many of these commodities were vital parts of the Jersey carrying trade.'[11] Some of these commodities were also important components of Guernsey's carrying trade. The minutes of meetings held by the Chambers of Commerce of Guernsey and Jersey show that the impact of depression was felt in both Islands. At the Annual General Meeting of March 1868, the Guernsey Chamber described the year 1867 as 'commercially a stagnant year, consequent on the crisis of 1866', the effects of which had been felt not just in the carrying trade but also in shipbuilding, which had almost come to a complete standstill.[12] Just two weeks earlier, the Jersey Chamber reported that this Island's commerce had been adversely affected by 'the General Stagnation throughout the World', and that shipbuilding, 'a most productive branch of industry', had also almost completely ceased.[13] The assessments of both Chambers illustrate clearly the close connection between trade and shipbuilding. The fortunes of the shipyards followed closely fluctuations in the freight market: a downward trend in the employment of vessels led to a lower demand for new tonnage, and a decline in the output of the shipbuilding yards.[14]

While at the end of the 1860s the worldwide depression in trade may have been the most immediate cause of concern to the merchants, shipowners, and shipbuilders represented by the Chambers of Commerce, other far more worrying long-term developments were also taking place. Crucially important for the Channel Islands, as for many other ports across the country, was the fact that these years coincided with a period of great technological change in British shipping, which would result in Britain as a whole becoming, by the 1890s, by far the most successful shipbuilding nation in the world.[15] Of greatest significance was the shift from sail to steam, which, whilst not occurring overnight, was to have serious implications for the future of both Islands' maritime activities.

The impact of the development of steam first began to be felt in the 1850s, but in these early years sailing ship technology was protected on most routes by the fact that steamships were more expensive to build and, because of the cost of fuel, were also more expensive to operate. Thus, in the 1850s, steamships were generally only employed in river and coastal navigation, where, as P.L.Cottrell explains, there was no need for large on-board fuel bunkers.[16] From the 1860s, following the development of a more economical high-pressure marine engine, the participation of steamships in the deep sea trades increased.[17] As the new technology improved—innovations occurred more rapidly than in sail—freight rates for steamships became more competitive and wooden sailing ships began to be forced out of some of their traditional trades. It was during the latter part of the decade of the 1860s that the greatest progress appears to have been made. In her study of Jersey's cod trade, Rosemary Ommer cites an editorial from *Mitchell's Maritime Register* commenting on the fact that in 1865 only 0.22% of total newly registered tonnage was built of iron; that by 1869, the total tonnage of steam vessels registered in Britain amounted to nearly half of the tonnage of new sailing vessels registered; and that, also by 1869, the total tonnage of newly registered wooden vessels had fallen to 38.8% of the total registered in 1863. As *Mitchell's* concluded, 'these returns disclose the revolution that is taking place in shipping, for iron-built vessels are slowly but surely superseding wood, and steam is supplanting sail ... We need not say that this employment of steamships must have tended to retard the increase of sailing tonnage and keep down freights.' Just three months earlier, in April 1870, *Mitchell's* had ominously warned that 'The Rivalry between steam and sailing vessels has fairly commenced ...'.[18] The magnitude of the changes taking place across the country is clear from P.L.Cottrell's figures

**6**  St Helier Harbour, Jersey, *c*.1870. © Société Jersiaise.

showing the growth of steam tonnage registered at Liverpool between 1820 and 1880. In 1820, total steam tonnage registered at Liverpool is estimated to have amounted to no more than 117 tons; in 1850, the official returns showed a total of 11,411 tons; in 1865, the figure stood at 186,313 tons; and by 1880, the total had risen to a spectacular 555,062 tons, accounting for 37.5% of total registered shipping. In London, steam shipping had grown even more impressively, relative to sail, by 1880. In 1850, steam-tonnage accounted for 10.1% of the total registered at the port; by 1880, its share had increased to 51.7%.[19]

These figures notwithstanding, the shift from sail to steam was neither sudden nor general in all trades throughout the country. In the years between the 1850s and the 1890s, shipowners took into account not just the state of the freight market but also the trades in which each was involved, so that in some trades—the bulk trades in particular—sail survived alongside steam.[20] Thus, Cottrell's figures on Liverpool also show that however spectacular the increase in registered steam tonnage between 1850 and 1880, sailing tonnage still accounted for more than 60% of the shipping of the port.[21] Cottrell's findings support Ommer's conclusion that it was not until the mid-1890s that, with a continuous reduction in fuel consumption, sail finally lost its competitiveness on longer hauls.[22]

The shift from sail to steam, then, was gradual rather than sudden, but the technological advances which were taking place in British shipbuilding did have damaging effects on countless large and small shipyards across the country. The development of steamships and the introduction of the iron hull led to important alterations to the complexity of ship construction and to the size of vessels built, transforming British shipbuilding from an industry composed mainly of small handicraft firms into one consisting of large, highly capitalized businesses, which employed not only craftsmen but also semi-skilled machine workers and labourers.[23] As wooden shipbuilding became increasingly obsolete, the number of ports involved in shipbuilding across the country contracted. In the first half of the 19th century, when timber sailing ships of some 200 tons burden were the standard output, shipyards could be found in all major and minor ports around the coasts of Britain and Ireland. Wooden ships required little in the way of equipment, and the industry could thus be sustained without vast amounts of capital. But during the second half of the 19th century, British shipbuilding became increasingly specialised: builders developed expertise in the construction of particular types of vessels and the needs of specific kinds of owners, enabling them, for instance, to minimize idle capacity in their yards by making it feasible to build 'on spec'—that is, before orders were placed. In addition, the industry became more and more concentrated in a small number of centres where all the requirements of the builders could be met: cheap supplies of labour, capital, raw materials (iron and coal), land, subsidiary industries (steel and engineering), and a large guaranteed market for ships and repair work. By the 1870s, the major shipbuilding centres were concentrated along the Clyde, Tyne, Wear and Tees rivers, with three other important regions—Belfast, Barrow and West Hartlepool—developing later.[24]

As the shipyards became increasingly clustered in a small number of centres, some of the older shipbuilding centres declined, including those hitherto as important as London and Liverpool. The large volume of traffic through these ports could do little more than delay the decline for a decade or so.[25] Against this background, smaller shipyards in many other parts of Britain—the south-west of England, for example[26]—which could not count on the requisite raw materials, or on the necessary capital and labour, or indeed on a large potential market, had little chance of survival. British shipbuilding had changed beyond all recognition.

Thus, from the crisis of the 1860s onwards, the shipowners and shipbuilders of the Channel Islands faced two grave problems. On the one hand, the growing complexity of shipbuilding made it virtually impossible for Island shipbuilders to make the transition from building wooden sailing ships to iron steamships. By the 1890s almost all the shipyards of Guernsey and Jersey had closed down.[27] On the other hand, the expansion of steamship navigation meant that owners of existing Island sailing tonnage began to face serious competition from faster, more regular steamers in many of their traditional trades. In Guernsey, for example, the editor of Ferdinand Brock Tupper's *History of Guernsey* anticipated as early as the mid-1870s the damage that steam would inflict on Island shipping, and warned that the future of the large fleet of good quality ships, brigs and schooners which enterprising shipowners had gradually built up over the previous two decades—

vessels which had found employment in the carrying trade to all parts of the world, including India, China and Australia—was now threatened by the advance of screw steam ships. The threat to Island shipping would be even more serious, he added, with the opening of the Suez Canal, which would afford ever greater advantages to steam.[28]

There is no shortage of evidence to confirm the accuracy of these observations. In February 1880, for instance, Abraham Bishop, President of the Guernsey Chamber of Commerce, talked at length to the members convened at their Annual General Meeting about the problems besetting that Island's shipping interest. Whereas in past years most people in Guernsey had some interest in the fortunes of shipping and trade, the situation had greatly changed in more recent times; trade had declined, and the attitude of islanders towards this once thriving sector of the local economy had shifted as a result: 'Formerly', Bishop observed, 'when a Guernsey vessel was lost there used to be much sorrow and regret, now if only the lives were saved, it appeared more a matter of rejoicing … This showed what a change had taken place.'[29] The President of the Chamber correctly attributed the decline of Island shipping to the advance of iron steamers which were gradually superseding wooden vessels in the foreign trade. But he also perceptively pointed out that Guernsey was not just witnessing the replacement of wooden sailing ships by steamers, but also a very real transformation in the nature of the foreign trade and in the way it was conducted. Earlier in the century ships from ports across the country had been able to participate in the expansion of maritime trade worldwide; by the 1880s, it was the larger ports, where iron ships abounded, that were taking the lion's share of foreign trade, carried by ships that were far more powerful than anything the Island could offer. For Guernsey, the implications of this transformation were painfully obvious: in the past, Island vessels had returned with 'rich cargoes'; now they often failed to make any profit, and indeed frequently made large losses.[30]

In fact, however, the effects of the changes occurring in British shipping were not identical in both Islands, and, much as in other parts of the country, their impact was not felt in all spheres of activity at precisely the same time. In Guernsey, the worst effects were cushioned by the growth, over the course of the 19th century, of granite quarrying in the Island. Granite was exported in vast quantities to London, and in the transport of stone, as the final section of this study shows, sailing vessels were able to compete at least until the end of the 1880s. It was to be many years before steam supplanted sail in the bulk trades. In other trades, however, especially those where speed was a crucial consideration, Guernsey was badly affected: the small fast schooners built for the purpose of servicing the fruit trade from Spain, Portugal and the Azores were losing out to steamers as early as the 1870s.[31] But in Jersey, the impact of the new technology on the sailing-ship carrying trade was swift and could almost be called catastrophic,[32] as the figures presented in Table 9 suggest.

Table 9 shows that Jersey's sailing fleet expanded steadily from the 1820s to the 1860s, but then began an equally steep and steady decline, although it

| | 1826 | 1845 | 1855 | 1865 | 1875 | 1885 | 1895 |
|---|---|---|---|---|---|---|---|
| *15-50* | 14 | 80 | 148 | 174 | 136 | 71 | 38 |
| *50-100* | 44 | 62 | 61 | 80 | 93 | 68 | 48 |
| *100-200* | 43 | 98 | 88 | 103 | 36 | 25 | 16 |
| *200-300* | 15 | 22 | 28 | 36 | 9 | 6 | 3 |
| *300-400* | 1 | 2 | 12 | 14 | 6 | 1 | |
| *400-500* | 1 | 3 | 4 | 5 | 6 | | |
| *500-600* | | | 1 | 2 | 1 | | |
| *600-700* | | | | 2 | | | |
| *700-800* | | | | 2 | | | |
| *800-900* | | | 1 | | | | |
| *900-1000* | | | | 1 | | | |
| *1000-1100* | | | | 1 | | | |
| *1100-1200* | | | | 1 | | | |
| **Total Vessels** | 118 | 267 | 343 | 422 | 288 | 171 | 105 |
| **Total Tonnage** | 14,022 | 27,714 | 35,400 | 48,628 | 24,792 | 12,596 | 7,786 |

**Table 9: Registered Tonnage: Jersey, 1826-1885 (by numbers registered in each tonnage range)** [33]

should be said that this comparison of figures on registered tonnage for the 19th century should be treated with some caution, given the frequent changes introduced over the course of the century in the methods of calculating tonnage: the purpose of the table is merely to illustrate the rapid growth of the Island's fleet and its subsequent vertiginous decline. Between 1865 and 1885, Jersey-registered sailing tonnage fell by approximately 75%—from 48,628 tons in 1865 to 12,596 in 1885. Over the next 10 years, registered tonnage fell again, by approximately 40%, to 7,786 tons. Vessels in the higher tonnage categories—all those over 400 tons and a very large proportion of those in the 100-400 ton ranges—were among the first casualties, a reflection of the Island's diminishing participation in the foreign trade. Then, between 1875 and 1885, the number of vessels in the lowest tonnage category (15 to 50 tons) also fell dramatically—perhaps in part as a result of the increasing use of steamers to carry perishable agricultural produce to the mainland. In 1885, the Jersey Chamber of Commerce was expressing its concern that it was becoming increasingly difficult even for the smallest vessels to find 'remunerative employment'.[34]

By the early 1880s, even the owners of vessels which remained on Jersey's register of shipping—many had either been lost and not replaced, or sold, or transferred to other ports—were finding it increasingly difficult to keep these in operation. The extent of underemployment of shipping is difficult to measure for any port, given the absence of sources upon which such an analysis might be based. But in this Island there is one set of records—those of the Jersey Merchant

Seamen's Benefit Society—which enable us to gauge, if only approximately, the magnitude of the problem faced by shipowners.

The Jersey Merchant Seamen's Benefit Society was established in 1835 for the purpose of protecting disabled sailors, and sailors' widows and children,[35] and most importantly for the purpose of this study, was funded by contributions from the seamen themselves, which were deducted from their pay at the end of every voyage and posted in the Society's ledgers against the name of the vessel from which each sailor had been discharged. The ledgers show that by the end of 1880 only a relatively small proportion of vessels still listed on the Island's register of shipping had returned seamen's contributions to the Benefit Society corresponding to voyages undertaken during that year. We know from the Shipping List published in the *British Press and Jersey Times Almanac* of 1880 that at the end of 1879, 258 vessels, adding up to a total tonnage of 17,990, were registered in Jersey. But of these, only 79 (30.6%) totalling some 7,100 tons (approximately 40% of registered tonnage) had returned crew lists and contributions to the Society by the end of the year.[36] The figures compare very unfavourably with those for 1850. The Shipping List published in the *British Press Almanac* of that year shows that 342 vessels[37]—a total of 32,755 tons—were registered in Jersey at the end of 1849, while the ledgers of the Benefit Society show that of these, 248 vessels (72.5%) totalling 23,308 tons (71.2% of the total registered) had returned crew lists and seamen's contributions before the end of 1850.[38] There may be several explanations for the absence from the ledgers of so many vessels, and we should not assume that underemployment was the only or even the principal reason. Some vessels may have been operating out of other British or even foreign ports and not returned to Jersey throughout the entire year, much like Guernsey's *Golden Spur*, which in 15 years of sailing, only once voyaged back to that Island.[39] Some may have been trading with the fisheries and staying away from the Island for long periods of time: in 1880, Jersey's connections with the Newfoundland and Canadian fisheries were still of enough importance to the trading community to merit discussion at Chamber of Commerce meetings.[40] And even in the early 1890s, according to Ansted, the Island carried on a much diminished but profitable trade with Newfoundland.[41] Or perhaps shipowners in Jersey had an incentive to avoid the Island. There are suggestions, reported in *Staddon and Grigg's Almanack* of 1876, published in Guernsey, that local rates of taxation on shipping and the Jersey Merchant Seamen's Fund were proving onerous to Jersey shipowners, making the cost of shipping far higher to them than to shipowners from other ports. According to the *Almanack*, many Jersey shipowners were choosing to transfer their vessels elsewhere, including Guernsey (where no comparable benefit society existed).[42]

Whatever the reasons for the absence from the ledgers of such a large proportion of shipping still registered in Jersey, the effects of falling contributions were felt keenly by the officers of the Merchant Seamen's Benefit Society: they were concerned that a fall in receipts would make it difficult to continue to support the retired and disabled seamen and their dependents who relied on pensions and allowances paid by the Fund. Their concerns were real enough, and provide further evidence of the impact of the decline of shipping on the Island. From 1852, the Society's Minute Books recorded annually the number of crew lists returned and income received, and from the mid-1860s, we see here, as in all other indicators, a sharp downward trend. 1863 was the peak year for Island shipping: 345 crew lists were returned, bringing in an income from seamen's contributions of £666. In 1894, just over 50 crew lists were returned, which brought in a much diminished income of £99.

On several occasions from the mid-1870s onwards, the officers of the Society discussed the reasons for, and consequences of, falling contributions.[43] In 1881, they attributed the problem 'chiefly ... to the great decrease in shipping', but 'also in a great measure owing to the large number of vessels registered at other ports',[44] confirming the observation advanced in *Staddon and Grigg's Almanack* that many Jersey shipowners were transferring their vessels out of the Island. By 1893, it was reported that in addition to a general decrease in shipping registered in Jersey, very few vessels which were lost were being replaced, and it was finally acknowledged 'that this reduction will be an annual one'.[45] The consequences of this, of course, spread wider than the shipowners, shipbuilders and active sailors: by the time the Annual General Meeting of July 1875 was held, the decision had already been taken to reduce, from July, the value of pensions to widows and retired seamen, since the Society was no longer able to meet its current obligations without encroaching on its capital.[46] By 1881, the continuing fall in seamen's contributions led the President of the Society, Raulin Robin, to advocate the introduction of annual subscriptions.[47] Little could be done to resolve the Society's difficulties, however. By 1890, its income was reported to be inadequate to meet its obligations,[48] despite allowances having been curtailed years earlier; and by 1894, it had ceased to collect seamen's contributions altogether.[49] Although the Society continued to meet its obligation to provide pensions and allowances until 1947, in reality, by the end of the 19th century, the Jersey Merchant Seamen's Benefit Society, together with Jersey's merchant sailing fleet, had effectively ceased to function.

In Guernsey, the impact of the changes occurring in British shipping was neither as fast nor as ruinous as it was in Jersey. Certainly, by the 1880s, the size of this Island's sailing fleet, much like that of its neighbour, had contracted, but between the mid-1860s and the mid-1870s, when total registered tonnage in Jersey fell by half, total registered tonnage in Guernsey actually increased. Table 10 shows that, in 1866, there were registered in Guernsey 133 vessels with a combined tonnage of 24,698; by 1876, 164 vessels were on the register, accounting for a surprisingly high aggregate tonnage of 30,029 (compared with 24,792 in Jersey in 1875). And although by 1885 total registered tonnage in Guernsey had fallen by 30%, to 19,361, this was still nearly 7,000 tons higher than that of Jersey.

The implications of the figures for our understanding of the varying impact of decline on the Islands' shipping fleets are important. At mid-century, Guernsey's merchant sailing fleet could not compare in size with that of Jersey. Nor could

|  | 1830 | 1845 | 1855 | 1866 | 1876 | 1885 | 1900 |
|---|---|---|---|---|---|---|---|
| 15-50 | 19 | 21 | 23 | 11 | 24 | 21 | 16 |
| 50-100 | 16 | 29 | 21 | 16 | 21 | 25 | 26 |
| 100-200 | 25 | 57 | 54 | 64 | 54 | 33 | 11 |
| 200-300 | 10 | 10 | 13 | 29 | 48 | 38 | 12 |
| 300-400 |  |  | 5 | 7 | 9 | 2 | 1 |
| 400-500 |  |  |  |  | 2 | 1 |  |
| 500-600 |  |  |  | 4 | 2 |  |  |
| 600-700 |  |  |  | 2 | 4 | 2 |  |
| Total Vessels | 70 | 117 | 116 | 133 | 164 | 122 | 66 |
| Total Tonnage | 7,547 | 13,268 | 15,315 | 24,698 | 30,029 | 19,361 | 7,518 |

**Table 10: Registered Tonnage: Guernsey, 1830–1900 (by numbers registered in each tonnage range)**[50]

Guernsey's trading relations compare in scale or complexity with those of Jersey. Guernsey had fewer ships, its largest vessels all measured under 700 tons, and its mercantile activities were less ambitious. Yet Guernsey's fleet was protected from the worst effects of decline precisely because it was less dependent on international trade. Even during the peak years of shipbuilding and foreign trade the Island concentrated at least part of its attention on the development of granite quarrying and of a granite export trade, an operation whose importance was not limited to the stone merchants and quarrymen but extended also to the shipowners, because the transport of granite provided employment to at least a proportion of local shipping. This was to be of great advantage to Guernsey, for the existence of an export trade from the island enabled shipowners to redeploy at least some of those vessels which had been pushed out of the international carrying trade by the development of steam shipping. In fact, the trade was significant enough, and more importantly as far as the shipowners were concerned, substantial enough, to convince many owners of wooden sailing vessels from Jersey and even other ports on the mainland, who were facing the same problems as shipowners in Guernsey, to transfer their vessels to the Island. *Guerin's Almanac* of 1885 shows that, by the mid-1880s, approximately one-fifth of total registered tonnage in Guernsey (nearly 4,000 tons of shipping) was owned by shipowners resident in Jersey, Bristol, Goole and Faversham. It must be said, however, that the granite trade, vital though it was until the late 1880s, was only capable of delaying the disintegration of Guernsey's sailing fleet in the short to medium term. The export of stone was not a long-term solution to the problems facing Guernsey shipping: by the mid- to late-1880s, steamships were rapidly displacing wooden sailing vessels even in the transport of granite, and, the shipowners repeatedly complained, were actually favoured by the stone merchants,[51] whose own interests were to dispatch as much stone as possible as quickly as possible. In 1900, only 66 vessels remained on the Guernsey register, amounting to a total registered tonnage of 7,518.

Moreover, however successful the granite trade may have been in protecting Guernsey shipowners from the difficulties which were so manifest in Jersey, it could not save Island shipbuilding—as opposed to ship repairing and refitting—even in the short term. Registered tonnage increased in Guernsey until the mid-1870s, but the figures on output from Guernsey's shipyards show a steep decline from the period 1870-4 onwards, as measured by number of vessels, aggregate tonnage, and average tonnage. In the quinquennium 1865-9, 26 vessels were launched from Island yards, totalling 5,388 tons—an average of 207. In the five years between 1875 and 1879, only 7 vessels were launched, amounting to a total 399 tons—an average of 57.[52] Thus, while in Guernsey shipowners may have been able to redeploy some of their existing larger ships to the transport of granite to the mainland, Table 11 indicates that demand for new large ships had fallen drastically and with it new investment in all but a few small vessels.

In this respect, there was little difference between the Islands, for the figures on output from Jersey's shipyards tell a similar story. The number, aggregate tonnage, and average tonnage of locally built vessels suffered a sharp fall, suggesting that here, too, demand for large vessels had declined, and that what little demand remained was principally for smaller vessels. In the quinquennium 1865-9, 101 vessels were built in Jersey, amounting to a total 12,013 tons and an average of 119 tons—output from the shipyards of this Island having already fallen compared with 1860-4. In the five year period between 1875 and 1879, 42 vessels were built, amounting to only 2,492 tons—an average of 59.[53] By 1885, according to Rosemary Ommer, there was no new investment in shipping at all.[54]

| Year | Jersey Built | | | Guernsey Built | | |
|------|---------|-------|---------|---------|-------|---------|
|      | *Vessels* | *Tons* | *Average* | *Vessels* | *Tons* | *Average* |
| 1815-19 | 17 | 1,040 | 61 | 20 | 2,285 | 114 |
| 1820-24 | 21 | 1,710 | 81 | 30 | 2,931 | 98 |
| 1825-29 | 47 | 4,343 | 92 | 15 | 1,607 | 107 |
| 1830-34 | 26 | 4,103 | 158 | 12 | 1,541 | 128 |
| 1835-39 | 77 | 9,467 | 123 | 54 | 4,830 | 89 |
| 1840-44 | 91 | 8,836 | 97 | 59 | 6,257 | 106 |
| 1845-49 | 78 | 7,750 | 99 | 18 | 2,125 | 118 |
| 1850-54 | 95 | 14,251 | 150 | 16 | 2,750 | 172 |
| 1855-59 | 115 | 16,743 | 146 | 16 | 3,439 | 215 |
| 1860-64 | 115 | 15,417 | 134 | 18 | 4,601 | 256 |
| 1865-69 | 101 | 12,013 | 119 | 26 | 5,388 | 207 |
| 1870-74 | 56 | 3,473 | 62 | 9 | 1,229 | 137 |
| 1875-79 | 42 | 2,492 | 59 | 7 | 399 | 57 |
|  |  |  |  |  |  |  |
| Total | 881 | 101,638 | — | 300 | 39,382 | — |

**Table 11: Quinquennial Figures of Vessels Built in Jersey and Guernsey, 1815-1879[55]**

**-II-**

From the end of the 1860s, the participation of Channel Island vessels in the deep sea trades declined, demand for new tonnage fell, and the output of Island shipyards contracted. The effects on employment were felt immediately in both Islands, but, for a variety of reasons, some of which have already been discussed, these were especially serious in Jersey, where many families were forced to emigrate from the Island altogether, in a complete reversal of earlier patterns. Misgivings were expressed in Guernsey, of course, especially when, towards the end of the 1860s, with no apparent signs of recovery in trade, doubts began to be voiced about the future prospects of the shipbuilding industry. In 1869, for example, Abraham Bishop, President of the Chamber of Commerce, called on the States to support the development of ship repairing facilities in the Island—'a most important consideration at the present time, and under present circumstances, when so many of the working class, and especially of the shipwrights, were wanting employment, and the means of procuring bread for themselves and families'.[56] But in Jersey, where the population had doubled between 1821 and 1851, the threat of large-scale unemployment was especially alarming. Shipwrights and other artisans, seafarers, and especially unskilled labourers all felt the impact of the depression in trade. In March 1870, the Chamber of Commerce, having expressed its 'deep sympathy with the labouring classes, on whom high prices for food, frequent suspension of employment, and exceptional severe weather have borne hardly', proceeded to report on the state of the local labour market, and concluded that since it was basically overstocked, unemployment was not likely to fall in the foreseeable future, 'and that much long continued suffering must follow'. While it was reported at that same meeting that several public works were being planned, which would create some jobs, these would only be short term, and would not absorb all unemployed hands. Completion of the projects would, in any case, again leave the labour market glutted. As the Chamber put it

> No subject more serious in all its bearings on the state and prosperity of the Island calls for consideration than this unfortunate and now little doubted fact, that the local supply of unskilled labour far exceeds the demand. Its natural and logical consequence is that the indigent portion of the Population will rapidly increase, unless remedial means be found.[57]

Emigration was one solution to the problem, and one that many people in Jersey resorted to in the years after 1870. The high rates of population growth, sustained by large-scale immigration, which had characterized the Island in the period 1821-51 had already begun to be reversed in the decade to 1861, the total population falling slightly from 57,155 (or 57,020) to 55,613.[58] Why the population fell during these years is not clear, but it is possible that at least part of the decrease may be accounted for by some emigration of shipwrights from the Island. Alan Jamieson found that during the Crimean War, when large government orders were placed for warships, London shipbuilders conducted a recruitment campaign for Jersey shipwrights, offering them, in 1856, 7s. to 10s. a day, compared with the 3s. 3d. they received in Jersey in 1853. According to Jamieson, there was no shortage of recruits.[59]

The decade 1861 to 1871 witnessed another slight increase, to 56,627, but the *British Press and Jersey Times Almanac* of 1875 attributed this rise to the arrival of French families seeking refuge in the Island during the Franco-Prussian conflict of 1870, who contributed to boosting the census figures of the following year. But they were only temporary residents, and they were concentrated mainly in the parishes of St Helier, St Saviour, St Brelade and St Lawrence. In seven other parishes, the population was falling as a result of emigration. This conclusion is confirmed by the census figures for the following decade. More people left the island between 1871 and 1881 than during any other single decade throughout the century: the total population dropped by over 7%, from 56,627 to 52,445. The two decades to 1901 witnessed further falls—of 2,073 between 1881 and 1891, and 1,942 between 1891 and 1901. According to John Kelleher, in the three decades between 1851 and 1881, as many as 14,000 people emigrated from the Island. Most were artisans and their families who had originally been migrants to Jersey, and who were now forced to leave the Island in search of work. But some local artisans also emigrated.[60] The records of the Chamber of Commerce provide confirmation that many emigrants had indeed been employed in trades connected with shipping. In December 1883, when the Chamber of Commerce discussed the possibility of developing ship repairing facilities within the Island (not for the first time), for which it had to obtain the States' agreement to release funds for the construction of a patent slip, it warned that 'this work should be pushed forward without delay as a great number of shipwrights and other skilled workmen Employed on the repairs of vessels have left, and are still leaving'.[61] By the early 1890s, again according to the records of the Chamber of Commerce, few remained in Jersey. In 1892, one J. Le Maistre spoke at the Annual General Meeting of the Chamber of 'the absence of shipwright artisans in the Island', which he attributed to the fact that no support had been obtained for the construction of facilities for repairing and refitting vessels in Jersey.[62]

The effects on Jersey's seamen are far harder to evaluate, not least because the censuses cannot provide reliable estimates of the size of the seafaring population: sailors were usually at sea when censuses were carried out. But through the records of the Jersey Merchant Seamen's Benefit Society, which will be analysed in greater detail in Part III, we can assess approximately the changes that had taken place in the size and composition of the Island's seafaring labour force during the 30 years between 1850 and 1880-1.[63] For reasons which have already been explained elsewhere, the conclusions derived from analysis of this source have to be treated with caution, because we cannot be sure how many Jersey vessels were avoiding or evading the payment of contributions to the Society. This possibility notwithstanding, the ledgers do show a significant fall in the number of seafarers finding employment on Jersey vessels by the early 1880s, as measured by the numbers paying contributions, and they also show that the composition of the labour force had changed. In 1850, 2,621 seamen paid contributions to the Seamen's Benefit Fund, of which 1,505 (57.42%) were Jersey-born. 1,116 (42.58%) came from outside the Island—principally from England (555), Ireland (98), Scotland (51), and Wales (27). However, some of the men who gave places other than Jersey as their place of birth were undoubtedly Island residents in 1851: it is not uncommon to find non-Islanders listed in the ledgers alongside their Jersey-born sons. This is to be expected, given the number of English families, in particular, who migrated to Jersey in the years before 1850.

By the early 1880s far fewer men were employed as seafarers in Jersey. In the two year period between 1 January 1880 and 31 December 1881, only 1,177 individual seafarers are recorded in the ledgers as having paid contributions to the Fund. The figure for this two year period is 53% lower than for the single year of 1850. Furthermore, important changes had taken place in the composition of the labour force. In 1880-1, 930 (79.1%) seamen whose names were entered in the Society's ledgers were Jersey-born, compared with only 245 (20.8%) who came from other places. Thus, while the total number of Jerseymen finding employment on Island-registered vessels had fallen quite significantly, by the 1880s masters appear to have been showing a preference for engaging Islanders as crews. The figures also suggest that fewer sailors from other parts of Britain were operating out of Jersey by this date, and that the Island had ceased to attract English migrants as it had done in earlier years.

Guernsey, on the other hand, did not experience rates of population growth as high as those of Jersey between 1821 and 1851, but equally, it did not suffer a similar exodus. In fact, despite the fears of widespread unemployment expressed by the President of the Chamber of Commerce in the late 1860s, Guernsey experienced a quite steady rate of population growth to 1891. Between 1851 and 1881, the population of Guernsey increased from 29,732 to 32,379. Over the following decade, from 1881 to 1891, the population increased again, by almost 9%, to 35,218. The rate of growth was particularly marked in the parish of St Sampson, the main quarrying area in the Island, where the population more than doubled between 1851 and 1891—from 2,006 in 1851, to 3,624 in 1881, and 4,493 in 1891.[64]

The records of discussions held by the Jersey Chamber of Commerce suggest that the growth in Guernsey's population could be attributed in part to some emigration from Jersey, especially of the unemployed from the shipbuilding industry: it was said that some of the artisans who were leaving were actually taking up residence in the neighbouring Island. At a General Meeting held by the Chamber in December 1883, for example, J. Le Maistre commented that many of Jersey's shipwrights were leaving for Guernsey and other places, 'where constant Employment was found owing to the existence of Patent Slips ...'.[65] It should be said, however, that Le Maistre was particularly interested in the construction of facilities for the repair and refitting of vessels in Jersey—he repeatedly brought up the subject in the Chamber's meetings—and it is therefore quite possible that his warnings regarding the emigration of shipbuilding workers were at least partly aimed at persuading the States to agree to financing the patent slips requested by the shipbuilders. Shipbuilding workers may have been leaving the Island for other places, but the census figures, published in *Parliamentary Papers*, do not confirm large-scale emigration from Jersey to Guernsey, at least not among the Jersey-born. The Census Reports show instead that the Jersey-born population enumerated in Guernsey during the 1881 census was only marginally larger than the Guernsey-born population enumerated in Jersey—958 Jersey-born residents in Guernsey, compared with 875 Guernsey-born residents in Jersey.[66] Admittedly, this was a reversal of earlier patterns of migration between the Islands. In 1851, almost 2% of Jersey's population originated in Guernsey or the other Islands in the bailiwick (a total of 1,080), but the Jersey-born do not even figure as a separate category in Guernsey's census figures for that year.[67] There was, therefore, some movement from the larger to the smaller Island between 1851 and 1881, but the numbers involved were quite small.

The increase in Guernsey's population cannot be attributed to migration from neighbouring Jersey. Nor can it be attributed to higher rates of immigration from other sources. The proportion of non-Islanders in the total population of the bailiwick of Guernsey in 1881 (21.5%) continued to be smaller than in Jersey (28.5%), and had fallen compared with 1850, when the percentage stood at 28.3%.[68] Was this difference, then, a result of lower rates of emigration from Guernsey? If so, do the figures confirm that Guernsey was less affected by the decline of both the carrying trade and shipbuilding during the later decades of the 19th century than Jersey was? We know from Alan Jamieson's work that Islanders and people of non-local origin emigrated in some numbers during the 19th century from Guernsey as well as Jersey, and that they went to Canada and the United States and, from the 1840s, to Australia.[69] But given the current state of comparative research on the Channel Islands during the 19th century, the extent to which the Islands diverged in this respect remains uncertain. Further research is required, especially on Guernsey's history, before these questions can be answered with any degree of certainty. It might be argued, however, that the development and growth of granite quarrying in Guernsey through the 19th century, which required a labour force of quarrymen, crackers, carters and sailors, absorbed at least some of the surplus labour—the stone trade became as significant to this Island, in employment terms, as the cod trade had been to Jersey during the heyday of Island shipping.

**–III–**

In some important respects, the Channel Islands responded differently to the difficulties they faced from the end of the 1860s—difficulties such as the technological improvements in British shipbuilding which, while making Britain in general unrivalled as a shipbuilding nation, pushed Island shipowners out of most of their traditional trades and led to the collapse of their once flourishing shipbuilding industries. In both Guernsey and Jersey other sectors urgently had to be either fostered or developed to replace merchant shipping, and these gradually contributed to changing the character of the local economies. In this period, as in earlier decades, the Islands did not follow absolutely parallel paths. Both promoted agriculture and tourism, but only Guernsey had any success in developing facilities for ship repairing and refitting, which assisted the shipbuilders in the short term, and only Guernsey capitalised on its exports of granite.

The discussion that follows is not aimed at providing a definitive study of the development of the Island economies during the closing decades of the 19th century. Such a study would involve a far wider-ranging analysis of Channel Island agriculture, cattle rearing, fishing and so on than has been attempted here.[70] The purpose of the remaining sections of this study is, instead, twofold: first, to compare the ways in which the commercial communities of the Islands, represented by their respective Chambers of Commerce, responded to the problems faced by the shipping and shipbuilding sectors, and to examine the extent to which efforts were made by the Chambers to find solutions that might assist those sectors; and secondly, to consider the role played by the granite trade in Guernsey in the survival of Island shipping during the closing decades of the century.

In Guernsey, when the first troubling signs of crisis in the Island's trading activities emerged, the Chamber of Commerce sought to exert its influence on the States of the Island to secure facilities for ship repairing, which would serve to alleviate the worst effects of a shipbuilding industry under pressure. In addition, due in part to the need to procure employment for Island shipping but also to the vigour of a group of stone merchants within the Chamber, it focused some of its attention on promoting exports of Guernsey granite. A third area of interest was the promotion of the Island's agricultural and horticultural exports. And finally, tourism, too, received some encouragement. In Jersey, on the other hand, the influence of the shipping community in the Island, and surprisingly even within the Chamber of Commerce, appears to have waned as maritime trade went into decline. Perhaps for this reason, the pressure brought to bear by the Chamber on the States of the Island in order to obtain its support for the construction of facilities for ship repairing similar to those of Guernsey failed to produce the desired results. Moreover, the efforts of at least some members of the Chamber to encourage the development of a stone trade like that of Guernsey made little progress. Instead, in Jersey, agriculture and tourism rapidly replaced shipping as the basis of the economy. This was perhaps inevitable, given that agriculture at least had clearly proved itself to be more solid and durable than the Island's commercial and maritime activities had been.[71]

In the early days, however, the construction of repairing facilities was one of the solutions sought by the Chambers of Commerce of both Guernsey and Jersey to alleviate the problems caused to their respective shipbuilding industries by the collapse of maritime trade. This was in fact one option that had been considered some time before the full impact of the shift from wooden sailing ships to iron steamships had been fully recognised. As early as the mid-1860s, when the largest and most powerful vessels ever built in Guernsey were launched, the Chamber of Commerce began to voice an interest in developing ship repairing facilities on a large scale. At the time, the reasons behind these discussions had little to do with the vulnerability of Island shipbuilding in the face of competition from iron and steam. Shipowners in particular began to examine the advantages of ship repairing locally not because of any fears about the future of shipbuilding, but because existing facilities were inadequate now that vessels were larger, because the cost of repairs in London and other ports was higher than in Guernsey, and because of the inconvenience experienced by owners when unable to supervise repairs. An appeal was thus made to the States: a good graving dock (or dry dock) should be constructed at St Peter Port, as well as a patent slip at St Sampson's. In return, the States would be assured of increased revenues from harbour dues, graving dock dues, and duties on timber consumed in the repairs. Labour would be employed, and the trade of the Island in general would prosper.[72]

Although in 1868 the proposal for the graving dock was rejected, the Chamber of Commerce did not abandon its efforts to persuade the States of the absolute necessity of constructing ship repairing facilities in the Island. The Chamber argued that it would represent a saving to Island shipowners because the difference in the rates of pay between England and Guernsey—workmen in England were paid 7s. 6d. a day while in the Island they received 3s. 6d.— would reduce costs. Furthermore, once the facilities were built, ships from Jersey and even from England would be taken to the Island for repair. 'The graving dock', the President explained, 'was absolutely required in the interest of the shipping of the Island'.[73]

Despite the Guernsey Chamber of Commerce's interest in exploiting new commercial opportunities in the late 1860s, there is no indication in the discussions held at this time of any fears for the future of the local shipbuilding industry. Even though their battle with the States coincided with a period of depression in the Island's trade, there appeared to be no reason for concern, since in the single year of 1866 fifteen new vessels had been added to the register.[74] 1866 was a year of depression, but there was always a gap of a year or two between a fall in trade or profits and the output of the shipbuilding yards. It was not until March 1869, with no apparent signs of recovery appearing, that doubts began to be voiced about the future prospects of Guernsey's shipbuilding industry, and with these indications of trouble ahead, there also emerged concerns about unemployment among the Island's shipbuilding workers. In his address to the Chamber, Abraham Bishop, echoing the warnings given in *Mitchell's* at about the same time,[75] suggested that it would probably be unwise for shipbuilders to invest much in shipbuilding in the future, given the growing importance of iron in ship construction. The prospects for ship repairing—presumably including refitting and lengthening—looked more promising and 'susceptible of great expansion': if the facilities requested by shipowners were provided, by which he meant the graving dock, many vessels would be sent to Guernsey for repair and large sums of money would be spent in the Island, which could not but benefit trade in general and the working classes in particular.[76] A month later, at a meeting held specifically to discuss the issue, Abraham Bishop returned to the same theme, arguing that ship repairing facilities would be of benefit to all classes and interests in Guernsey, 'to those of the town and to those of the country, through the large sums of money which would constantly be expended for native labour, and thereby give life and activity to the trade and agriculture of the island'. Here, as

**7**   St Peter Port Harbour, Guernsey, with Castle Cornet in the background, *c*.1870.
© Priaulx Library, Guernsey.

in Jersey at about the same time, the argument centred on the question of
employment. In calling for the States' support for these proposals, Bishop referred
to the shortage of employment and consequent poverty which were already
affecting Guernsey's working class, in particular the shipwrights. The chief cause,
he argued, was the absence of local accommodation for repair, which forced
shipowners to send their vessels to England for repair, although they would
'greatly prefer' to do this at home. 'It was clear', the president concluded, that
'the graving dock which the shipowners asked for, but which had been thus far
refused them was the very corner-stone of our well being and prosperity.'[77]

In June 1869 the Chamber's request was partly met by the States—approval
being given for the construction of a patent slip in St Peter Port. In the long-
term the construction of ship repairing facilities did little to halt the decline of
the shipbuilding industry or indeed the disintegration of the island's wooden
sailing fleet, which was much diminished by 1900.[78] But it may well have delayed
the worst effects, in the short term at least, of the decline of sectors that had for
decades been central to the Island economy. We have no evidence to indicate
whether the construction of the patent slip did attract vessels from other British
ports. But the fact that in 1874 the States voted to finance the construction of
a second patent slip, which was said to be for the purpose of providing additional
facilities for ship repairs—'a trade likely to assume larger proportions in consequence
of the moderate charges, and excellent workmanship of our ship carpenters'[79]—
suggests that existing facilities were already fully stretched. As for the patent slip
at St Sampson, the contributions which the shippers of stone made to the meetings

of the Chamber suggest that in that trade the facilities for ship repairing were utilised. In 1880, in informing the Chamber of the important contribution which the stone trade had made to the Island economy, John Hamley did not neglect to mention the men who were employed in fitting out vessels and keeping them in order.[80]

In Jersey, on the other hand, the efforts of the Chamber of Commerce to obtain from the States of that Island approval for a scheme similar to that of Guernsey met with complete failure. Here, too, doubts about the future prospects of shipbuilding had been voiced several years before the industry went into decline. In 1867, the Jersey shipbuilder Daniel Le Vesconte, for example, acknowledged that the future of shipbuilding did not look too promising, now that wooden ships were being overshadowed by vessels of composite construction or of iron. While believing that Jersey might be able to build iron vessels on a small scale, as it still had the advantage of cheap labour, Le Vesconte proposed that the Island should concentrate instead on ship repairing. As in Guernsey, graving docks and repairing slips would have to be built, but then British ship-owners would send their vessels to Jersey for repair, 'it being more to their advantage from the difference in the price of labour.'[81]

Over the next three decades, in spite of repeated failures, the Jersey Chamber discussed on numerous occasions the absolute necessity of a graving dock or patent slips, which may in itself suggest that this scheme was having some success in Guernsey. At the Annual General Meeting of March 1877, it was reported that 'this accommodation to the shipping interest would be of great general advantage to the Island as it would induce people to send their vessels here for repair, and thus furnish much desired employment to our Shipbuilders'.[82] Yet two years later, in 1879, the Minutes recorded that the proposal for the construction of graving docks, which the States had been urged to act upon, remained in abeyance.[83] Again in 1882, at the Chamber's AGM, J. Le Maistre spoke of 'the apathy and indifference of the States to the shipping interests in so long neglecting to provide patent slips, and graving docks in order to provide for the repair of vessels ...'.[84] The following year, the Chamber, still despairing of the situation, again declared that the patent slip was indispensable to the Island to prevent owners whose ships needed repair being driven away from Jersey.[85] This was precisely what appeared to be occurring: in December, at a General Meeting called to discuss the question of harbour improvements, it was reported that

> owing to the want of accommodation a great amount of work is lost to the Island, for not only are Jersey owners compelled to send their vessels elsewhere for repairs, but it is well known that if the necessary appliances existed Jersey vessels would be repaired here, and vessels would come from other ports for the same purpose.[86]

Despite frequent discussions in successive special meetings and Annual General Meetings held by the Chamber of Commerce, and the clear concern of many of its members that the Island's shipbuilders were facing certain ruin, their requests were not met. By 1895, the Annual Report presented to the Chamber stressed 'the just claims of sailing vessels to ... a graving dock or patent slip, not to mention a floating dock,[87] which has formed part of every scheme of Harbour improvements but on paper only ... In these respects, Jersey is at a great disadvantage compared with Guernsey.'[88]

Why the shipowners and shipbuilders of Jersey should have failed so utterly to influence the members of the States on the question of facilities for the repair of vessels, in view of the fact that it was upon these sectors that the prosperity of the Island between the 1820s and the 1860s largely rested, is not clear. Rosemary Ommer argues that the States of Jersey had from its inception been a governing instrument of the landed proprietors, and for this reason focused its endeavours on the agricultural economy.[89] John Kelleher confirms and expands Ommer's findings, arguing that Jersey's political structure had always been dominated by the landed interest, and that political power was never shared with the merchant sector, despite the latter's undoubted capital wealth and its crucial contribution to the development of the economy. The power of the rural bloc, based on land and agriculture, was reflected in a strong presence in the States; the urban bloc, on the other hand, composed of the merchant and commercial classes, had considerable wealth, but this was not translated into political power.[90] The collapse of the Island's maritime trades and associated industries, coupled with the financial collapses of the 1870s and 1880s, no doubt whittled away what little influence these sectors retained. At the same time as the importance to the local economy of the agricultural sector, and of an expanding tourism sector, increased, so too did their influence in the Chamber. Henceforth, the volume of agricultural exports and the numbers of tourists visiting the Island in the summer season or coming to take up residence in Jersey became central concerns of the commercial community. As the Chamber of Commerce acknowledged in 1884, 'The augmentation of wealth and prosperity must be connected with either the increase of exports or imports, the former having reference more especially to agricultural produce, and the latter to a larger arrival of passengers and families to take up their residence in the island.'[91]

The minutes of meetings held by the Chamber certainly do *suggest* that the influence of agriculturists and those involved in tourism grew as the fortunes of shipping and shipbuilding went into decline. If the influence of a sector can be measured by the coverage granted to it at the Chamber's meetings, then the contrast with Guernsey is clear. While the Minute Books of the Guernsey Chamber of Commerce record frequent discussions throughout the 1860s, 1870s, 1880s and even the 1890s about the needs of shipowners, shipbuilders and, increasingly, the exporters of granite,[92] in Jersey the Minute Books reveal a growing concern for the fortunes of livestock exports and more particularly the potato trade, and for ways of improving facilities for visitors to the Island. This was at the expense of the interests of the shipping community: it would appear that even the harbour improvements accomplished in Jersey, if not intended primarily for the purpose of facilitating agricultural exports and attracting larger numbers of tourists, were expected to assist these sectors. As the Chamber recorded in December 1882, in discussing the harbour improvements, 'the potato traffic has considerably increased

| Year | Tons | Value (£) |
|------|------|-----------|
| 1883 | 47,000 | 282,000 |
| 1884 | 50,000 | 343,756 |
| 1886 | 60,000 | n/av. |
| 1887 | 50,670 | 434,917 |
| 1888 | 60,527 | 242,110 |
| 1889 | 56,684 | 264,153 |
| 1890 | 62,599 | 293,651 |
| 1893 | 57,762 | 327,366 |
| 1894 | 60,605 | 462,895 |
| 1895 | 54,290 | 359,989 |
| 1897 | 53,555 | 402,274 |
| 1898 | 56,227 | 338,269 |
| 1899 | 65,040 | 380,357 |

**Table 12: Exports of Potatoes—Jersey, 1883–1899**

during the past few years, as also a great increase in the tonnage of steamers bringing passengers to the Island, and ... it is highly important, that there should be sufficient room for steamers taking in cargo, more especially during the potato season ...'.[93]

Agricultural and livestock exports—potatoes and cattle in particular—increased steadily and substantially in this Island after 1860. John Kelleher's study of Jersey's rural community during the 19th century shows that potatoes were already becoming an important export in the 1840s (having been introduced in the 1740s), but that sales plummeted over the next two decades as a result of the potato blight of 1845. The impact of the disease was immediate—reducing export volumes from 18,560 tons in 1843/4 to 3,822 tons in 1845/6—and persisted for the rest of the decade. The annual average of exports during the decade 1845/6 to 1856 reached only 4,900 tons, falling to 4,200 tons between 1856 and 1866, compared with an annual average of 13,500 tons during the decade 1834 to 1844. By the late 1860s, just as the Island's maritime trading activities began to decline sharply, export figures began to rise again, with cultivation now being concentrated on the trade in 'earlies'. In 1868, 10,184 tons of potatoes were exported, and in 1878, 27,626 tons.[94] As the table above shows, potato exports grew even more substantially thereafter, peaking at just over 65,000 tons in 1899.[95]

Just how crucial this trade had become to the Island becomes clear from the numerous reports presented to the AGMs of the Chamber of Commerce.[96] By the mid-1870s it had been recognised clearly that only the potato trade had served

to balance the losses sustained in other sectors of the economy, affected not just
by depression but also by the bank failures:

> Fortunately, as a set off against the prevailing depression, the success which
> attended the culture of the potato was very marked ... the harvest itself yielded
> an abundant return and there is reason to believe that the agricultural successes
> of the year went a great way to balance the losses sustained by individuals in
> connection with the Bank failures. Your Committee trusts that this will prove
> a permanent source of income as the climate offers exceptional advantages for the
> culture and early maturity of the potato.[97]

Potato exports had become for Jersey something of a safety net. Thus, throughout the 1880s the exporters were on occasion congratulated for expanding the
volume and improving the quality of this product, and urged to maintain the
prestige in which it was held in English markets. The trade was now of vital
importance to the Island, not least because it provided 'a vast amount of
employment' at a time when other sectors were in decline.[98] Indeed, according
to Kelleher, by the 1880s, capital returns from the potato trade matched those
from the cod trade of earlier years. But there was one crucial difference: whereas
profits derived from the cod trade were shared out between a small group of
merchant houses, profits from the export of early potatoes were divided between
a large number of producers.[99]

The specialisation which the expansion of the export trade in potatoes en-
tailed resulted in other changes to the agricultural economy, however. First, it was
achieved to the detriment of other crops—cereals, root crops, and apples for cider
production—which had previously formed an integral part of the Island's agricultural
production.[100] Secondly, it led to an increasing reliance on imports of agricultural
produce to supply the local population, including grain and maincrop potatoes.[101]
Indeed, by the end of the 1880s, the extent of the Island's reliance on potato
exports had begun to give some cause for alarm. In March 1889, it was reported
that the volume of exports for the year 1888 exceeded that of 1887 by 10,000
tons, but that returns had fallen by £190,000. This showed

> clearly and painfully that it is unsafe to trust to that one staple of production only.
> The increasing competition of other places and the sending of immature and
> inferior produce to market combine to render the culture of the potato in this
> island less and less profitable ... this Chamber should urge all connected with the
> potato trade, to consider whether they should not in their own interests, and in
> that of the growers, encourage quality, instead of quantity ... thus preventing a
> glut of the markets, and maintaining the good name of Jersey produce.[102]

It was perhaps in response to an excessive dependence on this export product
that horticulture and glass-house agriculture began to be developed towards the
end of the century—especially tomatoes, grapes and flowers (the cultivation of
tomatoes under glass had become a major industry in Guernsey by the early
1890s).[103] By the end of the 1890s, several large glass houses were reported to
have been built in Jersey, leading to a steady increase in exports of glass-house

8   Commercial grape growing, Jersey, *c.*1890. © Société Jersiaise.

produce.[104] By 1900, the Chamber was informed that 'a large number of land-owners have undertaken the cultivation of tomatoes, flowers, and other market produce for the English market. Glass houses are being built in several parts of the Island.' Significantly, the Chamber sought to encourage these developments amongst growers by suggesting that this new sector could in future bring to Jersey the same kind of prosperity that it had enjoyed in the 'balmy days of potato growing and cattle dealing'. No reference was made now to the undoubted prosperity which shipping and the carrying trades, or even the cod trade, had brought to the Island just a few decades earlier.[105]

Of course, it should not be assumed that only Jersey sought to promote exports of agricultural produce and a tourism industry. The potential of both agriculture and tourism were frequently discussed by the Guernsey Chamber of Commerce, and these sectors were encouraged here as well. The export of agricultural produce expanded considerably in both Islands during the second half of the 19th century and the importance of this trade to the economy was acknowledged in Guernsey as much as in Jersey. In 1869, for example, Abraham Bishop reported to the members of the Chamber, convened at their AGM, on the progress of agricultural exports during the previous year. In the spring of 1868, Guernsey exported to London potatoes to the value of £30,000 (compared

| Year | No. of Packages |
|------|-----------------|
| 1883 | 138,508 |
| 1884 | 184,800 |
| 1885 | 220,000 |
| 1886 | 240,300 |
| 1887 | 277,400 |
| 1888 | 330,200 |
| 1889 | 391,906 |
| 1890 | 493,398 |
| 1891 | 664,679 |
| 1893 | 1,048,171 |
| 1894 | 909,655 |
| 1896 | 1,403,945 |
| 1897 | 1,370,099 |

**Table 13: Exports of Fruits, Flowers,
Vegetables—Guernsey, 1883-1897**

with £70,000 exported from Jersey), as well as broccoli and fruits of various types, which could always be profitably sold because they ripened much earlier in the Channel Islands than in England, thus commanding good prices. 'This alone', Bishop acknowledged, 'must have a sensible effect alike on our industrial, commercial and financial interests.'[106]

In fact, the commercial community in Guernsey was as aware as the commercial community in Jersey that the Channel Islands could no longer depend on maritime trade of the kind conducted in earlier years and that other sectors had to be developed to take its place. In 1886, G.F.Carrington, by then President of the Chamber, advised that while the Guernsey economy had previously depended on its shipping, Islanders should in future concentrate on, and promote, their own exports.[107] Although Carrington was probably referring as much to the export of granite as to that of agricultural produce, there is no doubt that expansion in the agricultural and horticultural sector had been very substantial by this date, as demonstrated by the number of packages exported from the Island shown in Table 13.[108]

As for the composition of exports, figures for the years 1883-5 show that potatoes accounted for between 20% and 26% of the total, the remainder consisting of tomatoes, beans and radishes, broccoli, flowers, and grapes.[109] Yet it was the potato trade from the Island that was of particular interest to J.Stuart Blackie when, en route to Jersey in 1883, he witnessed the activity taking place at one of Guernsey's harbours:

The whole traffic of a country here passes bodily before [the observer] in the space of an hour; and what struck me most, when brooding over this process from the quarter deck, at Guernsey, was the interminable number of empty casks or barrels that came swinging up from the hold, relay after relay, floundering about in the air ... these casks had come from Covent Garden, where they have been disembowelled of their wealth of early potatoes to fit out London dinners, and were come to their native soil to be replenished with fresh stores ...[110]

By end of the 1880s, while there was regret among the shipowners for the loss of Guernsey's shipping interests, there was also a growing recognition that henceforth the agricultural sector was likely to be the mainstay of the economy: the balance between shipping and agriculture had simply shifted in favour of the latter, and since the results had clearly been satisfactory, all efforts should be made to foster and increase this trade in the future.[111]

Agriculture—and later horticulture—were not the only sectors to be developed in the Channel Islands during the decades when shipping and maritime trade were in decline. In fact, from the beginning of the 1870s the Jersey Chamber of Commerce put considerable pressure on the States to provide greater and better facilities for visitors, all with the intention of making the Island a more attractive summer resort, and improving Jersey's chances of competing successfully with other English and continental resorts. Progress in this sphere seems to have accelerated from the early 1870s, although as early as 1862 the Chamber of Commerce of Jersey did collaborate with the Guernsey Chamber and W.H.Smith in London to promote the Channel Islands as a holiday destination. For £150 W.H.Smith printed an advertisement, which was to be displayed at 100 railway stations in England and Wales, describing the attractions of the Islands and the cost of passages from Southampton and Weymouth.[112]

Despite these efforts, however, few facilities had been provided by 1870 to attract tourists to the Island, the Chamber of Commerce having observed 'that another year has passed away without the adoption of practical means of constructing a low water landing place for passengers ... so long as no action is taken for providing means to land passengers safely, numbers of visitors will be deterred from coming to Jersey at a moment when trade languishes ...'.[113] If Jersey was to compete with the most fashionable English and European summer resorts for the 'better class' of tourists, then it was 'imperative that something should be done to cause the better class of strangers to visit us and when here, that they should find attractions equal, at least, to those offered by the places of fashionable resort on the English coast and on the Continent.' Given its mild climate and its impressive scenery, Jersey could compete with any fashionable holiday resort. But if the Island was to make the most of its natural advantages, then amusements and pastimes would have to be provided for visitors.[114]

Ease of transport, cheap passenger rates, advertisements at railway stations in England, safe and comfortable landing stages—these were all measures sought by the Chamber to make the Island more appealing and encourage tourists to choose it as a holiday destination. As the AGM was informed in March 1884,

| Year | No. of Visitors |
|------|-----------------|
| 1875 | 22,816 |
| 1882 | 29,263 |
| 1883 | 30,836 |
| 1884 | 31,168 |
| 1885 | 31,842 |
| 1886 | 32,398 |
| 1887 | 29,412 |
| 1888 | 30,455 |
| 1889 | 32,125 |
| 1890 | 40,635 |
| 1891 | 42,803 |
| 1892 | 45,361 |
| 1894 | 48,568 |
| 1895 | 55,867 |

**Table 14: Visitors to Jersey, 1875–95
(Tourist Season, May–September)**

every opportunity should be taken to increase the number of visitors to Jersey, and incentives—in particular cheap passenger rates and easy landing stages—should be provided to attract them.[115] By the end of the century, suggestions were also being made to improve the appearance of St Helier, and to provide attractions for visitors to the town. In 1899 the Chamber stressed

> the absolute necessity of efforts being made to add to the attractions of this place
> as a seaside resort … the completion of the Victoria Avenue, erecting upon it
> shelters at suitable distances, and the immediate establishment of a Municipal
> Band to perform in the most attractive parts of the Town would go far to make
> the stay of visitors more agreeable.[116]

There is no doubt that the Chamber of Commerce considered the tourism sector to be of great importance to the Island. From the mid-1870s to the mid-1890s, it monitored and regularly recorded the number of tourists visiting Jersey during the summer season (May to September), and, as the figures presented in Table 14 show, this optimism was not misplaced.[117]

In Guernsey, too, at about the same time, similar moves were being made to encourage tourism, though figures showing the extent to which these were successful are not available. Unlike the Jersey Chamber of Commerce, the Guernsey Chamber did not regularly record the number of visitors arriving annually in the Island, although in 1891 it did report that in 1890 the number of visitors had increased by about several thousands over previous years, and that it was expected that with quicker sea passages the Channel Islands would increasingly be favoured by tourists. Also in 1890, a committee was established for the purpose of procuring musical entertainments for visitors during the summer evenings, the purpose being to ensure that 'every means should be fostered which has for its object the making of our Island more attractive to strangers'.[118]

Thus, from the mid-1870s onwards, the commercial communities in both Guernsey and Jersey made great efforts to further existing economic activities and create new ones, so as to offset the losses which were daily being made in shipping (to which we might add the cod trade in Jersey's case). Agriculture, horticulture, livestock exports, tourism, and, in Guernsey, ship repairing—all these became potential areas for development. But what contribution, if any, did these activities make to Island shipping? To what extent did Island shipowners, for example, benefit from the expansion of Island exports? Were these new or growing trades satisfactory substitutes for the carrying trade of earlier years, at least insofar as the shipowners were concerned? Or did steamships dominate these trades, too?

Although, as we have seen, agricultural/horticultural exports expanded considerably in the second half of the 19th century, becoming a significant source of income for both Islands, these could do little to assist Island shipping. The value of agricultural exports was high, but the volume was insufficient to employ more than a small proportion of the sailing fleets. As the 19th century progressed, moreover, steam came to overshadow sail in the transport of agricultural produce to the mainland as well. This was perishable produce, and where speed was at a premium steamers had a great advantage over sailing vessels. Thus, although in February 1874 the Guernsey Chamber of Commerce suggested that the export of agricultural and horticultural produce was increasing annually, that it had reached vast proportions, and was proving to be of great profit not just to the Island but also to the shipping interest,[119] it is not clear how far the owners of Guernsey's sailing tonnage were ever likely to benefit from this expansion. Even in 1840, non-Island vessels dominated this trade. Jamieson's analysis of the *London Customs Bills of Entry* shows that, in that year, 157,765 bushels of Guernsey potatoes and 14,905 tons of Jersey potatoes were transported from the Channel Islands to London in 215 shipments. Of these, just over two-thirds (144) were carried by non-Island vessels: Guernsey vessels took only 31 shipments; Jersey vessels, 40.[120] The participation of Island-vessels in this trade in later decades is unlikely to have increased much. The *Bills* for the years 1868, 1883 and 1887 show that produce exported to the port of Southampton during these years, for example, was also carried largely in non-Island steamers, principally those registered at Southampton itself.[121]

The records of discussions held by the Chambers of Commerce of both Islands confirm that steamers were greatly involved in this export trade. In Guernsey, as early as 1869, the Chamber's Annual Report indicated that steamers carried at least some of the Island's agricultural produce to market, and that speed of delivery was what made this form of transport particularly attractive: 'The export of other Island produce, such as vegetables, etc., has been large during the last six weeks by steamers to England, which ... has been effected in an incredibly short space of time.'[122] Agricultural and horticultural exports could not halt the decline of shipping in Jersey either, for much of the trade in potatoes appears also to have been carried in steamers: in December 1882, the Chamber of Commerce discussed the need to facilitate the arrival of steamers taking on cargo, most especially during the potato season, and particularly in view of the expansion of the 'potato traffic'.[123]

Figures showing the number and tonnage of steam and sailing vessels entering and leaving Guernsey's ports during four years in the 1890s suggest that steamers were becoming more and more prominent in trade. In 1893, 1,277 steamers totalling 237,918 tons entered Guernsey, compared with 877 sailing vessels totalling 93,109 tons; in 1894, 1,836 steamers arrived, amounting to 329,354 tons, compared with 702 sailing vessels amounting to 61,308 tons. These were vessels inwards with cargoes. As for outward vessels with cargoes, the figures show that in 1896, 1,884 steamers, representing 365,169 tons, left the Island, compared with 712 sailing vessels representing 75,046 tons of shipping; in 1897, 2,071 steamers, totalling 413,061 tons left, compared with 634 sailing ships, totalling 73,180 tons.[124]

These figures notwithstanding, it should be remembered that the decline of shipping was not felt as early or as dramatically in Guernsey as it was in Jersey. While it is certainly true that Guernsey's merchant fleet eventually met the same end as that of Jersey—by 1900 little remained of either—the smaller Island was not entirely dependent on agricultural and horticultural exports to keep its shipping in operation. As the following section will show, Guernsey's fleet survived for longer than that of its neighbour because, as locally-registered vessels were increasingly forced out of the international carrying trade, many shipowners were able to redeploy at least some of their vessels to the granite trade, where steam had as yet made little impact.

-IV-

Guernsey's shipping interest had a significant advantage over its counterpart in Jersey in the years after 1870. Over the previous half century, the smaller Island had developed one important activity—granite quarrying—that could be of great assistance to Island shipping. In this sector, the *volume* of exports was very large, peaking at almost 300,000 tons in 1897, the product was not perishable, and speed was less crucial. The granite trade consequently served to *postpone* for Island shipowners the worst effects of competition from steamships in the carrying trade. Of the two islands, only Guernsey had any success in developing a substantial export trade in granite, but there is evidence that at least in some quarters in Jersey there was considerable interest in following

Guernsey's lead. In March 1884, for instance, the Jersey Chamber of Commerce reported that it 'sees with satisfaction the extension of the Jersey Railway to La Moie and trusts that the stone trade, which it is intended to develop, will be fully successful as it would be of inestimable value to the island'.[125] The following year, the Chamber again stressed the benefits which the Island would derive from a stone export trade, but regretted that no specific measures had been taken to make the quality of Jersey stone—which compared favourably with stone from other sources—better known elsewhere.[126] Despite the efforts of some supporters of granite quarrying in Jersey, who clearly did see the potential benefits which the export of this product could bring to the Island, perhaps because they understood that it could ease the difficulties faced by shipowners and builders, in 1887, J. Le Maistre informed the members of the Jersey Chamber of Commerce that although Jersey's stone trade had made some progress during the previous year—the quality of their stone being 'quite equal to that of Guernsey'—'it hardly received the attention, and Encouragement it deserved'.[127] Le Maistre's comments on this issue are very interesting in view of the frequent contributions he made to the meetings of the Chamber, discussed in the previous section, lamenting the lack of facilities for ship repairing in the Island, and the indifference of the States to the plight of shipowners and shipbuilding workers. His comments suggest that he, and perhaps others in the Island, were keeping a close eye on developments in Guernsey, jealously watching the success of shipowners in obtaining the support of the States for the building of facilities for ship repairing, and of the stone merchants in expanding granite exports. Le Maistre obviously believed that Jersey could, with some support and encouragement, emulate the success of the stone merchants in Guernsey.

This does not mean, however, that Jersey did not develop a quarrying industry. In Mont Mado, in the parish of St John, pink syenite, said to be 'of great beauty', was quarried, and while it was not exported in great quantities, it was in demand in St Helier and other parts of the Island. Other quarries were also apparently worked near Mont Mado, and it was said that good granite was obtained from La Moye, in the parish of St Brelade.[128] Jersey stone was obviously in demand for domestic use. Stone exports, however, were insignificant compared with Guernsey's. Figures on Jersey's exports published in the *British Press and Jersey Times Almanac* of 1880 show that, in 1879, exports of stone from this Island reached only 1,414 tons, compared with 238,345 tons exported from Guernsey during the same year. The *Almanac* of 1885 published figures for 1883, showing total exports of 1,367 tons, compared with 259,816 tons from Guernsey. In the following year, only 315 tons of granite were exported from Jersey. And the *London Customs Bills of Entry* of 1887, a year for which all stone shipments leaving both islands for all ports included in the *Bills* have been analysed, show a total of 645 tons imported from Jersey into these ports, compared with 202,151 tons imported from Guernsey. Jersey also exported gravel, but volumes of this product, too, were small, amounting to 2,304 tons in 1879 and 3,359 tons in 1884.[129] At least some of those shipowners in Jersey who recognised that there were freights to be had in the transport of stone reacted by transferring their vessels over to Guernsey, plied the stone route to London, and operated entirely out of that Island instead.

In Guernsey, on the other hand, the granite trade received considerable encouragement—much more than it was ever given in Jersey—and this was no doubt at least partly owing to the fact that the stone traders of this Island were a vociferous group: their willingness to press their claims and have their importance recognised is clearly reflected in the minutes of meetings held by the Chamber of Commerce. They had good reason to expect some recognition and encouragement: of all the developments which emerged in the Island economy during the later decades of the 19th century, only stone exports, combined with the coal trade from Newcastle,[130] proved capable of assisting shipping to any great extent. In terms of value, it was reported in February 1883 that the sale and freight of Guernsey granite during the previous year, 1882, had amounted to some £150,000.[131] We have few figures to indicate the annual value of agricultural and horticultural exports from the Island, except for the years 1887 and 1888. In the first year, 1887, the total value of exports (including potatoes, fruits, and flowers) amounted to £100,550; in 1888, £146,950.[132] The values of both agricultural produce and granite exported from Guernsey were, therefore, comparable, at least during the years for which figures are available. They are far lower, however, than the value of Jersey's potato trade alone: export values in 1887 reached £434,917, falling back to £242,110 in 1888, and rising again to £462,895 in 1894.[133] But the importance of granite lay not only in the income derived by the Island from its sale, but also in that it provided occupation to a significant proportion of sailing vessels which would otherwise not have found employment. As Robin Craig observed, in referring to the study of maritime trades in general, 'the movement of raw materials is of particular importance because of their heavy demand for shipping'.[134] In Guernsey, the *volume* of exports in 1877 alone reached 256,050 tons, and 268,282 in 1896, although this trade was not entirely serviced by ships registered in Guernsey.

Guernsey granite, we have seen, began to be used for the paving of roads in London as an alternative to Aberdeen granite.[135]

Export volumes were small during the early decades of the 19th century. The *Almanac* of Guernsey of 1830 listed granite among the Island's exports in 1829: 13,547 tons for the construction of roads and a further 11,656 tons of paving stones.[136] Granite exports were probably also of little importance to Island shipping at this stage. As we saw in the final section of Part I, in 1840, according to Alan Jamieson, 39,502 tons of stone were transported from Guernsey to London in 264 shipments: of these, the vast majority—215, or 81%— were carried in non-Island vessels; only 44 (17%) were transported by Guernsey-registered vessels.[137]

By the late 1840s, however, the trade had begun to expand at a staggering rate—more than fifty quarries had been opened by the 1890s.[138] But in spite of the fact that granite quarrying was growing at a phenomenal speed, it was not until the mid-1860s that the importance of the industry to the Island in general, and to Island shipowners in particular, began to be recognised. Interestingly, after the mid-1860s, we begin to detect a marked change in the attitudes of the members of the Chamber of Commerce towards the trade and towards those involved in it. From 1863, total exports of stone from St Sampson's, the main area of quarrying, as well as from St Peter Port, were reported at almost every Annual General Meeting, suggesting a growing interest among the members in the fortunes of the quarries. But at the same time, fears were voiced about the effects the trade was having on the Island. Henry Tupper, President of the Chamber in the mid-1860s, reflected at the 1865 AGM that while the stone trade had materially benefited the owners of the quarries and others involved in stone exports, it was 'a positive disadvantage to the island generally'. The trade cost the States some £500 per year for the repair of roads 'ground to mud under the heavy traffic', and led to the 'permanent disfigurement of the island by the removal of its hillocks, converted into holes half filled with rubbish'. Furthermore, the trade resulted in widespread pauperism: 'the thousands of children born in the island, from the stone-cracking population, is a serious evil to the island generally'. Indeed, Henry Tupper added,

> People must not imagine that the stone trade is an unmitigated advantage, a boon conferred by St Sampson's on the island, that the island is to make sacrifices to foster. I wish the trade every prosperity, as such, and will do nothing to check it, but its evil consequences are equally apparent and much to be deplored.[139]

These remarks were made in the context of, and may therefore have been provoked by, a dispute with the quarry owners of St Sampson's over the amalgamation of the harbour dues of St Sampson's and St Peter Port, a plan to which those involved in the stone trade were opposed on the grounds that their harbour dues should not be used to finance improvements in the town harbour. But Tupper's attack on the granite trade may also, perhaps, have reflected the different backgrounds of those involved in the stone trade or the lower regard in which the trade itself was held in the Island. This is an impression which is difficult to substantiate, but in the mid-1850s, Ferdinand Brock Tupper, in his *History of Guernsey*, referred to the vessels engaged in the coal and stone trade as being 'of inferior value, many being old, and none coppered'.[140] The large number of poor immigrant labourers arriving in the Island to work in the quarries may also have been a source of concern for Islanders. In 1870, when the Chamber of Commerce reported a decrease in stone exports compared with previous years (exports had increased quite significantly in 1866 and 1867, and then fallen back again), it also reflected that this fall was to be regretted, 'the more so as ... this trade had drawn to the island a considerable number of work people who swelled the amount of the prevailing distress'.[141] As far as the Chamber was concerned, the situation was aggravated by the fact that, in 1869, much of the stone exported 'has been exported in 'spauls' as it came from the quarry, in order to secure employment to the London poor'. The stone, the Chamber claimed, was to be broken by the poor of London, thus depriving Guernsey 'of one means of our local industry'.[142] The analysis presented in Part III of this collection of studies shows the growth of the population of the parish of St Sampson, one of the main areas of quarrying[143] and the centre of the stone business,[144] and confirms that the quarries were drawing large numbers of people. The population of this parish grew, between 1841 and 1891, at a faster rate than any other in the Island—from 1,567 to 4,493.[145]

Despite such reservations, held by some influential men in the Island, it had been recognised by the mid-1860s that the stone trade was contributing in no small way to the Island's shipbuilding businesses. In 1866, just a year after Henry Tupper's outburst, the Committee of the Chamber of Commerce reported that it wished to note, with reference to another annual increase in the size of the Island's merchant fleet, the remarkable change which had taken place in the size and quality of Guernsey's coasting vessels, employed mainly in the coal and stone trades: these were now 'fine, large, well-built, well found, burthensome, and still fast-sailing vessels, a credit to their owners and to the island …'. Coasting vessels in the stone and coal trades were 'well employed', the Committee added, while a further development of the trade was to be expected.[146]

As Table 15[147] shows, further expansion did indeed occur (because, it was said, Guernsey granite was superior to other types for roadmaking)[148] just as the Island's participation in the international carrying trade began to decline. The importance of stone to the Island could now hardly fail to be noticed. By October 1879, when the Chamber held a special meeting to discuss the possible construction of a tramway to the quarries of St Sampson, the President observed that the issue 'deeply concerned the interests of the whole island … with its prosperity all prospered, and with its decline all must more or less suffer loss. The trade all experience showed had materially enriched the island, and its exportation had brought much money back … the stone trade was the staple commodity.'[149]

However, as we have already observed, the importance of the granite trade lay not only in the money brought back to the Island from its sale, but also from the harbour dues paid on vessels docking at Guernsey, and from the knock-on effect it had on other sectors of the economy, such as the business it gave to the local traders who supplied the ships. In addition, it was crucially important to the employment of many sailing vessels which had previously been fully engaged in the foreign trade, but which, by 1880, would have been laid up, transferred to other ports, or sold, had it not been for the possibility of redeployment to this growing domestic trade. As John Hamley, a vociferous defender of the trade, one of the largest quarry proprietors in the Island, and owner of several vessels employed in shipping granite to London, informed the members of the Chamber in 1880, whereas other trades in which the Island's shipping had previously found employment had declined, the reverse had occurred in the stone trade. As well as utilizing some of Guernsey's shipping tonnage, the stone trade had an impact on other Island trades and therefore on employment, too. Hamley claimed that he

| Year | St Sampson | St Peter Port | Total Exports |
|------|-----------|---------------|---------------|
| 1863 | 134,675 | 14,199 | 148,874 |
| 1864 | 134,406 | 15,670 | 150,076 |
| 1866 | 160,408 | 41,091 | 201,499 |
| 1867 | 186,876 | 49,255 | 236,131 |
| 1868 | 155,068 | 13,810 | 168,878 |
| 1869 | 161,316 | 25,249 | 186,565 |
| 1871 | 169,176 | 14,907 | 184,083 |
| 1872 | 152,677 | 17,348 | 170,025 |
| 1874 | 169,169 | --- | --- |
| 1875 | 173,055 | 14,176 | 187,231 |
| 1876 | --- | --- | 210,000 |
| 1877 | 230,688 | 25,362 | 256,050 |
| 1878 | 215,917 | 22,851 | 238,768 |
| 1879 | 217,535 | 20,810 | 238,345 |
| 1880 | 202,957 | 18,000 | 220,957 |
| 1881 | 180,472 | 18,056 | 198,528 |
| 1882 | 191,831 | 15,104 | 206,935 |
| 1883 | 244,275 | 15,541 | 259,816 |
| 1884 | 210,005 | 15,757 | 225,762 |
| 1885 | 197,045 | 17,782 | 214,827 |
| 1886 | 231,085 | 16,801 | 247,886 |
| 1887 | 217,725 | 15,727 | 233,452 |
| 1888 | 226,227 | 15,882 | 242,109 |
| 1889 | 229,525 | 14,994 | 244,519 |
| 1890 | 239,330 | 16,899 | 256,229 |
| 1891 | 212,057 | 10,952 | 223,009 |
| 1893 | 234,747 | 6,038 | 240,785 |
| 1894 | 257,046 | 6,538 | 263,584 |
| 1895 | --- | --- | 263,584 |
| 1896 | --- | --- | 268,282 |
| 1897 | --- | --- | 291,636 |

**Table 15: Stone Exports from Guernsey, 1863-1888 (tons)**

alone employed 105 sailors on his vessels. The sailors had to be fed and the vessels had to be fitted out and kept in order: many trades benefited as a result. Furthermore, he argued that wooden ships would not be pushed out of the stone trade—sailing ships remained competitive in some bulk trades until the mid-1880s[150] and in others until after the 1890s—but that the size of the fleet should actually grow as the trade revived. This last point was somewhat over-optimistic by 1880, but Hamley was clearly seeking recognition for the contribution the stone trade had made to the Island. 'The present merchants', he said, 'raised the stone trade to its large proportions.' Thousands of men employed in the trade were paid regularly every week, whereas in the past the numbers employed were small, and those who did find employment were often not paid for months at a time. The Island, Hamley insisted, 'must be greatly benefited by this trade, and everything should be done to encourage it'.[151]

By 1883, it was estimated that between two and three thousand people were employed in the stone trade.[152] This figure no doubt included quarrymen and crackers, the latter apparently employed by the shippers rather than the owners of the quarries, according to one Mr Stranger, referred to as a quarry proprietor— and probably the same Philip Stranger who owned several vessels employed in shipping granite.[153] In 1879, he informed the Chamber of Commerce that stone cracking was not carried out at the quarries, since these were not large enough for stone to be broken there. The crackers, he added, 'were different from the quarrymen, and each shipper had his yards properly arranged, where the stone was received, and where the crackers worked'. Another group was that of the men whose job was to prepare dressed stone, such as pitchers and kerb stones.[154] In addition, among the estimated two to three thousand people directly employed in the stone export trade were, of course, the sailors who shipped it out of the Island. Although precise numbers of sailors engaged in the trade are difficult to estimate, the *London Customs Bills of Entry* of 1868 show an average of 505 men employed on Guernsey-registered vessels plying the stone route to the mainland over the course of that year—a figure arrived at by adding the average number of men employed on each vessel.[155] These numbers were clearly sustained until the early 1880s: the *Customs Bills of Entry* of 1883 show an average of 508 seamen employed on Guernsey vessels in the granite trade during that year.[156]

Because the Channel Islands were outside the British Customs area, all arrivals of vessels from the Channel Islands to selected mainland ports—London, Liverpool, Bristol, Hull and Southampton—were recorded in the *London Customs Bills*. The fact that by far the largest proportion of stone exported from Guernsey was shipped directly to London means that, through the *Bills*, it is possible to examine the trade closely, and in particular the extent to which Guernsey vessels participated in it. The *Bills*, combined with the *Mercantile Navy List*, also enable us to consider the ownership of Guernsey vessels engaged in the trade (and to measure the participation of vessels owned by Guernseymen but registered at other ports). Do the Bills provide sufficient evidence to support the proposition advanced here that the stone trade became more important to Island shipowners during those years when the participation of Guernsey vessels in the foreign trades declined? Did the proportion of shipping tonnage employed in granite exports increase between the late 1860s and, say, the early 1880s? Were there any changes in the ownership of vessels engaged in the trade? And does the changing attitude of the Chamber of Commerce, so apparent in its records, reflect a growing participation of Island shipowners in it? To answer these questions we shall now turn to an analysis of all stone shipments arriving in the ports included in the *London Customs*

| Port of Registry | Vess | Shp. | Port of Registry | Vess | Shp. |
|---|---|---|---|---|---|
| Aberystwyth | 1 | 1 | Lynn | 2 | 2 |
| Arundel | 1 | 1 | Middlesbro' | 1 | 1 |
| Beaumaris | 1 | 1 | Padstow | 1 | 1 |
| Bideford | 1 | 1 | Plymouth | 2 | 2 |
| Boston | 5 | 5 | Poole | 3 | 3 |
| Bridport | 3 | 5 | Portsmouth | 5 | 5 |
| Colchester | 2 | 2 | Rochester | 2 | 2 |
| Cowes | 3 | 3 | Rye | 5 | 14 |
| Dartmouth | 2 | 3 | Southampton | 1 | 1 |
| Dundee | 1 | 1 | St.Andrews, N.B | 1 | 1 |
| Exeter | 13 | 26 | St.Ives | 1 | 1 |
| Falmouth | 2 | 2 | Stockton | 1 | 1 |
| Faversham | 29 | 45 | Sunderland | 3 | 3 |
| Fowey | 2 | 2 | Teignmouth | 5 | 6 |
| Goole | 29 | 32 | W.Hartlepool | 1 | 3 |
| Guernsey | 69 | 302 | Wells | 1 | 2 |
| Hull | 1 | 1 | Weymouth | 15 | 29 |
| Ipswich | 1 | 1 | Whitby | 1 | 1 |
| Jersey | 21 | 68 | Wisbech | 1 | 1 |
| Liverpool | 2 | 15 | Woodbridge | 1 | 1 |
| London | 11 | 14 | Yarmouth | 1 | 2 |
| Lowestoft | 1 | 1 | | | |
| Lyme | 1 | 1 | *Total* | 256 | 615 |

**Table 16: Port of Registry of Vessels Employed in Guernsey's Stone Trade with London, 1868**

*Bills of Entry* over the course of two sample years—1868 and 1883—and of the port of registration and ownership details of the vessels involved. An important point should be made at the outset, however. The paragraphs that follow focus specifically on assessing the importance of the stone trade to the survival of Island shipping. A distinction has to be made, therefore, between the trade itself, which all the evidence indicates prospered throughout the century, and the fortunes of the shipowners. As the Chamber of Commerce acknowledged in 1892, the prosperity of the former did not necessarily translate into prosperity for the latter: whereas the stone trade 'was in a healthy condition; the shipping unfortunately was not so …'.[157] Nevertheless, the evidence suggests that shipowners were becoming increasingly dependent on the trade until the late-1880s;[158] thereafter, they began to face growing competition from steamers, at which point, the interests of the stone merchants and the shipowners clearly diverged.

According to the figures published by the Guernsey Chamber of Commerce, 168,878 tons of stone were exported from the Island in 1868.[159] The *London*

*Bills* for that year show that 157,718 tons (93.39% of the total) were shipped directly to the ports of Southampton and London.[160] Only seven shipments, totalling 695 tons, went to Southampton. The remaining 615 shipments, a total of 157,023 tons (92.98% of all stone exports) were destined for the port of London. The transport of this product, exported in vast quantities from the Island, attracted shipping from ports across the country. As Table 16 shows, as many as 256 vessels from 44 ports were involved in transporting stone between Guernsey and London in 1868. But the table also shows that this was a trade largely dominated by Guernsey's own shipping tonnage, and, to a lesser but not insignificant extent, Jersey's. While many ships from many different ports appear in the table, few can be said to have found regular employment in the trade, since in most cases, their role was limited to the shipment of one or two cargoes over the course of the entire year, which may simply reflect the fact that ship-owners in many ports along the coast of Britain, aware that there were freights to be had in Guernsey, redeployed their ships to the Island when other freights were not available, or else carried cargoes to the Island and carried outward freights of stone. From Beaumaris and Padstow, for example, came the 131-ton *Glan Ogwen* and the 90-ton *Camilla*, both of which made single voyages from Guernsey to London, carrying shipments of 128 tons and 140 tons respectively. Five vessels came from Boston and another five from Portsmouth, but all these were registered to different owners, and all made no more than one voyage each in the trade. The only ports that figure prominently in the table, apart from Guernsey and Jersey, are Exeter, Faversham, Goole and Weymouth: vessels from these ports took 132 of the total 615 cargoes shipped to London in 1868. In some of these cases, the transport of granite may have been combined with their own traditional trades. Vessels from Faversham (Whitstable) and Goole, for example, were probably carrying cargoes of coal to Guernsey and returning, via London, with shipments of stone. Weymouth vessels, for their part, may have had some connection with the trade in Portland stone, another building material in demand in London.[161] However, most of the vessels registered at these four ports made one or at most two voyages in the trade in 1868—the only exceptions are the *Artaxerxes* and the *Wild Wave* from Exeter; the *Impetuous* from Faversham; and the *Belinda*, the *John Mowlem* and the *Louisa* from Weymouth. This did not amount to serious competition for Guernsey shipowners: despite the apparent widespread participation of vessels from many British ports as distant as Dundee and Fowey, therefore, the stone trade between the Island and London was essentially a trade dominated by Guernsey shipowners, except for the relatively important share that went to owners of vessels registered at Jersey, at least in 1868. Thus, 69 Guernsey-registered vessels transported to London in 1868 a combined total of 88,915 tons of stone (56.63% of total exports) in 302 separate shipments, and of these 54 made more than two voyages during the year. In addition, 21 Jersey-registered vessels transported a total of 19,729 tons (12.56% of exports) in 68 separate shipments. In 1868, the stone trade with London employed 90 Channel Island vessels, and they transported granite shipments amounting to just under 70 per cent of the total taken to London in that year.

But what of the ownership of the Guernsey vessels? How widespread among Island shipowners or shipowning firms was participation in this trade? And to what extent did the Island's most prominent shipowners—Le Lacheur, Dorey, Marquand, among others—participate in it? The evidence indicates that, by the late 1860s, a comparatively large proportion of Guernsey's shipping tonnage did take part, to a greater or lesser extent, in this important domestic trade. Almost half of all vessels over 50 tons which were included in the Shipping List published in *Barbet's Almanac* of 1870 are shown in the *London Customs Bills of Entry* to have transported shipments of granite in 1868—the trade gave employment to 62 out of a total 128 ships (48.4% of the Island's entire fleet). This represented a marked change compared with 1845. Of the 96 vessels over 50 tons listed in the *Almanac* of that year, only 29 (30.2%) had been employed in transporting granite to the mainland.[162]

The owners of vessels engaged in the granite trade in 1868 were not, however, a homogeneous group.[163] There were some—among whom we may count John Hamley, John Guilbert and Julia Williams[164]—who dedicated their entire fleets to the transport of stone. But small-scale owners could and did participate in the trade, too: William Newberry and P.O.Falla, for instance, both of whom were owners of single ships regularly employed on the stone route to London. As for Guernsey's principal shipowners, most assigned one or two vessels to the stone trade in 1868, including Lelean & Co., Thomas Domaille & Co., Peter Le Page & Co., J.Sebire, and Dorey & Co. For Peter Le Page & Co. this may be said to have been a crucial component of business: three out of five vessels registered to Le Page were regularly employed in granite in 1868. The others, at least in 1868, had fewer vessels plying the stone route: one of five registered to Thomas Domaille & Co., and one of four registered to Dorey & Co., and in this case, only one voyage was made. Although we cannot establish from the data for one year whether these were merely the first steps taken by the major shipowners in granite, this is certainly possible: by 1883, for example, all Dorey & Co. tonnage was fully employed in the trade. Very few of the Island's principal shipowners are absent from the list of those whose vessels were employed in shipping granite in 1868—G.F.Carrington & Co., John Marquand & Co., and William Le Lacheur & Co. In Le Lacheur's case, of course, his absence may be explained by the composition of his fleet. All Le Lacheur ships were large, ranging from 327 to 652 tons, whereas vessels normally associated with the granite trade were normally smaller, ranging from 47 to 277 tons in 1868.

Over the next 15 years, the granite trade continued to grow, but although Guernsey shipowners continued to be the main beneficiaries of it, troubling signs were beginning to emerge, as steam began to compete in this trade as well. The threat to Island shipowners was real indeed, not least because by the early 1880s it was generally acknowledged in Guernsey that many shipowners and others were now largely dependent on the stone trade for their livelihoods. As G.F.Carrington, shipowner and President of the Chamber of Commerce, was reported to have commented at the Annual General Meeting of February 1882, regarding the state of the stone trade:

The shipowners were particularly anxious that this prosperity might continue, and that nothing might occur to mar it in the future. Much depended upon it, for thousands were engaged in carrying it on. Owners of vessels and their crews, quarrymen, carters, crackers, workmen and labourers with their wives and numerous families were all deeply interested in it, and any material decline in the demand was felt all around.

The stone trade was crucial to the Island, Carrington concluded, for were it not for this trade, the Island's shipping fleet would be worthless. Without stone for the ships to transport, most would be laid up, as these were now largely unfit for the foreign trade.[165] But to what extent were Guernsey shipowners taking part in the shipment of granite to the mainland by the early 1880s? Had their involvement increased in the intervening 15 years? And what was the nature of the threat they faced from the steamers?

According to figures collected by the Guernsey Chamber of Commerce, 259,816 tons of stone were exported from the Island in 1883, compared with 168,878 tons in 1868. Through the *London Customs Bills of Entry*, we can identify the destination of some 757 shipments totalling 222,696 tons, or 85.71% of the total. Twenty cargoes—a total of 2,578 tons—were shipped to Southampton, but London continued to be the main destination: in 1883, 274 vessels transported 737 shipments amounting to 219,938 tons (84.65% of total exports). As Table 17[166] shows, vessels from 57 ports across the country—including the Channel Islands—were involved in the trade in 1883. Despite the fact that the table appears to show a growing participation of vessels from ports outside the Channel Islands in 1883, there had in fact been few changes in the nature of the granite trade over the previous 15 years. In 1883, just as in 1868, the granite trade from Guernsey attracted one or two ships from many different parts of the country, but most of these were undertaking single voyages: this did not amount to regular employment, nor did it constitute a serious threat to Island shipowners.

Indeed, the only ports which figure prominently by 1883, apart from the Channel Islands, were Faversham, Goole and London, and it was only the Faversham and London-registered vessels that were taking a significant share of the trade. In the case of Faversham and Goole-registered vessels, the transport of granite from the Island by this time is even more likely to have been combined with the transport of coal, since coal imports in Guernsey were increasing as the building of greenhouses in the Island expanded.[167] This combining of stone and coal worked for Guernsey vessels, too. In the mid-1890s Ansted described how 'sailing ships are employed in conveying the stone, and these ships, when unloaded, proceed to Newcastle for coals, thus making a round trip'.[168]

The threat to Guernsey shipowners did not come from these vessels, but from those registered at London, for it is here that we begin to see an important change emerging in the trade. While the 41 Faversham-registered vessels which appear in the table shipped 83 cargoes of stone totalling 27,125 tons (12.3% of all exports to London), 27 London-registered vessels carried between them 106 shipments of stone totalling 26,176 tons (11.9% of total exports). While the figures do not

| Port of Registry | Vess | Shp. | Port of Registry | Vess | Shp. |
|---|---|---|---|---|---|
| Aberysthwyth | 1 | 1 | Kirkwall | 1 | 2 |
| Ardrossan | 1 | 1 | Leith | 3 | 4 |
| Bideford | 1 | 1 | Littlehampton | 4 | 5 |
| Bo'ness | 1 | 2 | Liverpool | 1 | 1 |
| Boston | 2 | 8 | London | 27 | 106 |
| Bridport | 1 | 2 | Lynn | 1 | 1 |
| Bristol | 2 | 3 | Maryport | 1 | 1 |
| Brixham | 3 | 7 | Middlesbro' | 7 | 10 |
| Caernarvon | 3 | 3 | Montrose | 1 | 5 |
| Cardiff | 1 | 1 | North Shields | 1 | 5 |
| Chester | 1 | 1 | Newport | 2 | 7 |
| Colchester | 2 | 4 | Padstow | 2 | 2 |
| Cowes | 2 | 5 | Plymouth | 1 | 1 |
| Dartmouth | 2 | 9 | Poole | 1 | 1 |
| Dover | 2 | 2 | Portsmouth | 1 | 1 |
| Dublin | 1 | 1 | Rochester | 1 | 1 |
| Exeter | 4 | 7 | Runcorn | 4 | 4 |
| Faversham | 41 | 83 | Rye | 1 | 1 |
| Fowey | 4 | 4 | Shoreham | 1 | 1 |
| Glasgow | 2 | 2 | Stockton | 3 | 5 |
| Goole | 20 | 33 | Sunderland | 3 | 5 |
| Grangemouth | 1 | 4 | Teignmouth | 4 | 6 |
| Grimsby | 1 | 1 | W.Hartlepool | 2 | 3 |
| Guernsey | 67 | 323 | Weymouth | 3 | 7 |
| Harwich | 2 | 5 | Whitby | 1 | 1 |
| Hull | 3 | 6 | Whitehaven | 1 | 1 |
| Inverness | 1 | 1 | Wick | 1 | 1 |
| Ipswich | 1 | 1 | Yarmouth | 2 | 4 |
| Jersey | 20 | 24 | *Total* | *274* | *737* |

**Table 17: Port of Registry of Vessels Employed in Guernsey's Stone Trade with London, 1883**

appear to be dissimilar, there was a significant difference: two London–registered vessels alone—the steamers *Staperayder* and *Stannington*—made between them a total of 58 voyages in the trade over the course of 1883, carrying general merchandise and over 11,000 tons of stone.[169] As we shall see in the next few pages, when we return to the increasing role of steamships in the export of granite, these steamers had the capacity to make fast and regular voyages to and from the Islands, and it was this trend that gave Guernsey shipowners, especially those with large fleets entirely dedicated to servicing it, real cause for alarm. This was despite the fact that the *Stannington* was owned by C.M.Farquharson of Guernsey, and the *Staperayder* by M.C.Cheesewright of London, who had extensive Channel Island connections.[170]

However, in spite of the concerns to which the steamers were giving rise, in 1883, Guernsey-registered vessels continued to take the lion's share of the trade. Sixty-seven vessels transported 323 shipments of stone to London   115,005 tons of the total 219,938 imported into London in that year (52.3%). The proportion of the trade taken by Guernsey shipowners had fallen compared with 1868 (52.3% compared with 56.63%), as had the number of vessels involved (67 instead of 69), but the volume of stone shipped had increased substantially—115,005 tons, compared with 88,915 tons. Thus, the volume of exports had increased, and Guernsey ships had benefited. In addition, by the early 1880s, there had been some important changes in terms of the ownership of vessels registered in the Island, including those employed in the granite trade. Perhaps the principal change was that most prominent Guernsey shipowners by 1883 had transferred at least some of their tonnage to this trade, including some, like Dorey & Co., who had not been much involved in granite in 1868: only one of four Dorey vessels in 1870 made any voyages in the trade in 1868, and only one voyage at that. By 1883, all four Dorey vessels were fully employed in granite, making a total of 26 voyages. Another interesting case is that of G.F. Carrington, owner of twelve ships in 1870, none of which appeared among the granite vessels in 1868. By 1885, Carrington retained only four ships, and of these, two plied the Guernsey-London route. By this time, Carrington was serving as President of the Chamber of Commerce: the interest in and support for the stone trade which he repeatedly demonstrated during the years he discharged this role was clearly rooted in a personal understanding of the importance of granite to Island shipowners. It must be emphasised, however, that its importance was not limited to the large owners. Many small vessels were also entirely dependent for employment on the transport of granite: owners such as Charles Le Page, whose 39-ton cutter *Courier* made as many as 9 voyages between Guernsey and London in 1883.

However, the granite trade did not, or perhaps could not, prevent the break-up of the sailing fleets of all prominent Guernsey shipowners. According to *Barbet's Almanack* of 1870, six vessels were registered to Lelean & Co. at the end of the previous year, of which three we know to have been employed in the trade in 1868. *Guerin's Almanack* of 1885 shows Lelean & Co.'s fleet to have dwindled to just two vessels, both of which were employed in shipping granite in 1883. Of the major shipowners of 1870, only John Marquand & Co. appears to have found continued employment for his vessels in other trades, though this fleet was also somewhat reduced by 1885: of seven vessels registered to Marquand in 1870, only four remained. William Le Lacheur & Co.'s fleet had dwindled even more dramatically: of the six vessels registered to him in 1870, only one, the 652-ton *Barranca*, remained on the register by 1885—this one, of course, was not employed in granite.

Shipowners who had recognised the importance of granite to the future of wooden sailing ships in the early days of expansion, specialised in it, and built up a fleet of vessels intended specifically for the purpose of servicing it, appear, on the other hand, to have prospered considerably. John Hamley, quarry proprietor and shipowner, is the best example. In 1870, he owned four vessels—a combined total of 572 tons. By 1883, Hamley's fleet had grown to 11 vessels, totalling 2,344 tons—more than four times the tonnage registered to him 15 years earlier—although some of these appear to have been owned jointly with a London-based importer of granite, Frederick Manuelle. Despite the decline in the fortunes of sailing ships in most trades, John Hamley had prospered.

One other important change had occurred in the 15 years between 1868 and 1883. Perhaps because of the existence of the granite trade, a substantial proportion of the Island's shipping tonnage was now registered to owners who were not Guernsey residents—over 3,000 tons by 1885. Among these were Thomas Minter, of Whitstable, owner of the *Impetuous*; Charles Kellit, of Goole, owner of the *Whisper*; William Coward of Knottingley, owner and master of the *Edward*; Julia McMahon and Edwain McMahon, both of Newport, Monmouthshire, owners respectively of the *Julia* and the *Trio*; and Edwin Whitley, also of Newport, owner of the *Lilian*. Many Jersey shipowners also transferred their vessels to Guernsey. In 1883, George Allix and Richard Allix had five vessels registered here—the *Argo*, the *Clacknacuddin*, the *Robinsons*, the *Satellite*, and the *Spring*. Others included Francis Picot's *Happy Return*; Robert Youlton's *Lavinia*; John Winter Nicolle's *Ocean Bride*; William F.Stoke's *Alice Jane*; and Philip Gavey's *Firm*.[171] This trend continued into the next decade. In 1894, when even the granite trade could no longer be depended on to provide employment to Island vessels, it was reported that of 9,880 tons registered locally, more than half was owned elsewhere.[172]

Yet in spite of such widespread participation of sailing vessels owned by non-Islanders in Guernsey's domestic trade, the fears of shipowners were not at any time directed at these. While those vessels which were registered here but owned elsewhere obviously must have competed with Guernsey-owned vessels for freights, at least they were repaired and fitted out in the Island and provisioned by local traders. It was, instead, the steamers that gave owners such as John Hamley cause for alarm, because of the speed with which they could complete each voyage, the share of the trade they could take as a result, and principally because of the favour in which they were said to be held by the stone merchants. Indeed, Hamley anticipated the consequences of the increasing participation of steamers before they became serious competitors. Thus, when it was reported at the Chamber of Commerce's AGM of 1883 that during the previous year several steamships had arrived in the Island to carry away stone, apparently because there had not been enough sailing ships available, John Hamley offered a word of warning. He focused on one important difference between the steamships and Guernsey's own sailing ships—that of the extent to which the latter provided employment to local people. When one of his vessels sailed from the Island it had on board provisions to the value of between £30 and £40. Furthermore, his ships gave employment to carpenters and sailmakers. The steamers, on the other hand, sailed in and out in a day, brought no ballast, and were not provisioned locally—their crews bought nothing except, sometimes, 'a red herring and a loaf of bread'.[173]

As we have seen, it was certainly true that a small number of steamers had become involved in the stone trade by 1883, and that, though few in number, they had the capacity to carry off a quite large share of the trade. In 1883, 20 steamers participated in the transport of stone to London, carrying between them shipments totalling 20,269 tons (9.2% of the total). But it is very probable that Hamley's concern was directed specifically at the two London-registered steamers discussed above—the *Staperayder* and the *Stannington*. In 1868, only the 146-ton *Staperayder* was involved in the trade, making a total of 14 voyages over the course of the year, and taking shipments totalling 1,182 tons. By 1883, the *Stannington* and the *Staperayder* had together made as many as 54 voyages (28 and 26 respectively), carrying shipments totalling 11,082 tons (just over 5% of the total). The *London Customs Bills of Entry* show that sailing vessels, even when fully employed, could complete a maximum of six to eight voyages over the course of a whole year. Clearly, as one Mersey shipowner had observed in the mid-1880s, admittedly in a quite different context, 'steam tonnage will do probably three or three and a half times the work that sailing tonnage will do'.[174]

Losses began to be made by Guernsey shipowners soon afterwards, and these were attributed largely, if not entirely at this stage, to competition from the steamers. 1884 was a bad year for the shipowners, if not for the stone merchants. Insurance rates had been high, due to heavy losses, freights had been low, and the problem had been aggravated by the fact that the steamers were carrying away a significant proportion of the trade. At the Chamber's AGM of 1885, John Hamley intervened once again to express his fears about the threat posed by competition from steamers in the stone trade, as well as to demand, in recognition of the important role that the granite trade had played in the Island over the previous decades, that the States offer some relief to shipowners, at least in the form of reduced harbour dues. *The Star* reported Hamley's intervention in the meeting in considerable detail:

> These steamers did a great injury to the trade of the Island, for, as a rule, they only left about 30 shillings on a voyage here, and paid no Wharfage dues, whereas sailing ships, especially those belonging to the island, left about £40 for Harbour dues, provisions, repairs, insurance, and general outfit. The former also contributed a mere trifle to the dues; while the sailing vessels belonging to the island had to pay Harbour Dues on everything imported for their requirements, surely then they were entitled to the greatest consideration at the present time when freights were so low. No class were suffering more than the shipowners, and as they contributed so largely to the Harbour Revenues, they ought to be assisted by reduction of the Dues. When they considered that 40 years ago the only stone exported was spalls taken to Rochester, to be there cracked and sent to London, they would see how the trade had increased and as it brought in so much to the States it was the duty of that body to encourage it in every possible way, and relieve it from all unnecessary burthens ... Freights were so low that they had need to save every possible expense ... the shipping interest deserved much more help from the States to put it on a better footing.[175]

The Chairman of the Chamber of Commerce, G.F.Carrington, who claimed to have 38 years of experience in the shipping trade, echoed Hamley's concerns, and made two important points. Carrington's first point was one that Hamley, too, had often made—that is, that the steamers brought little benefit to other traders, given that they were not provisioned locally. This was to be regretted, taking 'into consideration the large amount of money brought into circulation, and the number of families who derive a benefit, directly or indirectly, from the success of our shipping trade'. His second point was that the steamers were actually operating at a loss, offering rates that were ruinously low—ruinous to their owners—so that all there was left to do was to 'wish them to find other and better employment, and allow us to continue our trade unmolested'.[176]

Carrington's point about the ruinously low freight rates offered by the steamers was an important one in the mid-1880s. As P.L.Cottrell explains in his study of steamships on the Mersey, freight rates were notoriously volatile, and when they moved down—as between 1874 and 1879—they caused the value of steamers to fall and favoured sailing ships whose operating costs were lower, to the extent that some shipowners who had purchased steamers during the early 1870s had these converted to sail. When freight rates rose at the end of the decade, the advantage swung back to steam, and many new orders were placed. When freight rates fell again in the mid-1880s—according to the Guernsey Chamber of Commerce by 1885 freight rates had fallen by 50%[177]—steamship owners again bore the brunt because of their higher operating costs, and many were laid up.[178] Clearly, it was because of the need to keep the steamers in operation that these were offering lower and lower rates, and this worked to the advantage of the stone merchants. In 1886, Carrington succinctly summed up the situation which Guernsey shipowners now faced:

> My opinion is, looking at the tonnage of the United Kingdom, that the cause arises to a great extent from the over building of steamers of large tonnage, driving the smaller boats out of their different trades, by running at such low rates of freight, in fact, accepting anything that can be had, in order to keep these large and expensive steamers moving. In most cases these steamers work at a great loss to the owners, leaving them not only without a dividend, but a heavy loss from depreciation in value ... the steamers referred to have driven most of us quite out of the Foreign Trade; the smaller class of steamers sharing the same fate, and in turn driving the coasting steamers out of their regular work, compelling the latter to fall back in many cases on our already depressed stone trade. Although these vessels do very little good to the Island, seeing that they do not provision here, or leave scarcely a shilling among the tradesmen, they are by some of the stone shippers treated with much greater consideration than our own ships in their dispatch of loading and unloading.[179]

By 1886, there was a growing recognition among Guernsey shipowners that the days of the sailing ship were numbered. The Annual Report presented by the Committee of the Chamber of Commerce indicated that a further decline 'in the employment of our sailing tonnage' had occurred, and that the final demise of this once important sector of the Island economy was to be expected. Steam would finally supplant sail: 'the consummation of this is only a question of time'.[180] Analysis of the *London Customs Bills of Entry* for the year 1887 shows that the number of steamers finding employment in the stone trade was increasing very rapidly—36 in 1887, compared with only 20 three years earlier—and so, too, was the volume of granite which they carried away—40,345 tons in 1887 (about one-fifth of the total), compared with 20,269 in 1883. Yet for all the warnings repeatedly given by the Chamber of Commerce, the steamers were not yet pushing Guernsey vessels out of this trade. Sixty-three Guernsey-registered ships carried 278 shipments totalling 100,258 tons of stone to London in 1887—this amounted to nearly half (49.6%) of all granite cargoes shipped to that port during the year. The share of the trade taken by Guernsey-registered vessels had fallen by less than 3%, and the number of ships finding employment in this trade had fallen by only four in the intervening three years—from 67 to 63. If the steamers were taking an ever-growing share of the stone trade, they were doing so mainly at the expense of sailing vessels from other ports. Furthermore, the Bills also show that, with the exception of the London-registered *Staperayder* and *Stannington*, the steamers were not conducting a larger number of voyages over the course of the year than sailing ships. Indeed, the vast majority—26 out of 36—were only casually employed in this trade, conducting one or at most two voyages.[181]

The final demise of Guernsey's shipping fleet did not occur, therefore, before the end of the 1880s. Although by this time the Island's sailing tonnage had diminished somewhat compared with the mid-1870s, and while some of the tonnage registered here was by now owned elsewhere, Guernsey's merchant fleet had survived, though admittedly perhaps not exactly prospered, for two decades longer than that of Jersey. That this was largely, or even, it could be argued, entirely, owing to the granite trade cannot be in doubt: it was not until falling freight rates in the mid-1880s forced steamship owners to seek out whatever trades were available so as to keep their vessels in operation that Guernsey's sailing ships began to lose their competitiveness in this bulk trade.[182] As the President of the Chamber of Commerce regretfully conceded in 1888,

> We all know the source of revenue that granite has proved to the island. It has employed our ships, and in various ways has been the means of giving employment to hundreds of men and boys, and adding to the prosperity of the island... we cannot close our eyes to the fact, that it is only a question of a few years, when sailing ships will be a thing of the past, and the class of trained seamen, of which our little island could boast of having, no longer to be found.[183]

# Part 3

# POPULATION, EMPLOYMENT AND MARITIME TRADE: JERSEY AND GUERNSEY, 1821–1881

## -I-

The participation of the Channel Islands in the international carrying trade peaked in the mid-1860s. Yet by the end of the decade, as the impact of the depression in world trade began to be felt across the country, the Islands' involvement in long-distance maritime activities entered a period of decline from which neither would recover. The effects of the depression were exacerbated by the fact that the years after 1870 coincided with a period of great technological change in British shipping—the transition from wooden sailing ships to iron-built steamships—which, while making Britain as a whole unrivalled as a shipbuilding nation, eventually brought in its wake the demise of the Channel Islands' shipping fleets and the collapse of once thriving shipbuilding industries. As Part II showed, however, the transformations taking place in British shipping did not affect both Islands and all trades at exactly the same time. In Jersey, the impact of the collapse of the carrying and cod trades, combined with the effects of the bank crash of 1873, were immediate and severe, and were compounded by the decline of local shipbuilding, and then by a second bank crash in 1886. In Guernsey, by contrast, the worst effects of the crisis in trade and shipping were ameliorated, in the short to medium term at least, by the development over the course of the 19th century of an important granite quarrying industry, based in the parishes of St Sampson and Vale. Stone quarrying in Guernsey reached vast proportions by the latter decades of the century, and the fact that this product had to be transported to export markets on the mainland—principally London—provided local shipowners, mariners, and those involved in the upkeep of the Islands' sailing tonnage, though not the builders of new ships, with some protection from the consequences of decline in other maritime trades.

Both Islands, however, proved remarkably resilient in overcoming the difficulties faced in their respective economies from the late 1860s onwards. As their shipping became less and less able to compete in many traditional trades, and as local shipbuilders saw orders for new tonnage plummet, great efforts were made to develop other economic activities, especially those in which the Islands held a competitive edge. Both Jersey and Guernsey, for example, demonstrated a renewed interest in agriculture: as potatoes, vegetables and fruits of various kinds ripened earlier in the Channel Islands, they commanded a good price on the mainland, and brought high profits to their growers. The Islands exploited their mild climate in other ways as well: by investing in improving the appearance of their principal towns, as well as in providing better facilities for tourists, they sought to compete with the most fashionable holiday resorts of England and the continent. Any discussion of the transformations taking place in the local economies during these years should, however, be based on an understanding of the impact of these extremely important shifts on the Island populations, and it is therefore to the consequences of economic change on population and employment in the Channel Islands during the 19th century that the remainder of this study now turns.

## -II-
## DEMOGRAPHIC PATTERNS:
## JERSEY AND THE BAILIWICK OF GUERNSEY, 1821-1881

Population trends in the Channel Islands during the 19th century followed closely the fortunes of their shipping and maritime trade. Jersey, where the expansion of trade as well as registered sailing tonnage and local shipbuilding had been particularly impressive during the half century after 1815, experienced very high rates of growth, at least until mid-century. Between 1821 and 1851, the Island's population virtually doubled, from 28,600 to 57,020.[1] In Guernsey, where trading activities were less ambitious and more limited in scope, and where the expansion of registered shipping tonnage and local shipbuilding, while impressive, never reached the scale of its neighbour's, the population grew by less than 50% over the same period—from an estimated 20,227 in 1821, to 29,732 in 1851.[2] In the Bailiwick as a whole, as Table 18 shows, the population increased by just over 60% during these decades, from 20,827 to 33,719.[3]

Immigration played an important part in both Islands' population growth during these years. John Kelleher's correlation of natural growth rates and total population change shows that in Jersey, 61% of the increase between 1821 and

| | Jersey | | Guernsey & Adjacent Islands | | Guernsey | |
|---|---|---|---|---|---|---|
| Year | Total | % Change | Total | % Change | Total | % Change |
| 1800 | | | | | 18,500 | |
| 1806 | 22,855 | | | | | |
| 1821 | 28,600 | 25.1 | 20,827 | | **20,227 | 9.8 |
| 1831 | 36,582 | 27.9 | 26,128 | 25.5 | 24,349 | **19.8 |
| 1841 | 47,544 | 30.0 | 28,521 | 9.2 | 26,750 | 9.9 |
| 1851 | 57,020 | 19.9 | 33,719 | 18.2 | 29,732 | 11.2 |
| 1861 | 55,613 | -2.5 | 35,365 | 4.9 | 29,804 | 0.2 |
| 1871 | 56,627 | 1.8 | 33,969 | -3.9 | 30,593 | 2.6 |
| 1881 | 52,445 | -7.4 | 35,257 | 3.8 | 32,379 | 5.8 |
| 1891 | 50,372 | -4.0 | 37,677 | 6.9 | 35,218 | 8.8 |

**Table 18: Population Growth, Jersey, Guernsey and Adjacent Islands, 1800-1891**[4]

1851 can be accounted for by immigration:[5] by the mid-19th century, immigrants constituted almost one-third of the Island's total population (32.8%, or 18,701 of 57,020). Fewer immigrants travelled to Guernsey and the smaller Islands, and here they comprised a smaller proportion of the population: by 1851 immigrants constituted 28.3% (9,556 of 33,719) of the total population of the Bailiwick (there are no figures showing the composition of the population of Guernsey alone). Most immigrants to all of the Channel Islands were of English and Irish origin. By the middle of the 19th century, 11,095 English and 2,766 Irish immigrants resided in Jersey, and these two groups together made up nearly one-quarter of the total population. In Guernsey and the smaller Islands, although the total number of English and Irish residents was smaller—6,959 and 1,219, respectively— in percentage terms the figures were almost identical, the two groups accounting for 24.26% of the total.[6]

From the mid-19th century onwards, however, and especially after the late 1860s, population statistics began to show distinctly different trends. The impact of the diminishing participation of Channel Island vessels in international trade, and of the subsequent fall both in demand for new tonnage and shipbuilding output, was serious for both Islands, but it appears to have been particularly damaging in Jersey, where thousands were forced to emigrate, in a complete reversal of earlier patterns. Misgivings were expressed in Guernsey, of course, especially when, towards the end of the 1860s, with no apparent signs of recovery in trade, doubts began to be voiced about the future prospects of the shipbuilding industry. Thus, when in 1869 the President of the Chamber of Commerce, Abraham Bishop, called on the States to support the development of ship repairing facilities in the Island, he insisted that this was 'a most important consideration at the present time ... when so many of the working class, and especially of the

| Place of Birth | Jersey | | Guernsey & Adjacent Islands | |
|---|---|---|---|---|
| | Total | % | Total | % |
| Total | 57,020 | 100 | 33,719 | 100 |
| Jersey | 38,319 | 67.2 | - | - |
| Guernsey & Adjacent Islands | 1,080 | 1.9 | 24,163 | 71.7 |
| England | 11,095 | 19.5 | 6,959 | 20.6 |
| Wales | 106 | 0.2 | 38 | 0.1 |
| Scotland | 567 | 1.0 | 217 | 0.6 |
| Ireland | 2,766 | 4.9 | 1,219 | 3.6 |
| Isle of Man | 4 | - | - | - |
| British Colonies/East Indies | 611 | 1.1 | 267 | 0.8 |
| Foreign Parts/British Subjects | 108 | 0.2 | 39 | 0.1 |
| Foreign Parts/Foreign Subjects | 2,329 | 4.1 | 809 | 2.4 |
| At Sea | 35 | 0.1 | 8 | - |

Table 19: Population—by Place of Birth, 1851[7]

shipwrights, were wanting employment … '.[8] It was also at precisely this time—1870—that the Chamber recorded its concern that the stone exported to London in 1869 had been broken there rather than in Guernsey, depriving the Island 'of one means of our local industry'.[9] At a time when increasing unemployment among shipbuilding workers seemed a distinct probability, unemployment among unskilled stone breakers in the quarries was a prospect to be avoided.

In Jersey, however, where the population had doubled between 1821 and 1851, the threat of mass unemployment seems to have been especially alarming. As we have seen, shipwrights and other artisans, seafarers, and especially unskilled labourers, all felt the impact of the depression in trade and its consequences.[10] In fact, the high rates of population growth which had characterised Jersey in the period 1821 to 1851 had already begun to be reversed in the decade to 1861—the population falling from 57,020 to 55,613—though at this time there were no indications of the crises which were yet to strike the Island economy.[11] Some of the decline between 1851 and 1861 may instead be attributed to the emigration of Islanders to Canada, the United States, and, following the discovery of gold in 1851, to Australia.[12] Jersey was not of course alone in losing some of its population to these regions: Ferdinand Brock Tupper reported many emigrants leaving Guernsey for New York in the early 1840s; and, according to Alan Jamieson, most Channel Island emigrants to Australia in the late 1840s came from Guernsey.[13] In Jersey, moreover, some of the decline during this decade may be accounted for by the emigration of a number of shipbuilding workers and their families to England, as a result of a recruitment campaign conducted by London shipbuilders producing warships for the Crimean War. Since vastly higher wages were offered in London—between 7s. and 10s. a day in 1856, compared with the 3s. 3d. secured in Jersey, and this only after an Island-wide strike in 1853—there was no shortage of recruits.[14] The decade 1861 to 1871 witnessed another slight increase in the total population, from 55,613 to 56,627—but this rise the *British Press and Jersey Times Almanac* attributed to the arrival of French families seeking refuge during the Franco-Prussian conflict of 1870, who contributed to boosting the census figures of the following year. But they were only temporary residents.[15]

It was during the following decade, however, when a succession of crises struck the Island, that Jersey was to suffer the largest population decline of the century, the total falling by over 7%, from 56,627 to 52,445. The two decades to 1901 witnessed further falls, of 2,073 between 1881 and 1891, and 1,942 between 1891 and 1901. Indeed, in the three decades between 1851 and 1881 alone, as many as 14,000 people left the Island—the most serious loss clearly occurring during those first years of crisis between 1871 and 1881. Most emigrants, Kelleher found, were artisans and their families who had originally been migrants to Jersey, and who were now forced to leave the Island in search of work elsewhere. Some local artisans did, however, also emigrate.[16] Figures on the distribution of population by parish show that all but two of the Island's parishes—St Saviour and St Lawrence—experienced population decline between 1851 and 1881, and in some cases losses were substantial: the population of St Martin fell by 32% between these dates, that of Trinity by 23%, St John's by 19%, and St Clement's by 15%.[17]

The minutes of meetings held by the Jersey Chamber of Commerce indicate that among the emigrants were many who had been made unemployed by the collapse of the shipbuilding trades. In December 1883, when the Chamber discussed the possibility of developing ship repairing facilities within the Island, it warned that 'this work should be pushed forward without delay as a great number of our shipwrights and other skilled workmen employed on the repair of vessels have left, and are still leaving.'[18] By the early 1890s it was reported that few remained in Jersey. In 1892, J. Le Maistre spoke at the Annual General Meeting of 'the absence of shipwright artisans in the Island', the result, he argued, of the fact that no support had ever been obtained for the construction of ship repairing facilities in Jersey.

Guernsey did not experience rates of population growth as high as those of Jersey between 1821 and 1851. But equally, while emigration had been taking place here as well since the early 1800s,[19] the Island did not suffer an exodus of the magnitude of that of its neighbour in the years after mid-century. Indeed, despite the fears of widespread unemployment expressed by Abraham Bishop in the late 1860s, Guernsey experienced a steady rate of population growth to 1881. Between 1851 and 1881, as the population of Jersey was falling, that of Guernsey actually increased by almost 10%—from 29,732 to 32,379. Over the following decade, total population figures show a further increase of nearly 9%—to 35,218. This does not mean, however, that all the Island's parishes experienced population growth throughout this period. Some parishes—St Peter Port, St Andrew, Castel, St Saviour and Forest—contained smaller populations in 1881 than they did in 1851, although in none of these parishes did losses compare with those of St Martin or Trinity in Jersey.[20] In the two granite quarrying parishes of St Sampson and Vale, however, the population increased markedly and consistently throughout these decades: between 1851 and 1891 the population of Vale grew by 87%, from 2,110 to 3,947; the population of St Sampson more than doubled, from 2,006 to 4,493.[21]

The records of discussions held by the Jersey Chamber of Commerce suggest that some artisans leaving that Island—especially those who had previously been employed in the shipyards—were actually taking up residence in Guernsey. Thus, at a General Meeting of December 1883, J. Le Maistre warned that many of Jersey's shipwrights were leaving for Guernsey and other places, 'where constant employment was found owing to the existence of Patent Slips ...'.[22] As we have seen, however, Le Maistre was particularly interested in the construction of ship repairing facilities in Jersey—he repeatedly brought up the subject at the Chamber's meetings—and it is quite possible that his warnings regarding the emigration of shipbuilding workers to the smaller Island were aimed at persuading the States of the absolute necessity of providing the patent slips which had so often been requested by the shipowners and shipbuilders and which had been built in Guernsey. Some shipbuilding workers had been leaving Jersey for Guernsey: when the 1881 census was taken, one Jersey-born shipsmith and two Jersey shipwrights were among the population enumerated in St Sampson's District No.2,[23] for instance, this being one of the two parishes where

| Place of Birth | Jersey | | Guernsey & Adj.Islands | |
|---|---|---|---|---|
| | Total | % | Total | % |
| Total | 52,445 | 100 | 35,257 | 100 |
| Jersey | 37,479 | 71.5 | 958 | 2.7 |
| Guernsey & Adjacent Islands | 875 | 1.7 | 27,665 | 78.5 |
| England | 7,039 | 13.4 | 4,445 | 12.6 |
| Wales | 48 | 0.1 | 74 | 0.2 |
| Scotland | 296 | 0.6 | 158 | 0.4 |
| Ireland | 1,263 | 2.4 | 528 | 1.5 |
| Isle of Man | 11 | - | - | |
| British Colonies/East Indies | 831 | 1.6 | 384 | 1.1 |
| Foreign Parts/British Subjects | 396 | 0.8 | 196 | 0.6 |
| Other (Foreign Subjects) | 4,175 | 8.0 | 840 | 2.4 |
| At Sea | 32 | 0.1 | 9 | - |

**Table 20: Population—by Place of Birth, 1881**[24]

a patent slip had been built. But the census figures do not provide confirmation of large-scale emigration from one Island to the other: as Table 20 shows, in 1881 the Jersey-born population in Guernsey totalled only 958. If there had been some movement from the larger to the smaller Island between 1851 and 1881, the numbers involved were small.

In fact, the high rates of immigration which had characterised the years of expansion had slowed down in both Islands: the proportion of immigrants in the population as a whole actually fell more sharply in the Bailiwick of Guernsey, perhaps due in part to the departure of almost 2,200 people from Alderney, following completion of the harbour building project, between the censuses of 1861 and 1871.[25] Whereas in 1851 immigrants comprised 32.8% of the total population of Jersey and 28.3% of that of Guernsey and the smaller Islands, by 1881 the figures had fallen to 28.5% (14,966 of 52,445) and 21.5% (7,592 of 35,257), respectively. Even more marked was the decline in the proportions of English and Irish residents within the Island communities. Whereas at mid-century the English and Irish-born comprised nearly one-quarter of the population of both Islands, by 1881 immigrants from these sources constituted less than 15% of the total—14.6% in Jersey (8,302 of 52,445) and 14.7% in Guernsey (4,973 of the total 35,257 recorded in the census report).[26] In Jersey, however, where, as explained in Part II, important changes were taking place in the economy, which shifted the balance away from maritime towards agricultural pursuits, French immigration began to increase just as the number of new arrivals from England and Ireland was falling. The number of French immigrants, most of whom Kelleher found to have been labourers seeking to become tenant farmers, more than doubled between 1851 and 1881, from 2,100 (3.7% of the total population), to 4,300 (8.2%).[27] By 1891, there were more than 5,000 French-born residents on the Island, raising concerns among many Jersey farmers that they were in danger of being overwhelmed by migrants.[28] Such shifts in the composition of the immigrant population were not taking place in the Bailiwick of Guernsey: the 729 people classified as French-born in the 1881 census comprised only 2.07% of the total population of the Island.[29] If French emigrants came to the Channel Islands seeking to farm, then they may well have favoured Jersey over Guernsey—in the early 1880s, in St Sampson at least, French immigrants, much like their English and Irish counterparts, were far more likely to become labourers in the quarries, or the shipyards or docks connected with the stone trade, than they were to become farmers.[30]

Demographic patterns in the two largest of the Channel Islands during the 19th century therefore differed in several important respects. Jersey's demographic history was characterised by exceptionally high rates of population growth to mid-century, but this was followed by population decline across almost all parishes, and by important shifts in the composition of the immigrant groups as agriculture regained the upper hand in the economy—French immigrants constituting a significant, and growing, proportion of the total population by 1881. In Guernsey, by contrast, population growth was less marked to mid-century but continued steadily thereafter; and while in this Island there were no major changes in the composition of the immigrant groups, figures on the distribution of the population by parish indicate that there had been considerable internal migration towards the centres of the quarrying industry in St Sampson and Vale.

Such contrasting experiences raise several crucial questions regarding the bases upon which the economies of the Channel Islands rested during this period. If it is assumed that the changes taking place in Jersey's demographic structure, especially during the decade 1871 to 1881, were a direct consequence of rising unemployment among those sectors of the working population worst affected by the reduction in the Island's international trading activities (including the cod trade), which had an immediate knock-on effect on the shipbuilding industry, why did Guernsey sustain continuing population growth until the 1890s, albeit at a lower level than in previous years, given that this Island was equally affected by the crisis in trade and shipping from the late 1860s onwards? Was Jersey's economy during those middle decades of the century more dependent on maritime activities than that of Guernsey, and therefore worse affected by the decline of its external trading connections? Or can it be argued that the growth of granite quarrying in Guernsey, an industry which required a workforce of quarrymen, crackers, carters and sailors, as well as providing an outlet for the shipping tonnage rendered redundant by the decline of the Islands' external trading links also absorbed a substantial proportion of the labour now surplus to the requirements of the shipping industry?

That shipbuilding and maritime trade were of far greater importance, and indeed profit, to Jersey than to Guernsey was certainly the impression of Ferdinand Brock Tupper, writing his *History of Guernsey* in the 1850s. In seeking to explain what at mid-century he saw as the inability or unwillingness of the smaller Island to match the success of its neighbour—using as an example the fact that at that time Guernsey had 'scarcely a vessel engaged in the carrying or freight trade of

Brazil, the River Plate and Havannah'—Tupper asserted that the origins of Jersey's preeminence lay in the years of war between 1775 and 1815. 'While the merchants of Guernsey were engaged in importing tobacco from Virginia, and spirits from various countries, for the supply of the illicit trade,' he argued, 'those of Jersey were employed in establishing fisheries in North America.' Jersey's greatest advantage, however, was its cheaper labour, for this 'extends its beneficial influence to every other commercial undertaking; and, in consequence, Jersey not only possesses her grand staple, the North American cod fishery, but the oyster fishery on the French coast, and the Honduras and African trades; and, above all, she is largely engaged in shipbuilding ...'. Conversely, Tupper continued, 'in none of these sources of employment can Guernsey be said to participate in any way ...'. Thus, while in June 1854 there were 19 vessels on the stocks in Jersey, amounting to a combined tonnage of 5,853, in Guernsey at the same time there were but four, a total of 1,050 tons.[31]

Offering a quite different interpretation of Jersey's economic development during the 19th century, Rosemary Ommer has recently argued that the undoubted success of the carrying and cod trades, both of which—and this is crucial to her argument—were *external* to Jersey, led to the neglect of other facets of the Island's domestic economy. Thus, in discussing the realization of the Jersey Chamber of Commerce in 1879 that the Island had no new source of industry to fill the gap created by the depression in trade and shipbuilding, Ommer came to the conclusion that Jersey 'was now reaping what it had sown, for the effective ocean harvest and ocean transport of the cod trade with its related shipbuilding and carrying trades implied a minimal interest in land harvest, land transportation and hinterland development ...'.[32]

The importance of the cod trade to the Island has been amply documented since the 19th century, and the analysis presented in the first part of this book confirms it. Thus, in December 1841, in a letter to the President of the Board of Trade, Philip de Quetteville, President of the Chamber of Commerce, noted the contribution which the fisheries made not just to the Island's industry, but also to employment: 'There are employed ... as seamen, fishermen and landsmen about 4000 persons. There are in this Island many families engaged in the making of worsted hose and mitts, wearing apparel, boots and shoes for the use of the fisheries.'[33] The role of the fisheries as employers of labour in Jersey had also been noted a few years earlier, in 1837. In an anonymous article published in the *Jersey and Guernsey Magazine*, the author claimed that 1,275 Jerseymen—including mariners, fishermen, and landsmen such as storekeepers and shipwrights—were employed in the fisheries around the Gulf of St Lawrence: 542 at Chaleur Bay and Gaspé Bay; 180 at Arichat; 298 in Labrador; and 255 in Newfoundland.[34] This is not an insignificant figure for an Island with a total population of under 37,000 in 1831.

The fisheries drew their workforce principally, though not exclusively, from Jersey, and as two rare crew lists, one showing a complete list of crew and passengers on a vessel beginning a voyage to Chaleur Bay in March 1845, and another on voyage to Gaspé in April of the same year indicate, migrants came

9  The Weighbridge, St Helier, Jersey, with hotels and statue of Queen Victoria, after 1883. © Société Jersiaise.

from across the Island to undertake a wide variety of tasks. The *Farrago*, a Robin-owned vessel of 163 tons, had a total 27 men on board when it left Jersey for Chaleur Bay in March. In addition to the master, John Balleine, and the mate John Giffard, 25 other passengers and crew were listed: three men described as second mates (John Le Blancq, Philip Dorey, and Edward de la Perelle), one agent (John Fauvel), one carpenter (Frank Le Marquand), one sailmaker (Peter Godel), one cook, one blacksmith, one lad, two apprentices, nine fishermen, two splitters, one net mender and two shoremen. Most of the 27 men on board came from Jersey—though four fishermen did come from Guernsey and another from Sark. The parish of origin of three of the Jersey-born men who left the Island on the *Farrago* is not specified, but of the 19 men for whom we have details, six came from St Helier, three each from St Clement and St Ouen, two from St Peter, and one each from St Mary, St Saviour, Trinity, St John and St Lawrence.[35]

The *St Anne*, a 139-ton vessel, left the Island for Gaspé in April 1845 with a total of 18 passengers and crew on board. In addition to the master George Le Marquand, the first mate Philip Dumaresq, and the second mate Thomas Fielding, the *St Anne* carried three mariners, five carpenters, one carpenter/caulker, two men described as mariner/fishermen, one fisherman/shoreman, two boys (sent out for a period of service to include two summers and one winter), and one man whose job was described as mariner/shoreman/blacksmith (also out for two summers and one winter). Apart from one Frenchman and one Englishman from Plymouth, all the remaining passengers and crew on this vessel were Jersey-born. No details were given in the crew list of the master's parish of birth, but as for the other 15 men, these, too, were drawn from across the Island: four came from St Mary, three each from St Peter and St Helier, two from St Ouen, and one each from St Clement, St Lawrence and St Brelade. All but the master and first mate of the *St Anne* were left at Gaspé, the homeward crew consisting presumably of men returning to Jersey after completing their period of service.[36]

The importance of the cod fisheries to the Island is therefore not in doubt: not only did they draw hundreds of men for seasonal work in the fisheries, but they also, as Philip de Quetteville indicated in 1840, had a direct impact on the Island economy—goods manufactured in Jersey were sold to the fisheries (clothing, boots and shoes, for example);[37] vessels built in Jersey for local owners found employment not just in the transport of this product to its markets, but also in the international carrying trade to which the need to export the fish gave shipowners an entry.[38] The extent of the trade, moreover, as Ferdinand Brock Tupper claimed in the mid-1850s, and as Ommer has recently confirmed, contributed to the phenomenal expansion of the Island's shipbuilding industry in the years after 1815.[39]

Less clear, however, are the consequences of the Island's involvement in the cod and carrying trades on local economic and demographic structures; even less clear is the extent to which Jersey differed in this respect from its neighbour. Had the expansion of these sectors led to more far-reaching transformations in Jersey than they had in Guernsey? Had there been, for instance, a greater movement of population from the parishes to the towns in the larger Island? Was it the case, as Ommer argued, that the very success of Jersey's external trade led to the neglect of other aspects of its domestic economy?

One means of gaining an understanding of the structure of the local economies during the years of expansion and decline of sectors connected with the Islands' international maritime activities lies in examining the occupational distribution of their populations, and it is therefore to a comparison of the occupational structures of Jersey and Guernsey that we shall now turn. The remaining sections of this study do not purport to provide a definitive study of labour in the Channel Islands, however; their aim is instead to offer some insight into the importance of shipping and trade in the Island communities in the mid- to late 19th century, in particular their contribution to employment, to assess the effects on employment of the shifts which had begun to take place in the Island economies by the early 1880s—the growth of agricultural exports and the development of tourism in both Islands, the expansion of granite quarrying in Guernsey—and to consider the consequences on the Islands' patterns of internal migration of the development of sectors that were central to the Islands' development in the years following 1815.

The analysis that follows is based on a wide variety of sources. All tables showing the occupational distribution of adult males in 1851 and 1881 are based on the occupational tables (the summary tables), abstracted by the census authorities from the manuscript returns of individual enumerators, and published in *Parliamentary Papers* after each of the censuses. In the absence of a full analysis of

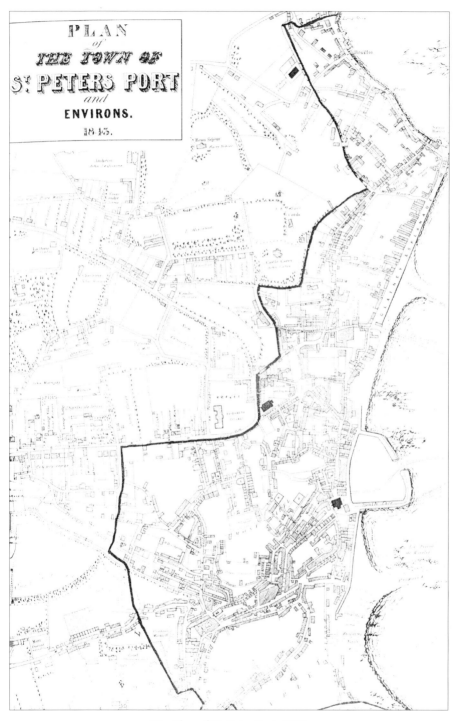

**10**   Plan of St Peter Port, 1843.

**11** Plan of St Helier, 1847.

all the enumerators' books corresponding to both Jersey and Guernsey, the published tables are the only accessible source for comparing the contribution of specific sectors to employment across the Islands as a whole from decade to decade. However, because of the inconsistencies of the data contained in the abstracted tables—the methodology applied by the authorities to classify the wide variety of occupations found in the enumerators' books were changed and refined after every census following that of 1851—it was imperative to adopt here a method of classification that could be applied consistently to the occupational tables corresponding to both Islands at each of the two censuses. The methodology adopted in this study is that first devised by Charles Booth in the 1880s, and recently refined by W.A. Armstrong.[40]

Patterns of internal migration, however, can be gauged only through the returns of individual census enumerators, and for this purpose, four districts of St Helier in Jersey (Districts 1, 2, 3 and 7) and four of St Peter Port (Districts 3, 4, 5 and 7—Canton No.1 North) have been selected from the 1851 census for detailed consideration. These will be referred to throughout this study as the St Helier sample and the St Peter Port sample. St Helier and St Peter Port were the administrative centres of the Islands, as well as the two largest towns, and it was these that experienced the highest rates of population growth to mid-century. The selected districts of St Helier comprised a total population of 3,256—representing 10.95% of the town's population of 29,741 in 1851—and encompassed some 770 households, among which were several hotels, inns and lodging houses.[41] The districts selected from St Peter Port comprised a total population of 1,850, divided into 480 households.[42] The proportion of the town's population included in this sample is almost identical to that of St Helier: it represents 10.85% of a total population of 17,047 in 1851.

The areas chosen for analysis, though small, were densely populated, and also contained higher proportions of non-local residents than the average across the Islands as whole. 39.3% of the population residing in the St Helier districts were born outside the Island, a figure which is considerably higher than in Jersey as a whole—32.8%. The proportion of non-Islanders in the St Peter Port districts was identical to that in St Helier—39.3%, compared with an average for the Island of 28.3%. Some of the streets selected for St Helier were among the most badly affected during the cholera epidemic of 1832: in his 1833 paper on the epidemic, George Symes Hooper, Secretary to the Jersey Central Board of Health, reported the existence of 'wretched hovels' in Parade Place; Cabot's Yard he described as filled with 'miserable tenements'.[43] Gregory Stevens Cox's analysis of a survey of male migrants in St Peter Port, compiled in 1830, shows that some of the streets included in the St Peter Port sample—Glategny for instance—'lay in the old quarter of the town, near the harbour, and offered cheap lodging houses, taverns and slum accommodation for labourers and poor artisans'.[44] Although such re-marks relate to the selected areas approximately twenty years before the 1851 census, it is probably safe to assume that few prosperous natives would have resided in these parts of the towns.[45] For these reasons, while on the one hand the districts chosen do seem to be especially comparable, on the other they were not entirely representative of the towns' populations, and the analysis presented here must therefore be subject to adjustment, or refinement, in the light of future research.

St Helier and St Peter Port, then, absorbed the lion's share of the population growth of the decades to 1851. The *British Press and Jersey Times Almanac* shows that, in 1851, St Helier housed some 52% of the Island's population, the other 11 parishes accounting for the remaining 48%. Between 1831 and 1851 the town's population grew by more than 85%, while the combined total of the other 11 parishes showed an increase of just over 33%.[46] While St Peter Port also housed more than half this Island's population by 1851—57.3%, compared with 42.7% in the other nine parishes—the population had grown less rapidly than that of St Helier—22.7% between 1831 and 1851, compared with 21.3% in the Island's other nine parishes.[47] In this Island, however, two other parishes—St Sampson and Vale—experienced high rates of growth in the decade 1841 to 1851, largely the result of the expansion of granite quarrying, which brought workers to these parishes and led to the development of the town of St Sampson. In the ten years between 1841 and 1851, the population of St Sampson grew by 28%, that of Vale by 24%. Thereafter, as the population of St Peter Port declined, that of the two granite quarrying parishes continued to grow steadily: between 1851 and 1891, the population of Vale increased by 87%, from 2,110 to 3,947; the population of St Sampson more than doubled, from 2,006 to 4,493.[48] Thus, in order to examine the extent to which the granite quarries were drawing migrants from the parishes of Guernsey by the early 1880s, one district of St Sampson (District No.2) has also been selected from the 1881 census for careful scrutiny. This will be referred to as the St Sampson sample.

Neither the manuscript returns, nor the occupational tables published in *Parliamentary Papers*, however, are entirely reliable sources for the study of that sector of the working population whose contribution to the success of Channel Island shipping was vital—that is, the seafarers. The seafaring population was a mobile—or 'floating'[49]—population, most often at sea, or at ports other than the home port, when the censuses were taken. According to tables published in *Parliamentary Papers*, more than 120,000 British and colonial seamen were on board ship and away from home on census night in 1851, of whom 2,747 were Channel Islanders. Of these, 1,910 were serving on vessels absent from the United Kingdom.[50] Of course, not all these men need necessarily have been Island residents, since sailors often operated out of ports other than their own; among the sailors employed on Guernsey and Jersey vessels, moreover, were many non-locals, some of whom were certainly Channel Island residents. Nevertheless, the figures illustrate the impossibility of measuring accurately, on the basis of the census statistics alone, the size of the workforce dependent on seafaring for their livelihoods in either of the Islands, not least because the figures published in the occupational tables included all sailors on board vessels in the port, regardless of their usual place of residence:[51] we know, for example, that the troops in Fort Regent and Elizabeth Castle as well as all sailors on board ship in the harbour (a total of 996) were amalgamated with the household schedules corresponding to St Helier; all sailors and fishermen at Mont Orgueil Harbour (559) were amalgamated with the figures for St Martin.[52]

For Jersey, however, there exists an excellent source for an examination of this Island's seafaring labour force in the records of the Jersey Merchant Seamen's Benefit Society, which was modelled on the old Greenwich Hospital and established in 1835 following the abolition of that fund at the end of the previous year.[53] The ledgers of the Society have not yet been exploited fully as a source for the study of Jersey's seafarers,[54] despite the fact that, because they record not just every contribution paid by sailors employed on Jersey-registered vessels but also their personal details, they are an exceptionally valuable source for analysing the composition and other characteristics of this sector of the Island's population.[55] It is for this purpose that the ledgers corresponding to the years 1850 and 1880-1 will be analysed in this study. But in addition to providing quite detailed information about the members of the crews serving on Jersey vessels, the ledgers of the Jersey Merchant Seamen's Benefit Society should serve to caution historians of communities such as those of the Channel Islands, so dependent on the sea (and in Jersey's case the cod trade) for their existence, of relying too heavily on census material which inevitably excluded such a sizeable sector of the working male population.

## -III-
## PATTERNS OF EMPLOYMENT:
## JERSEY AND THE BAILIWICK OF GUERNSEY, 1851

There can be little doubt that the great expansion of maritime trade and the growth of the Islands' shipping fleets—built mainly in the Islands and manned principally by Island-born sailors—provided a source of employment for hundreds of men: many men in varied occupations were required before a vessel could be put to sea. Shipbuilding alone required a wide variety of skills—shipwrights, ropemakers, sailmakers, mast and blockmakers, coopers, ship joiners, blacksmiths, sawyers, painters, riggers, chandlers, coppersmiths, brassworkers, plumbers and glaziers.[56] Many more men found employment in ports and harbours: pilots and boatmen, dockworkers, porters and labourers. Hundreds more were required to man vessels while at sea—masters and mates, carpenters and cooks, able seamen, ordinary seamen, apprentices and boys. Jersey's bases in the cod fisheries provided employment to hundreds more—mariners, shipwrights and carpenters, as well as fishermen. Many local merchants and traders were also dependent on the business generated by shipbuilding and maritime trade. Timber merchants, victuallers, hotel and innkeepers, lodging house keepers and publicans, among others, supplied the shipbuilders, provisioned the ships, and provided local and foreign mariners with food and lodging while on the Islands. Some may well have relied almost entirely on the trade generated by the arrival of foreign ships and catered specifically for it. On census night in 1851, for example, Berry's Boarding House, in Nelson Place, St Helier, gave lodging to 15 people, nine of whom were described as seamen. An unnamed pub in Caledonia Place, also in St Helier, listed 15 lodgers on census night, of whom nine were described as seamen, two as pilots, one as a shipbroker, and one as a rigger.[57] According to the *British Press Almanac*, there were 400 ale-houses in St Helier alone by 1855[58]—the crews of ships coming into the harbour would undoubtedly have frequented many of these. So, too, would they have frequented the taverns of St Peter Port, of which there were already over 100 by the 1780s, usually by the harbourside, providing accommodation to new arrivals.[59]

Many more men and women, of disparate backgrounds and occupations, had an interest in shipping and trade, derived from ownership of shares in Island vessels large and small. Among such men and women were those whom Sarah Palmer referred to as 'investors in shipping', people who had broad maritime or commercial interests, perhaps as merchants or shipbuilders.[60] But there were clearly many other individuals whose investments were modest and small-scale. The Ship Registers of Guernsey and Jersey show numerous such investors. While 42% of shares issued to individuals in Guernsey in 1851 were held by people designated as 'shipowners', the remainder were registered to people of varied occupations, some of whom were undoubtedly small shareholders. The majority certainly did have an obvious interest in shipping and trade, but in other cases the connections are less clear: mariners, master mariners and pilots accounted for 24% of shares; merchants, for 16%; shipbuilders and sailmakers, for 9%; others described as grocer, stonemason, plasterer, shoemaker, housekeeper, gentleman, farmer, law agent, and butcher, for a further 9%. In Jersey, shareholding in ships was even more widely spread. Only once does the description 'shipowner' appear in the 1851 registers (1%). In this Island, 42% of shares issued to individuals in that year were registered to merchants; the remainder to mariners and pilots (30%); and to numerous other individuals whose occupations were variously described as shipbuilder, shipwright, sailmaker and blockmaker (7%); coal merchant, corn merchant, trader (5%); yeoman (3%); master builder, fishmonger, mason, butcher, tailor, and druggist (6%); spinster, widow, gentleman (4%).[61] For all these people the fortunes of Island trade and shipping were of crucial importance. As the President of the Guernsey Chamber of Commerce commented in 1880, in describing with sadness the changing fortunes of that Island's maritime activities, there was a time when 'nearly everyone was more or less interested in shipping ...'.[62]

Neither the manuscript returns nor the published tables take account of those whose interest in shipping was indirect, but Table 21 below, which shows the occupational distribution of adult males by industrial sector in the Channel Islands in 1851, suggests that, as a source of *direct* employment for their adult male populations, occupations connected with merchant shipping (shipbuilding, seafaring, etc.) had become of considerably greater significance to Jersey than they had to Guernsey by the middle of the 19th century.

Several clarifications should be made at the outset, however, regarding the data contained in the table. First, the figures shown for Guernsey include not just

| Sector | Jersey | % | Guernsey | % |
|---|---|---|---|---|
| **Agriculture** | **2,629** | **17.9** | **2,294** | **25.8** |
| *of which fishing:* | *191* | *1.3* | *225* | *2.5* |
| *of which farming:* | *2,391* | *16.3* | *2,039* | *23.0* |
| **Mining/Quarrying** | **243** | **1.7** | **462** | **5.2** |
| *of which quarrying:* | *114* | *0.8* | *328* | *3.7* |
| *of which other stone/clay:* | *78* | *0.5* | *98* | *1.1* |
| **Building** | **1,755** | **12.0** | **1,241** | **14.0** |
| *of which carpenter/joiner:* | *834* | *5.7* | *452* | *5.1* |
| *of which painter/plumber/glazier:* | *149* | *1.0* | *38* | *0.8* |
| *of which mason/pavior:* | *457* | *3.1* | *386* | *4.3* |
| **Manufacturing** | **2,770** | **18.9** | **1,638** | **18.5** |
| *of which shipbuilding:* | *294* | *2.0* | *141* | *1.6* |
| *of which woodworkers:* | *145* | *1.0* | *116* | *1.3* |
| *of which furniture manufacturers:* | *209* | *1.4* | *118* | *1.3* |
| *of which shoemakers:* | *731* | *5.0* | *402* | *4.5* |
| *of which tailors:* | *264* | *1.8* | *200* | *2.2* |
| **Transport** | **1,809** | **12.3** | **531** | **6.0** |
| *of which seamen:* | *1,121* | *7.6* | *281* | *3.2* |
| *of which docks/warehouses:* | *43* | *0.3* | *42* | *0.5* |
| **Dealing** | **1,018** | **6.9** | **565** | **6.4** |
| *of which wine/spirits/hotels:* | *196* | *1.3* | *96* | *1.1* |
| *of which lodging houses:* | *21* | *0.1* | *10* | *0.1* |
| **Industrial Service** | **807** | **5.5** | **573** | **6.5** |
| *of which labourers:* | *743* | *5.1* | *551* | *6.2* |
| **Public Service/Professional** | **1,732** | **11.8** | **940** | **10.6** |
| *of which army/navy personnel:* | *1,111* | *7.6* | *562* | *6.3* |
| **Domestic Service** | **251** | **1.7** | **100** | **1.1** |
| *of which domestic servants:* | *153* | *1.0* | *42* | *0.5* |
| *of which inn servants:* | *25* | *0.2* | *14* | *0.2* |
| **Residual** | **1,643** | **11.2** | **533** | **6.0** |
| *of which property/shipowning/* | | | | |
| *independent/annuitants:* | *1,175* | *8.0* | *419* | *4.7* |
| *of no stated occupations:* | *344* | *2.3* | *82* | *0.9* |
| **Total** | **14,657** | | **8,877** | |

**Table 21: Occupations—by Industrial Sector, Males Aged Over 20, Jersey, Guernsey and Adjacent Islands, 1851**[63]

this but also adjacent Islands. Given that the harbour building project in Alderney was still in progress in 1851 we have to accept the possibility that the figures shown for the Bailiwick are slightly inflated, perhaps most especially in the Building and Industrial Services sectors: completion of the harbour and associated fortifications led to the departure of some 2,200 people from this Island between the censuses of 1861 and 1871.[64] Secondly, the table does not include all those fishermen and landsmen of various sorts who, by the time the census was taken at the end of March 1851, had already transferred out to the fisheries: as the crew lists of the *Farrago* and the *St Anne* in 1845 indicated, it was also not uncommon for migrants to be employed for periods of service exceeding one fishing season. And thirdly, the table does not take account of men who combined employments in one or more sectors, according to circumstance or season. The districts of St Helier selected from the 1851 census will suffice to show a few examples of this type:[65]

Thomas Bichard, of Seaton Place, for instance, described his occupation as ironfounder/plumber; Francis Perchard, of Parade Place, described himself as miller/plumber; William Guille, of Patriotic St., as shoemaker/miner journeyman; and George Roissier, of the Castle Inn, Esplanade, combined jobs as publican of the inn and plasterer.[66] Retired army and navy personnel, included in the Public Service & Professional sector, also frequently took jobs of various kinds to support their families: thus, among the seven Irish-born Chelsea pensioners identified in the districts selected from St Peter Port in 1851, three claimed to have some other form of employment: one was a basket maker, and two were labourers (one a stone labourer).[67] In all these cases, the clerks who compiled the abstracted tables counted only that occupation which seemed the most important, usually the first to be specified:[68] all occupations listed in second place in the returns, as well as the work of pensioners, would therefore remain unrecorded.

Nevertheless, if the occupational distribution of adult males can be utilised as one indicator of the bases upon which the Island economies rested at this one point in the mid-19th century, despite the deficiencies of the data, then the table demonstrates clearly that whilst there were marked similarities between the Islands in many of the industrial categories analysed—the Building, Manufacturing,[69] Dealing, Industrial Services,[70] and Public Service/Professional[71] sectors—there were also significant differences. Thus the table shows that manufacturing in general accounted for over 18% of all adult males in both Islands; even within the sub-categories chosen for comparison, the figures are remarkably close: the number of shoemakers in the sector, for example, was almost equally high in both Islands, although the importance of shoemaking is only clear in the case of Jersey, which, as De Quetteville and others noted, sold boots and shoes to the fisheries.[72] The table also shows, however, that in three sectors in particular—Agriculture, Quarrying and Transport—the Islands had diverged quite considerably by mid-century. In this respect, as in others which have been discussed throughout this study, the Islands did not follow absolutely parallel paths.

Table 21, then, shows that in 1851, the Mining and Quarrying sector in Guernsey (consisting mainly of men engaged in a variety of different jobs at the quarries) provided employment to 5.2% of the adult male population, compared with only 1.7% in Jersey. Jersey did have working quarries during the 19th century—pink syenite was mined in Mont Mado; good granite from La Moye, in St Brelade[73]—but not only did this industry contribute little to the Island's export trade or to its shipping, its contribution to employment was also low, and was to fall even further over the next three decades: by 1881, Mining and Quarrying absorbed only 1.3% of Jersey's adult males. In Guernsey, by contrast, the quarries were already an important source of employment by mid-century—though Henry Tupper's observations in the mid-1860s regarding the thousands of children born to the stone cracking population of St Sampson[74] was clearly somewhat exaggerated—and the industry was to become ever more significant as an employer of the male population of the Bailiwick as the century progressed. Almost 10% of all males aged over 20 were employed in some capacity in Guernsey's stone quarries by 1881.

The figures on the occupational distribution of adult males in the Channel Islands also show that, despite the expansion of maritime-related activities in Guernsey in the years after 1815, agriculture continued to be the major single source of employment for the male population in 1851, accounting for 25.8% of the total (of whom 225, or just under 10% of all men in this sector, were fishermen). In Jersey, on the other hand, a significantly lower proportion of adult males—17.9%, including 191 fishermen—were employed in occupations connected with agriculture: by 1851, fewer families in Jersey depended for their livelihoods on the land than in neighbouring Guernsey. What factors account for this divergence? Can the discrepancy be explained by reference to the Islands' inheritance laws?

Laws of inheritance and customary practices appear to have had similar aims in Guernsey and Jersey: in both Islands, the law sought to prevent excessive fragmentation. In Jersey, as Kelleher explained, the eldest son received not only the bulk of the inheritance—the house and farm buildings, and the entire unit if the land amounted to no more than 40 vergées—but he also claimed one-tenth of the rest of the property. Only what remained was divided between the younger children, the sons receiving larger shares than the daughters. It was customary, however, for younger sons to turn away from the land in order to avoid even the degree of fragmentation permitted by law and enable the eldest son to retain the family holding as a single unit; this often meant that the younger sons had to take up a trade, join the merchant navy, become clerks or labourers in the cod fisheries, or even emigrate from the Island altogether.[75]

Guernsey's inheritance laws combined the right to *préciput*, or right of primogeniture, and partible inheritance: only after the eldership was taken was the remaining real property divided, one-third among the daughters, two-thirds among the sons.[76] Yet by the 18th century, land had already become extremely sub-divided in Guernsey, and land holdings were barely large enough to support a small nuclear family, despite more intensive agricultural practices: younger siblings and children who could not be supported on these diminished farms were driven to St Peter Port either to find work or to seek alms, to the extent that in 1759, for example, the inhabitants of the town were driven to complain that the streets were 'daily crowded by the poor of the country, who do not subsist but by alms which they receive from charitable persons …'.[77] Indeed, according to Gregory Stevens Cox, it was this rural-urban shift that led to the growth of St Peter Port, which by the end of the 18th century housed over half the population of the Island.[78] Guernsey, therefore, appears to have been equally subject to factors encouraging out-migration from the countryside as Jersey.[79]

Given that the summary tables published in *Parliamentary Papers*, upon which Table 21 are based, include the population of Alderney and the smaller Islands with those of Guernsey (a problem which cannot be resolved), it is of course possible that the figures shown for the Bailiwick in that table are skewed in favour of agricultural occupations. However, Tables 22 and 23 below, which show the composition of the populations of the four districts of St Helier and four districts of St Peter Port selected for analysis from the 1851 census, tend to support the

| Place of Birth | No. | Place of Birth | No. |
|---|---|---|---|
| *Total Jersey-Born* | *1,975* | *Total non-Jersey* | *1,281* |
| *% Jersey-born* | *60.66%* | *% non-Jersey* | *39.34%* |
| of which: | | of which: | |
| St Helier | 1,424 | England | 751 |
| St Lawrence | 102 | Ireland | 267 |
| Trinity | 57 | Scotland | 17 |
| St John | 54 | Wales | 7 |
| Grouville | 50 | Guernsey | 88 |
| St Brelade | 45 | Alderney | 10 |
| St Martin | 41 | Sark | 3 |
| St Saviour | 41 | | |
| St Peter | 37 | France | 63 |
| St Ouen | 29 | | |
| St Mary | 22 | Other British Subjects | 19 |
| St Clement | 21 | Other Foreign | 51 |
| Jersey | 52 | Not Known | 5 |

**Table 22: Population of St Helier, 1851—Districts  1, 2, 3, 7**[80]

conclusion, insofar as concerns employment, that Jersey had not only become more reliant on shipping-related occupations, but that the expansion of sectors connected with maritime activities had also precipitated considerably higher levels of migration from the countryside to the town in that Island than they had in Guernsey.

Of the 3,256 people enumerated in the four districts which comprise the St Helier sample, over 39% (1,424) were born outside Jersey, a figure which is considerably higher than the average of 32.8% for the Island as a whole. In keeping with the general make-up of the town, the returns from these districts show a multiplicity of backgrounds and nationalities. Although the vast majority of non-locals in these four districts originated in England and Ireland—79.47% of all immigrants (58.63% and 20.84%, respectively)—there were also natives of Guernsey and the other Islands of the Bailiwick (7.88%), France (4.92%), Scotland and Wales (1.87%), and of a wide variety of other places including Barbados, Belgium, Ceylon, Corfu, Germany, Gibraltar, Italy, Jamaica, Malta, Newfoundland, Poland, Portugal, Quebec and Spain (a total of 5.85%). St Helier had clearly become home to a large and heterogeneous population.

The percentage of the population in the St Peter Port sample who came from outside the Island (39.3%) was identical to that in St Helier, this being a substantially higher proportion than the average of just over 28% across Guernsey as a whole. The composition of the immigrant population was generally similar to St Helier's, although the proportions did vary slightly. Most immigrants, for instance, were of English or Irish origin (81.29%), but in these districts of St Peter

| Place of Birth | No. | Place of Birth | No. |
|---|---|---|---|
| | | | |
| *Total Guernsey-born* | *1,123* | *Total non-Guernsey* | *727* |
| *% Guernsey-born* | *60.70%* | *% non-Guernsey* | *39.30%* |
| of which: | | of which: | |
| St.Peter Port | 1,021 | England | 549 |
| St.Sampson | 19 | Ireland | 42 |
| Vale | 22 | Scotland | 7 |
| Catel | 18 | Wales | 1 |
| St.Saviour | 5 | Alderney | 19 |
| Torteval | 0 | Sark | 4 |
| St.Peter | 0 | Jersey | 52 |
| Forest | 2 | Isle of Wight | 1 |
| St.Martin | 18 | France | 10 |
| St.Andrew | 2 | | |
| Not Known | 16 | Other British Subjects | 24 |
| | | Other Foreign | 18 |

**Table 23: Population of St Peter Port, 1851—Districts 3, 4, 5, 7**[81]

Port the English formed a larger proportion of the total than the Irish (75.52%, compared with 5.78%). In addition, again as in St Helier, there were here, in 1851, natives from other parts of the Bailiwick (2.61% from Alderney, 0.55% from Sark), from Jersey (7.15%), Scotland and Wales (1.10%), France (1.38%), and from various other places including Barbados, Belgium, Ceylon, Germany, Gibraltar, Italy, Java, Newfoundland and Quebec (a combined total of 5.77%). By the middle of the 19th century, therefore, St Peter Port, much like St Helier, had a large and heterogeneous immigrant population.

More significant for our purposes, however, is the local population in the samples. For these figures show that the extent of internal migration, as measured by the number of Islanders enumerated in these districts who gave parishes other than St Helier or St Peter Port as their place of birth, differed quite markedly between the Islands. Of the 1,975 Jersey-born individuals residing in the four districts which comprise the St Helier sample, more than one-quarter (499, or 25.27%) we know definitely to have consisted of migrants to the town (a further 52 gave 'Jersey' as their place of origin and are therefore included in the 'Not Known' category in the table). All the Island's parishes are represented among the population of these four districts alone by 1851. Conversely, of the 1,123 Guernsey-born individuals included in the St Peter Port sample, only 7.66% (86 individuals) consisted of migrants from the Island's other parishes, a further 16 being classified as 'Not Known'. In these four districts of St Peter Port in 1851, there were no migrants from Torteval or St Peter, and only a total of nine individuals had migrated from St Andrew, Forest and St Saviour. The figures suggest that although the expansion of maritime activities in Guernsey by the middle of the 19th century had been on a far more modest scale than they had been in Jersey, as all the indicators discussed in this and other studies show, it had not resulted in major movements of population from the rural areas to the town.

Indeed, analysis of the composition of this group—the internal migrants—also shows important differences. Of 86 migrants from Guernsey's parishes who resided, in 1851, in the districts included in the St Peter Port sample, the largest proportion (60, or 69.77%) were women;[82] only 26 (30.23%) were men. Of these, 16 were adults aged over 20: two were retired, leaving only 14 adult males in the sample. The occupational breakdown of these 14 migrants from the parishes to St Peter Port shows fairly varied activities—one florist, one gardener, two fishermen, one chicory manufacturer, one tailor, two shoemakers, one plasterer, two carpenters (one a master), one ropemaker, one shipowner and one sailor. Thus, of a total Guernsey-born population of 1,123 in the four districts analysed, only two of the adult males who had migrated from other parishes depended for their livelihoods on occupations clearly connected with the Island's maritime activities—the ship-owner and the sailor.

In Jersey, by contrast, 499 people in the sample of 3,256 (25.27%) were identified as having originated in other parishes, of whom 292 (58.2%) were women, and 207 (41.48%) were men. Of the 207 male migrants resident in St Helier in 1851, 145 (almost ten times the figure for Guernsey) were adults aged over 20. The occupational breakdown of these 145 men shows an array of occupations as varied as those in St Peter Port, but here, in St Helier, there were many more men from outlying parishes whose occupations were connected with the Island's external trade and shipping—amounting to almost one-third (47 or 32.41%) of the total. Of these, two were shipowners, and the remaining 45 worked either as mariners or in the shipbuilding trades: there were 25 sailors, two shipbuilders, 14 shipwrights, two ship-riggers, one ship carpenter, and one ship caulker.[83] It might be argued, therefore, that while the expansion of Guernsey's maritime trade and shipbuilding industry were less dramatic and less substantial than they were in Jersey, the impact of these activities on the Island community, as measured by movements of population from rural areas to the town, was correspondingly far less disruptive.

Although we should be cautious of drawing too many conclusions from figures drawn from a study which covers only a small proportion of the populations of St Helier and St Peter Port, figures on the contribution which shipping-related occupations made to adult male employment in the Channel Islands in the mid-19th century tend to support the argument advanced above. Merchant shipping, of course, does not constitute a separate industrial category in the classification scheme adopted in Table 21, since the jobs required to build, pilot, provision and man ships cut across several industrial categories. Seafarers, pilots, and boatmen, as well as dockworkers, are to be found in the transport sector; shipbuilders, shipwrights, and others engaged in the building and fitting of ships, in the manufacturing sector; shipowners are classified as people of independent means and are therefore to be found among the property owning sub-category in the

| Occupation | Jersey | Guernsey |
|---|---|---|
| Ship Agent | 11 | 6 |
| Boatmen/Bargemen | 398 | 28 |
| Shipowner | 46 | 17 |
| Seaman | 1,121 | 281 |
| Pilot | 25 | 50 |
| Others connected with sea navigation | 6 | 8 |
| Shipwright, Shipbuilder | 266 | 129 |
| Boat, barge builders | 7 | 2 |
| Others engaged in fitting ships | 21 | 10 |
| Sailcloth manufacture | 4 | - |
| Total | 1,905 | 531 |
| *Total All Occupations* | *14,657* | *8,877* |
| *Percentage Shipping-Related* | *13.0* | *6.0* |

**Table 24: Shipping-Related Occupations: Jersey and Guernsey, 1851**

sector referred to here as residual. For the purpose of comparison, therefore, Table 24 above is based on figures, drawn from the same summary tables, of men employed in occupations clearly identifiable as dependent on the Islands' shipping and maritime trade.

Table 24, then, shows numbers of adult men directly employed in the Channel Islands, in 1851, in shipping-related occupations: 1,905 in Jersey (13% of all adult males), and 531 in Guernsey (6%)—figures which include ship agents, shipbuilders, shipwrights and fitters, pilots and sailors. Several important points should be borne in mind, however, in interpreting the figures, which are presented solely for the purpose of comparison and should not be understood as reflecting accurately the size of the labour force required to build, maintain, and man the Channel Islands' shipping fleets. First, the table includes only adult males, yet all the evidence indicates that a significant proportion of the workforce employed in shipbuilding and especially in seafaring were under 20 years of age: of the 105 employed males aged between 15 and 19 identified in the four districts of St Helier analysed above, for instance, 10 were employed in the shipbuilding trades—one as a blockmaker, two as ship carpenters, three as shipwrights and four as sailmakers. Of 63 employed males in the same age group enumerated in St Peter Port's districts 3, 4, 5 and 7, three were sailors, one was a pilot, and eight were engaged in various capacities in the shipbuilding industry—two as ship carpenters, five as shipwrights, and one as a shipbuilder. Furthermore, there would have been many younger men employed at sea: lads aged between 13 and 14 were frequently taken on as apprentices and 'boys'.

Secondly, many of the jobs required to sustain a shipping industry—not just in the Channel Islands but in all other 19th-century British ports—were required

**12**   Deslandes Shipbuilding Yard, First Tower, Jersey, 1870. © Société Jersiaise.

in other industries, too. In analysing the occupational information drawn from the 1841 census, for example, Sarah Palmer found it impossible to identify and quantify precisely all the trades that contributed to British shipbuilding: as she explained, ropemakers met more than the demands of shipping.[84] The same can be said of many other trades as well, such as the carpenters and joiners who met the demands of the building sector as well as shipbuilding, or the sawyers who could well have been employed in any one or more of the many trades connected with woodworking. These observations should help explain why three Jersey shipbuilders alone, all of whom were enumerated in St Helier's District No.7 for the 1851 census—Matthew J.Valpy, Frederick C.Clarke, and George Deslandes, of Deslandes & Sons—claimed to employ a total of 443 men in their shipyards, when Table 24 shows a total of only 298 men in Jersey employed in all the shipbuilding trades.[85]

Thirdly, because the tables (which are themselves based on the manuscript returns of the census enumerators) can only take account of the population present in the Island at the time the census was taken, they are not an entirely reliable source for estimating the size of the seafaring labour force. As we have seen, sailors were frequently away from their usual place of residence at the time of the census. Sarah Palmer found that of the 184,071 seamen enumerated during the 1841 census, for example, as many as 138,156 (75%) were at sea on census night; only 45,915 were classified as seamen on shore.[86] According to tables published in *Parliamentary Papers*, on census night in 1851, 120,000 British and colonial seamen were on board ship and away from home, and of these 2,747 were Channel Islanders.[87] Indeed, the St Helier and St Peter Port samples provide ample evidence that many mariners were away from the Islands when the census was taken.[88] Of the 770 households in the districts selected from the St Helier census returns, 87 (11.3%) were headed by married women whose husbands were absent from home (though not all need necessarily have been absent from Jersey). The returns do not indicate the occupations of all absent husbands: in 42 of the 87 households no such details were provided. But of the 45 women who did specify their husbands' occupation, 26 (57.8%) claimed to be mariners' wives, of whom eight were married to master mariners.[89] Similarly, of the 480 households included in the St Peter Port sample, 58 (12.08%) were headed by women whose husbands were absent from home. Twenty-seven of the married women enumerated here gave details of their husbands' occupations: all but one were wives of mariners, five of whom were master mariners; one was married to a ship carpenter.[90]

The seafaring population, of course, included carpenters and, from time to time, even sailmakers. Ship carpenters, though rarely employed on short-distance voyages, frequently formed part of the crews of vessels engaged in the long-distance trades. Thus, 67 carpenters appear in the crew lists and agreements corresponding to voyages made by 150 Jersey-registered vessels in 1845— approximately one-quarter of these formed part of crews on ships sailing out to the fisheries; the remainder were taken on board ships sailing to destinations as distant as St Petersburg, Mauritius and the River Plate.[91] Carpenters were as likely to be taken on as members of crews on Guernsey-registered vessels: 35 were identified in the crew lists and agreements corresponding to voyages made by 81 vessels from this Island in 1845, sometimes on coasting voyages, but most usually, as in Jersey's case, in the long-distance trades.

The Channel Islands' participation in maritime activities during the 19th century, then, meant that any one time a quite sizeable proportion of both Islands' populations were away from home. In the absence of supporting evidence, however, it is impossible to estimate with any certainty how many men were at sea when the census was taken: households headed by wives of absent mariners fail to take account of unmarried mariners; the figures on the number of Channel Islanders at sea on census night fails to take account of immigrant seafarers; none of the sources show mariners who had transferred out to the fisheries.[92] The census, therefore, is a decidedly unreliable source for calculating just what proportion of the male populations of the Islands depended on seafaring for their livelihoods. For this we have to turn to other sources.

For Guernsey, we have the returns of the Registrar of Shipping, published annually in *Parliamentary Papers*, which show figures of 16,743 tons of shipping registered in the Island at the beginning of 1850 and a workforce of 1,049 men.[93] More reliable are the figures, presented by the Guernsey Chamber of Commerce at its Annual General Meeting of January 1865, showing the number of ships on the shipping register, their tonnage, and the total size of the labour force over the previous four years. The minutes of the AGM thus recorded that in 1861, 123 vessels were on the Island's register of shipping, amounting to 19,261 tons, and manned by 1,115 seamen; in 1862, the figures stood at 128 vessels, 19,679 tons, and 1,053 men; in 1863, 127 vessels, 19,831 tons, and 1,048 men; and finally, in 1864, 129 vessels, 21,187 tons, and 1,115 men. The point that was being made at the meeting was that although the Island's shipping tonnage had increased over that four-year period, the number of sailors required to man the fleet had fallen[94]—a trend that was also occurring in other parts of the country.[95] Man-ton ratios (measured as the number of men per hundred tons of shipping) had indeed fallen in Guernsey, from an average of 5.79 in 1861 to an average of 5.11 in 1864, and may of course have fallen between 1850 and 1861. But if we apply the ratios of 1861 to the tonnage registered at Guernsey in 1850—16,984 tons according to the Shipping List published in *Henry Broaurd's Almanack*—we can calculate *roughly* that a workforce of approximately 978 was required to man this Island's shipping fleet in 1850. The figure is closely in line with the returns of the Registrar of Shipping.

While useful for the purpose of comparing the size of the workforce required by both Islands to man their respective shipping fleets—the Registrar's returns showed 32,331 tons on the shipping register in Jersey and a total of 2,981 men[96]—the figures provide no further details to indicate the composition of the workforce: they do not show, for example, the ratio of Island to non-Island crews or the contribution of the various parishes to the labour force. For Jersey, however, we have the records of the Jersey Merchant Seamen's Benefit Society—an incomparable source for the study of the Island's seafaring labour force.

We know that at the end of 1849, there were registered at Jersey a total of 342 vessels with an aggregate tonnage of 32,755.[97] The 1850 ledgers show, however, that only a proportion of vessels on the register in that year returned crew lists and seamen's contributions to the Society: 72.5% of all vessels (248), corresponding to 71.2% of total registered tonnage (23,308).[98] In addition, a further twelve vessels not included in the *British Press Almanac's* Shipping List, some of which had come on to the register during that year, were also entered in the Society ledgers.[99] A total of 3,175 separate entries were made in the Society's ledgers between 1 January and 31 December 1850. After extracting from the analysis all those sailors whose names had been entered more than once (having served in two or more voyages and/or vessels over the course of the year) a total of 2,621 individuals were identified as having formed part of the crews manning some three-quarters of Jersey's sailing fleet in 1850.[100]

Of the 2,621 individual sailors who contributed to the Jersey Merchant Seamen's Benefit Society (contributions were collected from all men serving on Island-registered vessels, regardless of their place of residence), a total of 1,116 (42.58%) gave places other than Jersey as their place of birth, of whom the majority (65.5%) came from other parts of the United Kingdom and Ireland: 555 from England, 98 from Ireland, 51 from Scotland and 27 from Wales.[101] Because the ledgers record only place of birth rather than place of residence, it is not possible to estimate what

| Parish of Origin | Number | % of Total |
|---|---|---|
|  |  |  |
| St Helier | 338 | 22.46 |
| St Clement | 35 | 3.65 |
| St Peter | 118 | 7.84 |
| St John | 79 | 5.25 |
| St Mary | 55 | 3.65 |
| St Saviour | 43 | 2.86 |
| Grouville | 132 | 8.77 |
| St Ouen | 133 | 8.84 |
| St Brelade | 117 | 7.77 |
| St Martin | 150 | 9.97 |
| St Lawrence | 78 | 5.18 |
| Trinity | 87 | 5.78 |
| Not Known | 120 | 7.97 |
|  |  |  |
| **Total** | **1,505** | **100** |

**Table 25: Jersey Sailors, by Parish of Origin, 1850**

proportion of those who were not native to the Channel Islands were in fact local residents, and therefore formed part of the local labour pool. Many non-natives who served on Island vessels certainly were residents of Jersey (and may indeed have been part of the great influx of immigrants who moved to the Island during the boom years of the cod and carrying trades)—though the ledgers of 1881 are a better source than those of 1850 for showing some examples. In 1881, for instance, the crew of the vessel *Dart* included George W. Young, aged 40, of Portsmouth, and George W. Young, undoubtedly his son, aged 20, of Jersey. The crew of the *London* listed the Frenchman Frank Dinan, aged 44, and his two sons—Francis, aged 21, and Sydney, aged 14, both of Jersey. The *Robert and Hannah* included among the crew Jonas Sheppeck, aged 41, of Bridport, Charles Sheppeck, aged 21, of Newfoundland, and William Sheppeck, aged 13, of Jersey.[102]

While unreliable for estimating the number of *immigrant* men dependent on the Island's maritime activities at mid-century, the records of the Society are sufficiently detailed to enable us to examine the composition of the Jersey-born workforce. The ledgers show that a total of 1,505 Jersey-born men served on just three-quarters of the sailing fleet registered at the port in 1850. As Table 25 above shows, the largest single group of seafarers, predictably, came from St Helier, but almost 70% of the total 1,505 men identified in the ledgers came from the other Island parishes.

With such a phenomenally large seafaring population (it must be remembered that the ledgers recorded contributions made by sailors serving on only some three-quarters of the shipping registered at Jersey in 1850, that perhaps as many as several hundred immigrants also depended on seafaring for their live-lihoods, and that Jersey's trade and shipping continued to expand until the mid-1860s), the job losses which Jersey could potentially sustain following the collapse of the cod and carrying trades were enormous—and this does not of course include the job losses that would inevitably follow in the shipbuilding industry. The importance of understanding the effects on the Island's seafarers of Jersey's withdrawal from international trading activities could not be clearer. Thus, the emigration suffered by this Island in the years after 1870 was not linked just to the loss of jobs among the artisan class—though the repeated representations made by the Chamber of Commerce regarding the construction of ship repairing facilities to prevent the continuing emigration of shipbuilding workers suggest that losses were high among this class—but among its seafarers, too.

-IV-
## PATTERNS OF EMPLOYMENT:
## JERSEY AND THE BAILIWICK OF GUERNSEY, 1881

By the mid-1870s, important shifts had begun to occur in the Island economies, partly the result of the urgency with which the commercial communities in both Jersey and Guernsey sought to develop new activities to replace the central role formerly occupied by shipbuilding and the carrying trade. Guernsey, faced with the decline of the carrying trade, sought to develop local ship-repairing facilities; the granite trade, which in earlier years had given rise to criticism of the immi-grant stone-cracking population and to complaints that the stone quarries were destroying the countryside, was now recognised to be vital to the Island economy. As G.F.Carrington, President of the Chamber of Commerce, explained in 1885, it was imperative that in future Guernsey should concentrate on promoting its own exports.[103] Jersey, too, now recognised the importance of its own export trade: the potato trade was seen to be of particular significance—providing 'a vast amount of employment' at a time when other sectors were in decline.[104] But to what extent were the changes which we know to have occurred in the local economies reflected in the occupational distribution of the Island population by the early 1880s? Do the census statistics show a shift, for example, towards agricultural occupations as a result of the expansion of agricultural exports? Do the figures show a perceptible rise in occupations connected with a newer branch of industry—namely, tourism—as a result of the promotion of the Channel Islands as holiday resorts? Does the rapid and substantial growth of the population of St Sampson and Vale, in Guernsey, reflect the increasing importance of the granite quarrying industry in this Island?

Table 26, which compares the occupational distribution of adult males in Jersey in 1851 and 1881, shows that, by 1881, the Island's adult male population had fallen by almost 9%. In addition, significant shifts had taken place in the local economy. The principal readjustment which the figures demonstrate is that,

| Sector | 1851 | % | 1881 | % |
|---|---|---|---|---|
| **Agriculture** | **2,629** | **17.9** | **2,996** | **22.4** |
| *of which fishing:* | *191* | *1.3* | *138* | *1.0* |
| *of which farming:* | *2,391* | *16.3* | *2,817* | *21.1* |
| **Mining/Quarrying** | **243** | **1.7** | **168** | **1.3** |
| *of which quarrying:* | *114* | *0.8* | *122* | *0.9* |
| **Building** | **1,755** | **12.0** | **1,414** | **10.6** |
| *of which carpenter/joiner:* | *834* | *5.7* | *553* | *4.1* |
| *of which painter/plumber/glazier:* | *149* | *1.0* | *187* | *1.4* |
| **Manufacturing** | **2,770** | **18.9** | **1,925** | **14.4** |
| *of which shipbuilding:* | *294* | *2.0* | *242* | *1.8* |
| *of which woodworkers:* | *145* | *1.0* | *110* | *0.8* |
| *of which furniture manufacturers:* | *209* | *1.4* | *112* | *0.8* |
| *of which shoemakers:* | *731* | *5.0* | *\*381* | *2.8* |
| *of which tailors:* | *264* | *1.8* | *196* | *1.4* |
| **Transport** | **1,809** | **12.3** | **1,198** | **9.0** |
| *of which seamen:* | *1,121* | *7.6* | *809* | *6.0* |
| **Dealing** | **1,018** | **6.9** | **1,059** | **7.9** |
| *of which wine/spirits/hotels:* | *196* | *1.3* | *188* | *1.4* |
| *of which lodging houses:* | *21* | *0.1* | *8* | *0.05* |
| **Industrial Service** | **807** | **5.5** | **929** | **6.9** |
| *of which labourers:* | *743* | *5.1* | *726* | *5.4* |
| **Public Service/Professional** | **1,732** | **11.8** | **1,567** | **11.7** |
| *of which army/navy personnel:* | *1,111* | *7.6* | *783* | *5.9* |
| **Domestic Service** | **251** | **1.7** | **648** | **4.8** |
| *of which domestic servants:* | *153* | *1.0* | *66* | *0.5* |
| *of which inn servants:* | *25* | *0.2* | *47* | *0.3* |
| **Residual** | **1,643** | **11.2** | **1,473** | **11.0** |
| *of property/rank:* | *1,175* | *8.0* | *1,473* | *11.0* |
| **Total** | **14,657** | | **13,377** | |

\*Figures for 1881 include shoemakers and dealers.

**Table 26: Occupations—by Industrial Sector, Males Aged Over 20, Jersey, 1851, 1881**[105]

although by 1881 the number of men classified as fishermen in the census statistics had fallen, overall there had been a very large rise in the proportion of the population that was now dependent on the agricultural sector—22.4% of the total, compared with 17.9% in 1851. The rise was in fact even more marked than the figures here suggest: due to the peculiarities of the classification method applied by the census authorities to compile the summary tables, gardeners, who had in 1851 been classified as a single group and counted within the agricultural sector, had been divided by 1881 into two groups—one of which (the domestic gardeners) had been transferred to the Domestic Services sector. The increase shown in the agricultural sector in 1881, moreover, does not reflect a massive increase in the numbers of agricultural labourers or farm servants. There had been an increase in this group between 1851 and 1881—from 827 to 935—but the real increase was in the sub-category defined as farmers/graziers. This group (which includes sons, grandsons and nephews of farmers) increased by almost 36% between these dates—from 1,350 to 1,833. There was also a small increase in the number of nurserymen recorded in the statistics—from 7 in 1851 to 24 in 1881—perhaps reflecting the beginnings of the expansion of flower exports from the Island.

The growing importance to the Island of land-based occupations was at the expense of sectors which had in earlier decades been of crucial importance to the Island economy. The Building sector, and most especially the Manufacturing sector, for instance, show a quite considerable fall—in both cases no doubt reflecting in part job losses connected with the decline of the shipbuilding industry: the carpenters and joiners of the Building sector, the sawyers included among the woodworkers in the Manufacturing sector, as well as those referred to specifically as shipbuilding workers. Shoemakers also represented a much smaller proportion of the sector by 1881 than they had in 1851, and this may perhaps be attributed to Jersey's diminishing involvement in the cod fisheries.

The Transport sector, on the other hand, shows a less dramatic fall than might have been expected, given that this sector consisted largely of sailors. As we have seen, however, the census statistics are far too unreliable a source for assessing the changes taking place among this sector of the working population: the 809 seamen shown in the 1881 column of Table 26 would have included all sailors in the harbours, regardless of their usual place of residence, and excluded all local sailors absent from the Island on the night of the census. It is, again, only through the records of the Jersey Merchant Seamen's Benefit Society that we can estimate the effects of the decline of shipping on the Island's seafarers.

By the early 1880s, Jersey shipping had entered a period of irreversible decline. The number of vessels completing voyages over the course of a single year and returning crew lists and seamen's contributions to the Society had fallen dramatically: while this may have been in part the result of widespread evasion, the fact that the officers of the Society, faced with an ever-decreasing income, and increasingly unable to meet its obligations, finally took the decision to cease collecting contributions altogether, thus bringing the Benefit Society to an end, suggests that under-employment of vessels lay at the root of the problem. Over a two-year period stretching from 1 January 1880 to 31 December 1881, contributions were collected from seamen serving on 124 Jersey-registered vessels (48% of the total 258 registered at the port at the end of 1879), representing a combined tonnage of 10,295 (57% of the total 17,990 tons).[106] Only 1,700 separate entries were recorded in the Society's ledgers over those two years (equivalent to 53% of the number recorded in the single year of 1850). After extracting all names which had been entered more than once, a total of only 1,177 men remained. Analysis of this group shows, moreover, that the composition of the Island's seafaring labour force had changed in the intervening period. Whereas more than 40% of all sailors contributing to the Society in 1850 were non-natives, by 1880-1 only 20% of all mariners engaged as crews on Island-registered vessels came from outside the Island, most from other parts of the United Kingdom. Almost 80% of the total 1,177 individuals paying contributions to the Jersey Merchant Seamen's Benefit Society in 1880-1 were natives to the Island. Whether this reflects a growing preference on the part of masters to engage Islanders as crews, the decreasing number of immigrants in the Island, or perhaps the growing

| Parish of Origin | Number | % of Total |
|---|---|---|
| St Helier | 142 | 15.27 |
| St Clement | 17 | 1.83 |
| St Peter | 49 | 5.27 |
| St John | 34 | 3.66 |
| St Mary | 13 | 1.40 |
| St Saviour | 15 | 1.61 |
| Grouville | 57 | 6.13 |
| St Ouen | 86 | 9.25 |
| St Brelade | 59 | 6.34 |
| St Martin | 165 | 17.74 |
| St Lawrence | 18 | 1.93 |
| Trinity | 28 | 3.01 |
| Not Known | 247 | 26.56 |
| *Total* | *930* | *100* |

**Table 27: Jersey Sailors, by Parish of Origin, 1880-1**[107]

availability of local labour now that shipping was in decline, remains unclear, given our limited knowledge of the period. And while, as Table 27 above shows, seafaring continued to attract sailors from across the Island's parishes (quite size-able numbers from some parishes, such as St Martin) the contribution which seafaring made to the employment of the adult male population had fallen quite significantly compared with 1850.

Jersey, then, was shifting from being an economy based largely on the sea—on trade, shipbuilding, and manufactures, some for sale to the fisheries—to one based to a great extent on agriculture. Less marked, however, is the increase in the dealing sector, where we would expect to see reflected the growing importance of tourism. The most superficial examination of the occupational distribution of the female population, however, suggests that it was perhaps on the employment of women that tourism had the greatest impact. Thus, the occupational tables show that in 1851, there were 37 female innkeepers and 49 lodging house keepers in Jersey. By 1881, the figures had risen to 63 innkeepers, and 150 lodging house keepers; in addition, a new category had appeared in the statistics by this time—the washing and bathing service, which absorbed a female labour force of 708 in this Island alone.

Some of the shifts which had taken place in Jersey's economy are also evident in the occupational statistics of Guernsey and the smaller Islands, although here, unlike in Jersey, the total adult male population had increased by almost 10% between 1851 and 1881. The extent of employment provided by the Manufacturing and Building sectors, for instance, fell even more sharply in the Bailiwick than in Jersey. Some of the decline must be attributed to the collapse

| Sector | 1851 | % | 1881 | % |
|---|---|---|---|---|
| **Agriculture** | **2,294** | **25.8** | **2,138** | **22.0** |
| *of which fishing:* | *225* | *2.5* | *237* | *2.4* |
| *of which farming:* | *2,039* | *23.0* | *1,883* | *19.4* |
| **Mining/Quarrying** | **462** | **5.2** | **944** | **9.7** |
| *of which quarrying:* | *328* | *3.7* | *921* | *9.5* |
| **Building** | **1,241** | **14.0** | **1,014** | **10.4** |
| *of which carpenter/joiner:* | *452* | *5.1* | *372* | *3.8* |
| *of which plumber/painter/glazier:* | *38* | *0.4* | *73* | *0.7* |
| **Manufacturing** | **1,638** | **18.5** | **1,194** | **12.3** |
| *of which shipbuilding:* | *141* | *1.6* | *148* | *1.5* |
| *of which woodworkers:* | *116* | *1.3* | *51* | *0.5* |
| *of which furniture manufacturers:* | *118* | *1.3* | *78* | *0.8* |
| *of which shoemakers:* | *402* | *4.5* | *\*196* | *2.0* |
| *of which tailors:* | *200* | *2.2* | *127* | *1.3* |
| **Transport** | **531** | **6.0** | **803** | **8.3** |
| *of which seamen:* | *281* | *3.2* | *496* | *5.1* |
| **Dealing** | **565** | **6.4** | **567** | **5.8** |
| *of which wine/spirits/hotels:* | *96* | *1.1* | *73* | *0.7* |
| *of which lodging houses:* | *10* | *0.1* | *9* | *0.1* |
| **Industrial Service** | **573** | **6.5** | **519** | **5.3** |
| *of which labourers:* | *551* | *6.2* | *445* | *4.6* |
| **Public Service/Professional** | **940** | **10.6** | **1,331** | **13.7** |
| *of which army/navy personnel:* | *562* | *6.3* | *1,002* | *10.3* |
| **Domestic Service** | **100** | **1.1** | **415** | **4.3** |
| *of which domestic servants:* | *42* | *0.5* | *32* | *0.3* |
| *of which inn servants:* | *14* | *0.2* | *10* | *0.1* |
| **Residual** | **533** | **6.0** | **797** | **8.2** |
| *of property/rank:* | *419* | *4.7* | *797* | *8.2* |
| **Total** | **8,877** | | **9,722** | |

*Figures for 1881 include shoemakers and dealers.

**Table 28: Occupations—by Industrial Sector, Males Aged Over 20, Guernsey and Adjacent Islands, 1851, 1881.**[108]

of shipbuilding (despite the efforts of shipbuilders to redirect their efforts to ship repairing): although the shipbuilding category in the table actually shows a very slight rise between these dates, in all other trades that might have contributed to the industry—woodworkers and carpenters and joiners, for example—the figures show a decline.

Table 28 shows, however, that in this Island, there was no major shift towards agricultural activities by 1881 (the fall in numbers by this date should be attributed only to the fact that domestic gardeners had been moved to the Domestic Services sector). Nor was there here a perceptible rise in occupations connected with tourism. In this Island, however, just as in Jersey, the occupational tables suggest that it was in the employment of women that the development of this new branch of industry had the greatest effect. Thus, in 1851, there were 14 female innkeepers in Guernsey, and 69 lodging house keepers; by 1881, the census records a total of 20 innkeepers, 82 lodging house keepers, and 331 women employed in the washing and bathing service.

**13**    Granite Quarry, St Sampson, Guernsey, *c.*1880. Priaulx Library, Guernsey.

In Guernsey, however, the Mining and Quarrying sector had become of far greater importance as an employer of adult males by 1881. The proportion of the male population accounted for by this sector almost doubled—from 5.2% in 1851 to 9.7% in 1881—but the number of men accounted for by the quarries themselves almost trebled—from 328 to 921. Can it be argued, therefore, that it was the quarries in Guernsey, rather than agriculture, that absorbed the labour force that had become surplus to the requirements of manufacturing by 1881?

Analysis of the 1881 census returns corresponding to St Sampson's District No.2 indicates that there had been in Guernsey, by this time, some movement of population from the Island's other parishes to the centres of the granite quarrying industry. District No.2 comprised a total population of 1,312 in 1881—equivalent to about one-third of the total for the parish as a whole. Less than 50% of the population of the district were natives of St Sampson itself.[109]

The quarries were the single largest employers of the male population of St Sampson's. Of a total 327 men aged over 20 enumerated in District No.2, almost half (156, or 48%) were employed in occupations directly connected with the quarrying industry—carter, 20; stone labourer, 10; quarryman, 56; stone breaker, 50; stone cutter, 7; stone dresser, 9; stone trader, 1; granite merchant, 2. The importance of the quarries was, moreover, greater than these figures suggest, for they also had a knock-on effect on other sectors of the economy. In the 1870s,

| Place of Birth | No. | Place of Birth | No. |
|---|---|---|---|
|  |  |  |  |
| *Total Guernsey-born* | *948* | *Total non-Guernsey* | *364* |
| *% Guernsey-born* | *72.2* | *% non-Guernsey* | *27.7* |
| of which: |  | of which: |  |
| St Sampson | 648 | England | 214 |
| Vale | 88 | Ireland | 30 |
| St Peter Port | 152 | Scotland | 2 |
| Catel | 24 | Wales | 7 |
| St Saviour | 5 | Alderney | 10 |
| Torteval | 2 | Sark | 4 |
| St Peter | 4 | Jersey | 37 |
| Forest | 7 | Herm/Jethou | 2 |
| St Martin | 13 | France | 39 |
| St Andrew | 4 |  |  |
| Not Known | 1 | Other | 19 |

**Table 29: Population of St Sampson, 1881—District 2**[110]

the editor of Tupper's *History of Guernsey*, for example, noted the establishment, in 1876, of 'The St Sampson's Improved Dwelling-House Company Limited', set up for the purpose of building some 30 to 40 houses 'to accommodate captains of merchant vessels trading from St Sampson's', and the modernisation of the harbour, surrounded, by 1875, 'by commodious and handsome granite quays, and provided with a patent slip and various accommodations' and costing the States of Island some £20,000.[111] And, as John Hamley reminded the members of the Chamber of Commerce on several occasions, not only did the quarries directly employ a workforce of quarrymen, stone crackers and carters, but they also provided a source of employment for the sailors who manned the ships that transported the stone, and to the shipwrights and other artisans engaged in the upkeep of the tonnage employed in the trade.[112] The St Sampson sample confirms that, indeed, shipbuilding workers (shipwrights, sailmakers, etc.) and carpenters accounted for 7.3% of the adult male population enumerated in this one district; mariners and pilots, for a further 8.2%. The figures do indicate, therefore, that the development of the granite quarrying industry in Guernsey through the 19th century did serve to ameliorate the worst effects of the decline of shipping and maritime trade, not just in terms of the employment of Guernsey vessels, but also on the employment of Guernseymen.

The analysis presented in this study does not seek to offer any definitive conclusions regarding the impact of the rise and later decline of maritime-based activities in the Channel Islands during the 19th century. As explained throughout these pages, the difficulties of analysis inherent in the data mean that the conclusions presented may well be reassessed in the light of future research. There is, indeed, considerable scope for further research on the maritime history of the islands even during these years when the wooden sailing ship fleets went into decline. This study, for example, has not discussed those shipowners who migrated to other British ports, and perhaps continued to employ Channel Island seafarers, or those Island shipowners who embraced steam with considerable success, or indeed those joint-stock shipping companies which operated steam packets to the islands and which, though registered elsewhere, incorporated Channel Island capital and/or management. The purpose of the essays offered here is instead much more limited. It seeks to make a contribution to the history of the Channel Islands during the 19th century, and in particular to explain the ways in which the two largest of the Islands diverged during those years when shipbuilding and maritime trade were of central importance to the local economies. In addition, it aims to show how the commercial communities of each of the Islands sought to overcome the difficulties which arose in these important economic sectors when sailing ship technology began to lose its competitiveness in the face of the advent of steam, as well as to demonstrate the impact of the readjustments which inevitably followed on the Islands' populations, most especially in terms of immigration and employment. If it succeeds in generating further interest in the study of the history of Guernsey and Jersey, and in raising enough questions to encourage historians to make further use of the materials available in British and Channel Island archives, then its principal objective will also have been achieved.

# APPENDIX I.1

## Guernsey Shipping, 1812-1850

| Year | No. | Tons | Men | Year | No. | Tons | Men |
|------|-----|------|-----|------|-----|------|-----|
| 1812 | 76 | 8312 | 751 | 1832 | 80 | 9158 | 647 |
| 1813 | 84 | 9755 | 869 | 1833 | 79 | 9075 | 637 |
| 1814 | 65 | 6928 | 529 | 1834 | 77 | 9309 | 650 |
| 1815 | 61 | 6662 | 508 | 1835 | 78 | 9186 | 638 |
| 1817 | 63 | 6758 | 446 | 1836 | 87 | 9494 | 675 |
| 1818 | 65 | 7776 | 510 | 1837 | 90 | 9280 | 678 |
| 1819 | 69 | 7900 | 539 | 1838 | 98 | 10025 | 725 |
| 1820 | 66 | 7827 | 538 | 1839 | 105 | 11775 | 832 |
| 1821 | 65 | 8285 | 562 | 1840 | 118 | 13298 | 940 |
| 1822 | 64 | 7991 | 544 | 1841 | 133 | 15396 | 1103 |
| 1823 | 68 | 8288 | 571 | 1842 | 131 | 15129 | 1094 |
| 1824 | 70 | 7281 | 529 | 1843 | 125 | 14572 | 1051 |
| 1825 | 79 | 7298 | 556 | 1844 | 120 | 13277 | 974 |
| 1826 | 74 | 7130 | 543 | 1845 | 120 | 12898 | 939 |
| 1827 | 75 | 7879 | 580 | 1846 | 120 | 13263 | 914 |
| 1828 | 74 | 8364 | 594 | 1847 | 129 | 14084 | 952 |
| 1829 | 75 | 7672 | 574 | 1848 | 142 | 15474 | 1032 |
| 1830 | 77 | 8096 | 593 | 1849 | 141 | 16013 | 1031 |
| 1831 | 75 | 7906 | 578 | 1850 | 143 | 16743 | 1049 |

Sources: PP Vols:VIII (1814-15); XI (1816); X (1820); XIII (1821); XVI (1822); XII (1823); XV (1824);XVII (1825; XIX (1826); XIV (1826-7); XVI (1828); XV (1829); XV (1829); XXXVI (1837-8); XXX (1839); XXIX (1840); XIII (1840); XIII (1841); XXVI (1842); XXX (1843); XXXII (1844); XXVIII (1851); XXV (1846); XXXIV (1847); XXXIX (1847-8); XXX (1849); XXXIII (1850); XXXI (1851).

Note: Until 1824, these figures correspond to vessels registered in Guernsey as of 31 September of each year; from 1825, they correspond to vessels registered as of 31 December.

# APPENDIX I.2

## Jersey Shipping, 1812–1850

| Year | No. | Tons | Men | Year | No. | Tons | Men |
|------|-----|------|-----|------|-----|------|-----|
| 1812 | 54 | 5369 | 519 | 1832 | 216 | 20250 | 1895 |
| 1813 | 64 | 6379 | 708 | 1833 | 228 | 21799 | 1978 |
| 1814 | 62 | 6794 | 643 | 1834 | 231 | 21861 | 1975 |
| 1815 | 69 | 7519 | 626 | 1835 | 243 | 23221 | 2023 |
| 1817 | 79 | 8167 | 589 | 1836 | 235 | 20826 | 2034 |
| 1818 | 85 | 8967 | 636 | 1837 | 245 | 21107 | 2165 |
| 1819 | 84 | 9021 | 645 | 1838 | 241 | 20338 | 2222 |
| 1820 | 96 | 9883 | 860 | 1839 | 246 | 20763 | 2198 |
| 1821 | 103 | 10183 | 1043 | 1840 | 269 | 23529 | 2413 |
| 1822 | 107 | 10593 | 1076 | 1841 | 293 | 25868 | 2566 |
| 1823 | 114 | 11265 | 1062 | 1842 | 308 | 27304 | 2621 |
| 1824 | 116 | 11477 | 1164 | 1843 | 295 | 27003 | 2508 |
| 1825 | 142 | 13756 | 1330 | 1844 | 311 | 28078 | 2717 |
| 1826 | 171 | 15650 | 1518 | 1845 | 311 | 27690 | 2623 |
| 1827 | 183 | 16582 | 1658 | 1846 | 321 | 28783 | 2790 |
| 1828 | 196 | 17552 | 1750 | 1847 | 328 | 29714 | 2856 |
| 1829 | 200 | 18217 | 1761 | 1848 | 324 | 30569 | 2723 |
| 1830 | 205 | 18601 | 1754 | 1849 | 340 | 32056 | 2949 |
| 1831 | 212 | 19700 | 1907 | 1850 | 347 | 32331 | 2981 |

Sources: PP Vols:VIII (1814-15); XI (1816); X (1820); XIII (1821); XVI (1822); XII (1823); XV (1824);XVII (1825; XIX (1826); XIV (1826-7); XVI (1828); XV (1829); XV (1829); XXXVI (1837-8); XXX (1839); XXIX (1840); XIII (1840); XIII (1841); XXVI (1842); XXX (1843); XXXII (1844); XXVIII (1851); XXV (1846); XXXIV (1847); XXXIX (1847-8); XXX (1849); XXXIII (1850); XXXI (1851).

Note: Until 1824, these figures correspond to vessels registered in Guernsey as of 31 September of each year; from 1825, they correspond to vessels registered as of 31 December.

# APPENDIX I.3

**Guernsey-Registered Vessels, 1830-1876—by tonnage ranges (according to the Shipping Lists published in the Annual Almanacs)**

|  | 1830 | 1845 | 1855 | 1866 | 1876 |
|---|---|---|---|---|---|
| 15-50 | 19 | 21 | 23 | 11 | 24 |
| 50-100 | 16 | 29 | 21 | 16 | 21 |
| 100-200 | 25 | 57 | 54 | 64 | 54 |
| 200-300 | 10 | 10 | 13 | 29 | 48 |
| 300-400 |  |  | 5 | 7 | 9 |
| 400-500 |  |  |  |  | 2 |
| 500-600 |  |  |  | 4 | 2 |
| 600-700 |  |  |  | 2 | 4 |
| *Total Vessels* | 70 | 117 | 116 | 133 | 164 |
| *Total Tonnage* | 7,547 | 13,268 | 15,315 | 24,698 | 30,029 |
| *Average Tonnage* | 108 | 113 | 132 | 185 | 183 |

Note: These figures are drawn from the Annual Almanacs (1830, 1845, 1855, 1866 and 1876) held at the Priaulx Library, St Peter Port Guernsey, and they do not necessarily correspond exactly to figures given in Parliamentary Papers. In cases where Old measurement and New measurement tonnages are given, only New measurement tonnage has been used.

# Appendix I.4

**Jersey-Registered Vessels, 1826-1875—by tonnage ranges (according to the Shipping Lists published in the Annual Almanacs)**

|  | 1826 | 1845 | 1855 | 1865 | 1875 |
|---|---|---|---|---|---|
| 15-50 | 14 | 80 | 148 | 174 | 136 |
| 50-100 | 44 | 62 | 61 | 80 | 93 |
| 100-200 | 43 | 98 | 88 | 103 | 36 |
| 200-300 | 15 | 22 | 28 | 36 | 9 |
| 300-400 | 1 | 2 | 12 | 14 | 6 |
| 400-500 | 1 | 3 | 4 | 5 | 6 |
| 500-600 |  |  | 1 | 2 | 1 |
| 600-700 |  |  |  | 2 |  |
| 700-800 |  |  |  | 2 |  |
| 800-900 |  |  | 1 |  |  |
| 900-1000 |  |  |  | 1 |  |
| 1000-1100 |  |  |  | 1 |  |
| 1100-1200 |  |  |  | 1 |  |
| Total Vessels | 118 | 267 | 343 | 421 | 288 |
| Total Tonnage | 14,022 | 27,714 | 35,400 | 48,561 | 24,792 |
| Average Tonnage | 119 | 103 | 103 | 115 | 86 |

Note: These figures are drawn from the Annual Almanacs (1826, 1845, 1855, 1865, and 1875) held at the Société Jersiaise, St Helier, Jersey, and they do not necessarily correspond exactly to figures given in *Parliamentary Papers*. In cases where Old measurement and New measurement tonnages are given, only New measurement tonnage has been used.

# Appendix I.5

**Shipments of Goods from Jersey to London—1845 (carried in Jersey-registered vessels)**

| Vessel | Tons | Men | Cargo |
|---|---|---|---|
| *Adelaide* | 79 | 4 | Potatoes (106 tons) |
| *Alert* | 53 | 6 | Potatoes (55 tons) |
| *Alpha* | 58 | 5 | Potatoes (85 tons) |
| *Anna* | 39 | 4 | Potatoes (45 tons) |
| *Bartlett* | 52 | 3 | Potatoes (72 tons) |
| *Champion* | 126 | 6 | Cider/Vinegar/Boots/Cigars/Varnish |
| | | 5 | Lead/Wine/Brandy/Blubber |
| | | 6 | Lemons/Skins/Cod oil/Olives/Wine |
| | | 6 | Wine/Vinegar/Cordage/Metal/Glass |
| *Dart Packet* | 42 | 4 | Potatoes (47 tons) |
| *Eliza* | 35 | 3 | Potatoes (45 tons) |
| *General Don* | 40 | 4 | Apples (1300 bush) |
| *Grace* | 44 | 3 | Potatoes (64 tons) |
| *Herbert* | 57 | 4 | Potatoes (45 tons)/Wine |
| | | 3 | Potatoes (85 tons) |
| *John* | 48 | 3 | Potatoes (70 tons)/Carrots |
| *Lord Nelson* | 45 | 4 | Potatoes (70 tons) |
| | | 3 | Potatoes (70 tons) |
| | | 3 | Potatoes (72 tons) |
| | | 4 | Potatoes (75 tons) |
| *Mary* | 58 | 3 | Potatoes (98 tons)/Sails/Sailcloth |
| *Neptune* | 88 | 5 | Potatoes (130 tons) |
| *Ninus* | 59 | 4 | Potatoes (90 tons) |
| *No Joke* | 20 | 3 | Potatoes (25 tons) |
| | | 3 | Potatoes (25 tons) |
| *Patriot* | 95 | 6 | Potatoes (140 tons) |
| *Providence* | 31 | 3 | Potatoes (43 tons) |
| *Sarah* | 35 | 3 | Potatoes (45 tons) |

# Appendix I.5 (cont'd)

| Vessel | Tons | Men | Cargo |
|--------|------|-----|-------|
| *Siren* | 113 | 8 | Potatoes (155 tons) |
| *Trial* | 39 | 3 | Potatoes (42 tons)/Beef |
| | | 3 | Potatoes (47 tons) |
| *Virginia* | 29 | 3 | Potatoes (47 tons) |
| | | 3 | Potatoes (50 tons) |
| *Water Witch* | 58 | 4 | Apples (2100 bush) |

Source: *London Customs Bills of Entry*,  1 January - 31 December, 1845

# Appendix I.6

**Shipments of Goods from Guernsey to London—1845**
**(carried in Guernsey-registered vessels)**

| Vessel | Tons | Men | Cargo |
|--------|------|-----|-------|
| *Agnes* | 94 | 5 | Granite (145 tons) |
| | | 5 | Granite (145 tons) |
| | | 5 | Granite (145 tons) |
| | | 5 | Granite (145 tons) |
| | | 5 | Granite (150 tons) |
| *Albion* | 134 | 8 | Granite (200 tons) |
| *Alert* | 36 | 2 | Granite (50 tons) |
| *Alice* | 146 | 8 | Granite (225 tons) |
| *Apollo* | 125 | 6 | Granite (202 tons) |
| | | 6 | Granite (210 tons) |
| | | 6 | Granite (210 tons) |
| *Brilliant* | 77 | 4 | Granite (130 tons) |
| | | 5 | Granite (130 tons) |
| | | 6 | Granite (130 tons) |
| | | 5 | Granite (130 tons) |
| | | 5 | Granite (130 tons) |
| | | 5 | Granite (130 tons) |
| | | 5 | Granite (130 tons) |
| | | 5 | Granite (130 tons) |
| | | 5 | Granite (130 tons) |
| *British Queen* | 154 | 7 | Granite (240 tons) |
| | | 7 | Granite (245 tons) |
| | | 7 | Granite (250 tons) |
| | | 7 | Granite (250 tons) |
| | | 7 | Granite (250 tons) |
| *Clara* | 99 | 6 | Granite (175 tons) |
| | | 5 | Granite (175 tons) |
| | | 5 | Granite (175 tons) |

# APPENDIX I.6 (CONT'D)

| Vessel | Tons | Men | Cargo |
|---|---|---|---|
| | | 5 | Granite (180 tons) |
| Comet | 33 | 2 | Granite (14 tons)/Chicory |
| Concordia | 119 | 6 | Granite (200 tons) |
| | | 6 | Granite (200 tons) |
| | | 6 | Granite (200 tons) |
| | | 6 | Granite (200 tons) |
| | | 7 | Granite (205 tons) |
| Daniel Brock | 131 | 7 | Granite (208 tons) |
| | | 7 | Granite (208 tons) |
| | | 7 | Granite (208 tons) |
| | | 7 | Granite (215 tons) |
| | | 7 | Granite (208 tons) |
| Elizabeth | 59 | 4 | Potatoes (1850 bush) |
| | | 4 | Potatoes (3000 bush) |
| | | 4 | Potatoes (3000 bush) |
| Falcon | 59 | 5 | Potatoes (3300 bush) |
| George | 112 | 6 | Granite (170 tons) |
| Georgiana | 38 | 3 | Potatoes (1800 bush) |
| | | 3 | Potatoes (1800 bush) |
| Hannah | 198 | 8 | Granite (290 tons) |
| | | 8 | Granite (290 tons) |
| | | 8 | Granite (290 tons) |
| | | 8 | Granite (290 tons) |
| | | 8 | Granite (290 tons) |
| | | 8 | Granite (290 tons) |
| Herald | 88 | 4 | Granite (110 tons) |
| Hostilina | 120 | 7 | Granite (190 tons) |
| Ino | 128 | 6 | Granite (220 tons) |
| | | 6 | Granite (223 tons) |
| | | 6 | Granite (224 tons) |

| Vessel | Tons | Men | Cargo |
|--------|------|-----|-------|
|  |  | 6 | Granite (225 tons) |
|  |  | 6 | Granite (225 tons) |
|  |  | 6 | Granite (225 tons) |
| *Jane* | 35 | 3 | Potatoes (50 tons) |
| *Julia* | 173 | 8 | Granite (270 tons) |
|  |  | 8 | Granite (275 tons) |
|  |  | 8 | Granite (275 tons) |
|  |  | 8 | Granite (280 tons) |
|  |  | 8 | Granite (280 tons) |
| *Juliana* | 168 | 8 | Granite (250 tons) |
|  |  | 8 | Granite (250 tons) |
|  |  | 8 | Granite (250 tons) |
|  |  | 8 | Granite (250 tons) |
| *Lady Douglas* | 139 | 7 | Granite (230 tons) |
|  |  | 7 | Granite (240 tons) |
|  |  | 7 | Granite (240 tons) |
|  |  | 7 | Granite (240 tons) |
|  |  | 7 | Granite (240 tons) |
|  |  | 7 | Granite (240 tons) |
| *Lady Robilliard* | 53 | 4 | Granite (90 tons) |
|  |  | 4 | Granite (91 tons) |
| *Liberty* | 30 | 2 | Granite (50 tons) |
|  |  | 3 | Granite (50 tons) |
|  |  | 2 | Potatoes (1600 bush) |
| *Lively* | 62 | 4 | Granite (117 tons) |
|  |  | 4 | Granite (120 tons) |
|  |  | 3 | Granite (56 t.)/Potatoes (800 bush) |
|  |  | 3 | Granite (80 tons) |
|  |  | 3 | Granite (80 tons) |
|  |  | 3 | Granite (83 tons) |
|  |  | 4 | Granite (83 tons) |

| Vessel | Tons | Men | Cargo |
|--------|------|-----|-------|
| *Margaret* | 200 | 8 | Granite (295 tons) |
| | | 8 | Granite (300 tons) |
| | | 8 | Granite (300 tons) |
| | | 8 | Granite (300 tons) |
| | | 8 | Granite (300 tons) |
| *Marys* | 59 | 4 | Granite (40 tons)/Wine/Brandy/Rum |
| | | 4 | Potatoes (2500 bush) |
| | | 5 | Potatoes (25 tons)/Wines/Spirits |
| | | 4 | Potatoes (46 tons)/Wine/Biscuit |
| | | 4 | Potatoes (47 tons)/Wine/Spirits |
| | | 5 | Wines/Brandy/Cordials/Vegetables |
| *Matilda* | 105 | 7 | Granite (184 tons) |
| | | 6 | Granite (184 tons) |
| | | 6 | Granite (184 tons) |
| *Mellona* | 106 | 5 | Granite (175 tons) |
| | | 6 | Granite (175 tons) |
| | | 5 | Granite (180 tons) |
| | | 5 | Granite (180 tons) |
| | | 5 | Granite (180 tons) |
| | | 5 | Granite (180 tons) |
| | | 5 | Granite (185 tons) |
| | | 5 | Granite (185 tons) |
| *Navarino* | 104 | 5 | Granite (145 tons)/Brandy/Silks |
| | | 6 | Granite (35 tons)/Brandy/Fruit/Wine |
| | | 6 | Granite (94 tons) |
| | | 6 | Potatoes (60 t.)/Rosewood/Iron/Wine |
| | | 6 | Wine/Brandy |
| | | 6 | Wine/Spirits/Chicory/Books |
| *Neptune* | 148 | 7 | Granite (270 tons) |
| | | 7 | Granite (270 tons) |

| Vessel | Tons | Men | Cargo |
|---|---|---|---|
| | | 7 | Granite (270 tons) |
| | | 7 | Granite (270 tons) |
| | | 8 | Granite (280 tons) |
| *Prince Albert* | 58 | 4 | Cider/Vegetables/Shells |
| | | 3 | Cordial/Vinegar/Oil/Biscuit |
| | | 4 | Granite (44 t.)/Wine/Brandy/Fruit |
| | | 4 | Granite (60 tons)/Wine |
| | | 3 | Granite (76 t.)/Sausages/Vegetables |
| | | 3 | Potatoes (1250 bush)/Wine/Brandy |
| *Sarnia* | 74 | 5 | Potatoes (2000 bush)/Wine/Ink |
| | | 5 | Potatoes (41 t.)/Mahogany/Wine |
| | | 5 | Potatoes (700 bush)/Brandy/Wine |
| | | 5 | Wine/Onions/Cutlery |
| | | 5 | Wines/Brandy/Seed/Mercery |
| *Sertum* | 167 | 7 | Granite (290 tons) |
| | | 8 | Granite (290 tons) |
| | | 8 | Granite (290 tons) |
| | | 7 | Granite (290 tons) |
| | | 7 | Granite (290 tons) |
| *Sir William Collings* | 151 | 8 | Granite (250 tons) |
| | | 8 | Granite (250 tons) |
| | | 8 | Granite (255 tons) |
| | | 8 | Granite (260 tons) |
| *Speculator* | 96 | 5 | Granite (148 tons) |
| | | 5 | Granite (151 tons) |
| | | 5 | Granite (165 tons) |
| *Susan* | 171 | 8 | Granite (270 tons) |
| | | 8 | Granite (270 tons) |
| | | 8 | Granite (275 tons) |
| | | 8 | Granite (280 tons) |

| Vessel | Tons | Men | Cargo |
|---|---|---|---|
| *Trusty* | 150 | 7 | Granite (190 tons) |
| | | 7 | Granite (230 tons) |
| | | 7 | Granite (240 tons) |
| | | 7 | Granite (245 tons) |
| | | 7 | Granite (255 tons) |
| | | 7 | Granite (238 tons) |
| *Veritas* | 153 | 7 | Granite (255 tons) |
| | | 7 | Granite (255 tons) |
| | | 7 | Granite (255 tons) |
| | | 7 | Granite (255 tons) |
| | | 7 | Granite (260 tons) |
| *Victoria Regina* | 107 | 5 | Granite (170 tons) |
| | | 5 | Granite (70 tons) |

Source: *London Customs Bills of Entry,*      1 January – 31 December, 1845

# APPENDIX I.7

**Ratio of Jersey to Non-Jersey Crews, Foreign Trade—1845**
**(According to Port of Departure)**

| Port of Departure | No. Voy. | No. Men (A) | Jsy-born | % | Non-Jsy | % | Other C.I | % | Not Known | % |
|---|---|---|---|---|---|---|---|---|---|---|
| Jersey (B) | 76 | 611 | 492 | 80.5 | 103 | 16.9 | 15 | 2.4 | 1 | 0.2 |
| Liverpool | 37 | 333 | 183 | 54.9 | 139 | 41.7 | 10 | 3.0 | 1 | 0.3 |
| London | 29 | 288 | 120 | 41.7 | 161 | 55.9 | 7 | 2.4 | - | - |
| Cork | 6 | 49 | 29 | 59.2 | 19 | 38.8 | 1 | 2.0 | - | - |
| Other (C) | 21 | 159 | 84 | 52.8 | 70 | 44.0 | 5 | 3.1 | - | - |
| Total | 169 | 1440 | 908 | 63.0 | 492 | 34.2 | 38 | 2.6 | 2 | 0.1 |

Source: PRO BT 98/678, 98/956, 98/957, 98/959

Notes: (A) Figures include entire crews
(B) Includes all voyages beginning in Jersey, although many vessels proceeded to other British ports before sailing outwards
(C) Several ports, including Glasgow, Newport and Newcastle

# Appendix I.8

**Ratio of Guernsey to Non-Guernsey Crews, Foreign Trade—1845**
**(According to Port of Departure)**

| Port of Departure | No. Voy. | No. Men (A) | Gsy-born | % | Non-Gsy | % | Other C.I | % | Not Known | % |
|---|---|---|---|---|---|---|---|---|---|---|
| Guernsey (B) | 59 | 432 | 327 | 75.7 | 96 | 22.2 | 8 | 1.8 | 1 | 0.2 |
| Liverpool | 18 | 132 | 57 | 43.2 | 67 | 50.8 | 7 | 5.3 | 1 | 0.7 |
| London | 7 | 52 | 27 | 51.9 | 24 | 46.1 | 1 | 1.9 | - | - |
| Bristol | 4 | 22 | 12 | 54.5 | 10 | 45.5 | - | - | - | - |
| Glasgow | 5 | 35 | 9 | 25.7 | 25 | 71.4 | - | - | 1 | 2.9 |
| Other (C) | 8 | 66 | 42 | 63.6 | 22 | 33.3 | 2 | 3.0 | - | - |
| Total | 101 | 739 | 474 | 64.1 | 244 | 33.0 | 18 | 2.4 | 3 | 0.4 |

Source: PRO BT 98/664, 98/937, 98/938

Notes: (A) Figures include entire crews
(B) Includes all voyages beginning in Guernsey, although many vessels proceeded to other British ports before sailing outwards
(C) Several ports, including Leith, Newcastle and Newport

# Appendix I.9

## Vessels Built by George Deslandes & Son (of Jersey)

| Year | Rig | Name | Tonnage | | |
|------|-----|------|-----|-----|------|
| | | | *Old* | *New* | *Last* |
| 1824 | Brigantine | *Aurora* | 107 | - | - |
| 1825 | Brig | *Nameless* | 148 | - | - |
| 1825 | Schooner | *Antelope* | 138 | - | - |
| 1826 | Barque | *Swift* | 177 | - | - |
| 1827 | Brig | *Tiphys* | 111 | - | - |
| 1827 | Brigantine | *Judith & Esther* | 84 | - | - |
| 1828 | Brigantine | *Royal George* | 55 | - | - |
| 1830 | Brigantine | *Jolly Tar* | 166 | - | - |
| 1830 | Cutter | *Pilot Boat* | 31 | - | - |
| 1831 | Schooner | *Loyal William* | 70 | - | - |
| 1831 | Schooner | *Adelaide* | 70 | - | - |
| 1832 | Barque | *Amelia* | 235 | - | - |
| 1833 | Brig | *Secret* | 202 | - | - |
| 1834 | Schooner | *Alexander* | 93 | - | - |
| 1834 | Brig | *Temperance* | 132 | - | - |
| 1834 | Barque | *Good Luck* | 232 | - | - |
| 1834 | Schooner | *Amelia* | 104 | - | - |
| 1835 | Schooner | *Caesar* | 110 | - | - |
| 1835 | Schooner | *Guillelmo* | 118 | - | - |
| 1835 | Schooner | *Charles Buchan* | 129 | - | - |
| 1835 | Schooner | *Lord Anson* | 133 | - | - |
| 1836 | Schooner | *Master* | 137 | - | - |
| 1836 | Schooner | *Lydia* | 75 | - | - |
| 1837 | Schooner | *Deslandes* | 153 | 143 | - |
| 1837 | Cutter | *Jersey Packet* | 63 | - | - |
| 1837 | Schooner | *Rollo* | 75 | - | - |
| 1837 | Schooner | *Campbell* | 96 | - | - |
| 1838 | Schooner | *Judith* | 105 | - | - |
| 1838 | Barque | *Iris* | 254 | - | - |

# APPENDIX I.9 (CONT'D)

| Year Built | Rig | Name | Tonnage | | |
|---|---|---|---|---|---|
| | | | Old | New | Last |
| 1838 | Schooner | *Victoria* | 120 | - | - |
| 1839 | Barque | *British Merchant* | 278 | - | - |
| 1839 | Schooner | *George* | 58 | - | - |
| 1839 | Schooner | *Janus* | 105 | - | - |
| 1839 | Brig | *Fifteen* | 269 | - | - |
| 1840 | Schooner | *Astrea* | 164 | - | - |
| 1840 | Brigantine | *North Star* | 169 | - | - |
| 1840 | Brigantine | *Harriet L.* | 177 | - | - |
| 1840 | Schooner | *Flamer* | 110 | - | - |
| 1840 | Barque | *Julia* | 296 | - | - |
| 1840 | Schooner | *Prince* | 73 | - | - |
| 1840 | Schooner | *Agenoria* | 116 | - | - |
| 1840 | Schooner | *Ninus* | 71 | - | - |
| 1841 | Schooner | *Diadem* | 160 | - | - |
| 1841 | Schooner | *Spy* | 172 | 170 | - |
| 1841 | Schooner | *Phillipe* | 72 | - | - |
| 1841 | Cutter | *7 Brothers* | 20 | - | - |
| 1841 | Schooner | *Ann* | 58 | - | - |
| 1842 | Schooner | *Rachael* | 188 | 186 | - |
| 1843 | Schooner | *St.Helier* | 148 | 134 | 123 |
| 1843 | Schooner | *Victoria* | 135 | 120 | 111 |
| 1843 | Cutter | *Caroline* | 31 | - | - |
| 1843 | Cutter | *Trial* | 39 | - | - |
| 1845 | Schooner | *Mary* | 59 | - | - |
| 1846 | Barque | *Jane* | 360 | - | - |
| 1847 | Cutter | *Fairy* | 52 | - | - |
| 1847 | Brigantine | *Stratton* | 181 | - | - |
| 1847 | Brigantine | *Louisa* | 199 | - | - |
| 1848 | Brigantine | *Perseverance* | 194 | 194 | - |

| Year Built | Rig | Name | Tonnage | | |
|---|---|---|---|---|---|
| | | | Old | New | Last |
| 1848 | Brig | Corbiere | 249 | 227 | 214 |
| 1848 | Barque | Royal Sovereign | 570 | - | - |
| 1849 | Barque | Willing | 244 | 243 | 229 |
| 1849 | Schooner | Gulnare | 83 | - | - |
| 1849 | Schooner | Modeste | 87 | - | - |
| 1850 | Schooner | Brasdor | 109 | - | - |
| 1850 | Schooner | Acis | 113 | - | - |
| 1850 | Schooner | Mentor | 124 | 102 | 99 |
| 1851 | Schooner | Token | 126 | 107 | - |
| 1851 | Schooner | Blonde | 131 | 108 | - |
| 1852 | Brig | Exact | 220 | 204 | 186 |
| 1853 | Brigantine | Nox | 162 | 152 | - |
| 1853 | Barque | Loyal | 250 | 222 | 203 |
| 1854 | Brigantine | Foreman | 169 | 154 | - |
| 1855 | Barque | Glory | 270 | 250 | - |
| 1855 | Brigantine | Youth | 190 | 168 | - |
| 1856 | Brigantine | Pride | 226 | - | 176 |
| 1857 | Brigantine | Accra | 139 | - | 108 |
| 1857 | Barque | Hertha | 311 | 281 | 257 |
| 1858 | Brig | Hasty | 209 | - | 171 |
| 1858 | Schooner | Zeal | 144 | - | 107 |
| 1858 | Barque | Obey | 318 | - | 271 |
| 1859 | Brig | Kite | 245 | - | 188 |
| 1859 | Schooner | Just | 159 | - | 122 |
| 1860 | Barque | Reflect | 390 | - | 321 |
| 1861 | Brig | Offor | 220 | - | 172 |
| 1862 | Barque | Crown | 370 | - | 298 |
| 1862 | Brig | Firm | 189 | - | 140 |
| 1862 | Barque | Anne Kay | 287 | - | 209 |

# APPENDIX I.9 (CONT'D)

| Year Built | Rig | Name | Tonnage | | |
|---|---|---|---|---|---|
| | | | *Old* | *New* | *Last* |
| 1863 | Brigantine | *Guide* | 165 | - | 131 |
| 1864 | Barque | *Desdemona* | 664 | - | 581 |
| 1863 | Schooner | *Whydah* | 140 | - | 106 |
| 1864 | Brig | *Quick* | 280 | - | 228 |
| 1863 | Barque | *Courier* | 438 | - | 361 |
| 1864 | Brigantine | *Free* | 192 | - | 146 |
| 1865 | Brig | *Queen of the Seas* | 243 | - | 185 |
| 1865 | Brigantine | *Juventa* | 186 | - | 151 |
| 1867 | Barque | *Virgilia* | 540 | - | 512 |
| 1867 | Barque | *Brave* | 502 | - | 408 |
| 1868 | Brigantine | *Nerio* | 200 | - | 147 |
| 1869 | Brig | *Guess* | 246 | - | 175 |
| 1870 | Brig | *Hundredth* | 256 | - | 190 |
| 1871 | Brigantine | *Vitula* | 202 | - | 146 |
| 1872 | Schooner | *Providencia* | 91 | - | 59 |
| 1873 | Schooner | *Bulla* | 128 | - | 87 |
| 1873 | Schooner | *Lilian* | 91 | - | 58 |
| 1875 | Brig | *Cygnus* | 285 | - | 213 |
| 1880 | Schooner | *Trust* | 111 | - | 79 |

(Source: Société Jersiaise, St Helier)

# Appendix II.1

Ownership of Guernsey Vessels in the Stone Trade, 1868 (including tonnage, number of voyages made by each vessel, and totals carried)

| Owner | Vessel | Tons | Cargoes | Total |
|---|---|---|---|---|
| John Hamley | Admiral Nelson | 183 | 8 | 2,582 |
| | Ann | 156 | 6 | 1,530 |
| | Don Colino | 168 | 7 | 2,100 |
| | Wave | 65 | 2 | 200 |
| Julia Williams | Anglo-Saxon | 262 | 2 | 970 |
| | Countess Leicester | 171 | 2 | 620 |
| | Douglas | 168 | 4 | 1,160 |
| | Elizabeth & Cicely | 190 | 4 | 1,340 |
| John Guilbert | Jubilee | 188 | 5 | 1,625 |
| | Julia | 210 | 5 | 1,850 |
| | Bertha | 230 | 4 | 1,100 |
| | Kate | 226 | 2 | 820 |
| | Reward | 178 | 5 | 1,550 |
| Peter Le Page | Alice | 168 | 6 | 1,710 |
| | Wave | 98 | 7 | 1,176 |
| | William & Mary | 188 | 5 | 1,540 |
| Robert C.Whicker | Albion | 165 | 5 | 1,430 |
| | General Slade | 206 | 3 | 1,050 |
| | Ocean Bride | 220 | 1 | 390 |
| T.G.Reynolds | Prosperine | 180 | 5 | 1,600 |
| | Trial | 188 | 4 | 1,440 |
| | Triumph | 189 | 6 | 2,160 |
| Richard M.Lelean | Progress | 257 | 1 | 500 |
| | Reaper | 204 | 3 | 1,170 |
| George J.Coles | Anglo-Norman | 277 | 1 | 500 |
| | Sarnia | 97 | 4 | 655 |

| Owner | Vessel | Tons | Cargoes | Total |
|---|---|---|---|---|
| Abraham Collenette | Caroline Sainty | 191 | 6 | 2,070 |
|  | Livonia | 199 | 6 | 2,151 |
| A.J.Prevot | Adelaide | 233 | 2 | 761 |
| Auguste Goupillot | Cheval de Troie | 104 | 4 | 744 |
| Thomas Domaille | Lavinia | 145 | 5 | 1,150 |
| Betsy Langlois | Ellen | 90 | 7 | 1,193 |
| George Godfrey | Aliwal | 190 | 6 | 1,920 |
| William Newberry | Concordia | 125 | 9 | 2,115 |
| James Upson | Crescent | 107 | 5 | 909 |
| C.H.Barnett | Edissa | 175 | 5 | 1,651 |
| William Smith | Edward | 88 | 1 | 121 |
| F.J.Grandin-Jersey | Ellen | 156 | 1 | 270 |
| Daniel Mariette | Emma Eden | 125 | 5 | 1,080 |
| J.E.Lath | Iris | 103 | 9 | 1,694 |
| H.Arthur | Jessy | 191 | 5 | 1,620 |
| William Potter | Lily | 192 | 5 | 1,706 |
| P.O.Falla | Mellona | 125 | 5 | 1,120 |
| T.H.Flére | Ocean Monarch | 228 | 2 | 829 |
| John Martel | Recompense | 197 | 7 | 2,420 |
| Isaac Marquand | Renown | 227 | 6 | 2,520 |
| Josiah Dorey | Rescue | 207 | 1 | 380 |
| Robert Stonelake | Rhoda | 47 | 1 | 80 |
| John Helman | Rifleman | 226 | 1 | 420 |
| William Brown | Rosa | 190 | 4 | 1,340 |
| W.W.Bird | Shealtiel | 152 | 6 | 1,573 |
| James Renouf | Speedwell | 148 | 6 | 1,650 |
| Richard Peek | Surprise | 185 | 3 | 965 |
| Charles Le Page | Thomas & Elizabeth | 48 | 1 | 45 |

# Appendix II.1 (cont'd)

| Owner | Vessel | Tons | Cargoes | Total |
|---|---|---|---|---|
| Touzeau & Martel | Two Friends | 131 | 5 | 1,150 |
| Joseph Mauger | Unition | 145 | 5 | 1,250 |
| James Sebire | Veritas | 188 | 3 | 990 |
| Thomas Le Roy | Vibilia | 178 | 5 | 1,540 |
| Daniel Rougier | Wheatsheaf | 108 | 3 | 570 |
| William T.Brown | Zuma | 180 | 4 | 1,220 |
| Mary Le Lacheur | Hannah | 177 | 6 | 1,760 |
| Cheeswright/Miskin (London) | Dublin Lass | 170 | 3 | 925 |
| | Elizabeth | 184 | 4 | 1,280 |
| | Jane Lakey | 264 | 6 | 2,640 |
| | Mermaid | 147 | 5 | 1,225 |
| F.Welford-N'castle | Durham Packet | 172 | 6 | 1,795 |
| | Mary Garland | 227 | 5 | 1,735 |
| W.Swanston-N'castle | Friedrick William | 200 | 5 | 1,650 |
| | St.George | 182 | 6 | 1,920 |

Sources: *London Customs Bills of Entry* (1868) and the *Mercantile Navy List* (1868 and 1869).

# Appendix II.2

**Ownership of Guernsey Vessels in the Stone Trade, 1883 (including tonnage, number of voyages made by each vessel, and totals carried)**

| Owner | Vessel | Tons | Cargoes | Total |
|---|---|---|---|---|
| John Hamley | Augia | 199 | 6 | 2,220 |
| | Boatswain | 228 | 6 | 2,400 |
| | Flora | 249 | 7 | 3,020 |
| | Obey | 258 | 7 | 3,150 |
| | St.George | 182 | 5 | 1,600 |
| Philip Stranger | Agilis | 285 | 1 | 440 |
| | Aliwal | 190 | 5 | 1,600 |
| | Britannia | 217 | 5 | 1,840 |
| | Fearless | 229 | 7 | 2,730 |
| | Lord Strangford | 178 | 5 | 1,610 |
| | Sagitta | 282 | 7 | 3,331 |
| | William & Mary | 171 | 2 | 625 |
| John Guilbert | Bertha | 217 | 6 | 2,400 |
| | Isabel | 186 | 6 | 2,162 |
| | Kate | 212 | 6 | 2,400 |
| | Reward | 166 | 5 | 1,550 |
| Josiah Dorey | Ocean Monarch | 215 | 8 | 3,270 |
| | Sarnian Gem | 183 | 5 | 1,475 |
| | St.Devenick | 246 | 6 | 2,670 |
| | Star of the West | 202 | 7 | 2,475 |
| G.F.Carrington | Carrington | 225 | 7 | 2,800 |
| | Result | 242 | 6 | 2,768 |
| William Potter | Agenora | 215 | 7 | 2,730 |
| | Islander | 186 | 7 | 2,625 |
| Richard M.Lelean | Contest | 253 | 5 | 2,395 |
| | Progress | 245 | 3 | 1,425 |

| Owner | Vessel | Tons | Cargoes | Total |
|---|---|---|---|---|
| Richard H.Peek | Unition | 185 | 5 | 1,815 |
| | Surprise | 185 | 5 | 1,650 |
| Robert C.Whicker | Catherine | 186 | 6 | 2,120 |
| Samuel Winterflood | Alarm | 146 | 1 | 265 |
| George J.Coles | Jane Lakey | 243 | 4 | 1,720 |
| Palmire Prevot | Adelaide | 220 | 6 | 2,280 |
| James G.Williams | Bengairn | 256 | 5 | 2,450 |
| C.H.Newbury | Juan | 129 | 7 | 1,500 |
| Mourant Touzeau | Two Friends | 170 | 5 | 1,500 |
| Joseph Toms | Ocean Bride | 220 | 6 | 2,250 |
| Isaac Marquand | Renown | 215 | 7 | 2,900 |
| John Helman | Rifleman | 213 | 8 | 3,204 |
| W.W.Bird | Shealtiel | 140 | 5 | 1,229 |
| George Parsons | Teaser | 131 | 6 | 1,392 |
| William Wetherall | Minnie Eaton | 188 | 6 | 2,045 |
| John Ogier | Mellona | 115 | 1 | 220 |
| Charles Le Page | Courier | 39 | 9 | 564 |
| Albert De la Mare | Rapid | 43 | 8 | 501 |
| Clement M.Brouard | Dispatch | 28 | 2 | 62 |
| George Allix (Jersey) | Argo | 224 | 7 | 2,940 |
| | Spring | 225 | 1 | 420 |
| Richard Allix (Jersey) | Clacknaccuddin | 224 | 8 | 3,310 |
| | Robinsons | 188 | 6 | 2,190 |
| | Satellite | 245 | 6 | 2,700 |
| Robert Youlton (Jersey) | Lavinia | 215 | 5 | 2,090 |
| J.W. Nicolle (Jersey) | Ocean Bride | 224 | 2 | 1,000 |
| W.F. Stokes (Jersey) | Alice Jane | 198 | 2 | 740 |
| Francis Picot (Jersey) | Happy Return | 184 | 5 | 1,715 |
| William Steel (Jersey) | Freedom | 39 | 1 | 70 |

| Owner | Vessel | Tons | Cargoes | Total |
|---|---|---|---|---|
| Daniel Cooper (Jersey) | Friend of the Isles | 47 | 1 | 71 |
| Philip Gavey (Jersey) | Firm | 126 | 1 | 235 |
| N.P.Le Cocq (Alderney) | Edissa | 175 | 5 | 1,540 |
| W.Coward (Knottingley) | Edward | 88 | 1 | 150 |
| T.Minter (Whitstable) | Impetuous | 162 | 3 | 840 |
| C.Kellitt (Goole) | Whisper | 95 | 2 | 340 |
| A.McMahon (Newport) | Trio | 72 | 1 | 136 |
| J.McMahon (Newport) | Julia | 57 | 1 | 100 |
| E.Whitley (Newport) | Lilian | 58 | 1 | 100 |
| F.Mansell (London) | Monarch | 285 | 4 | 2,060 |
| F.Manuelle (London) | Never Despair | 230 | 5 | 2,180 |
| | Prince Alfred | 256 | 6 | 2,700 |

Sources: *London Customs Bills of Entry* (1883), the *Mercantile Navy List* (1883 and 1884), and *Lloyd's Register* (1884)

# APPENDIX II.3

**Exports from St Sampson Harbour, 1840-1853**

| Year | Stone (Tons) | Other Produce (Tons) |
|------|-------------|---------------------|
| 1840 | 47,777 | 373 |
| 1841 | 37,551 | 279 |
| 1842 | 55,992 | 543 |
| 1843 | 56,320 | 90 |
| 1844 | 57,544 | 15 |
| 1845 | 60,259 | 28 |
| 1846 | 66,829 | 47 |
| 1847 | 83,338 | 67 |
| 1848 | 97,660 | 128 |
| 1849 | 90,473 | 367 |
| 1850 | 82,593 | 221 |
| 1851 | 108,176 | - |
| 1852 | 103,820 | 120 |
| 1853 | 119,508 | 390 |
| | | |
| **Total** | **1,067,840** | **2,668** |

Source: *Henry Brouard's Almanack of Guernsey* (1855)
Note: Years run from 1 February to 31 January

# Appendix II.4

**Principal Agents Receiving Shipments of Guernsey Granite in London in 1883**

| Consignee | No. of Shipments | Total (Tons) |
|-----------|------------------|--------------|
| A Nicholson | 221 | 69,176 |
| A & F Manuelle | 236 | 64,137 |
| R.L & J Fennings | 77 | 23,328 |
| C Ross & Sons | 14 | 4,009 |
| S Trickett & Sons | 16 | 2,823 |
| J Mowlem & Co. | 5 | 1,560 |
| Nowell & Robson | 4 | 1,017 |
| Tomes & Wimpey | 7 | 977 |
| E Downs, Kennedy & Co. | 4 | 787 |
| S Genesi & Co. | 3 | 673 |
| Nicholson & Allen | 2 | 650 |
| Robson & Co. | 1 | 346 |
| J Paton | 1 | 120 |

Source: *London Customs Bills of Entry*, 1 January – 31 December 1883

# Appendix II.5

**Income and Expenditure, Jersey Merchant Seamen's Benefit Society, 1836-1865 (Jersey Pounds)**

| Year | Society Funds | Crew Lists In | Total Income From Lists | Total Expen. | Year | Society Funds | Crew Lists In | Total Income From Lists | Total Expen. |
|------|---------------|---------------|-------------------------|--------------|------|---------------|---------------|-------------------------|--------------|
| 1836 | 452   |     |     |     | 1851 | 6,950 |     |     | 628 |
| 1837 | 880   |     |     |     | 1852 | 7,068 | 325 | 679 | 729 |
| 1838 | 1,240 |     |     |     | 1853 | 7,060 | 315 | 629 | 833 |
| 1839 | 1,771 |     |     |     | 1854 | 7,162 | 313 | 634 | 682 |
| 1840 | 2,180 |     |     |     | 1855 | 7,275 | 325 | 655 | 700 |
| 1841 | 2,706 |     |     |     | 1856 | 7,409 | 308 | 675 | 680 |
| 1842 | 3,214 |     |     |     | 1857 | 7,495 | 301 | 672 | 739 |
| 1843 | 3,654 |     |     |     | 1858 | 7,567 | 341 | 637 | 719 |
| 1844 | 4,163 |     |     | 118 | 1859 | 7,663 | 327 | 689 | 751 |
| 1845 | 4,638 |     |     | 151 | 1860 | 7,695 | 345 | 646 | 783 |
| 1846 | 5,211 |     |     | 151 | 1861 | 7,674 | 325 | 666 | 856 |
| 1847 | 5,727 |     |     | 221 | 1862 | 7,628 | 341 | 637 | 853 |
| 1848 | 6,241 |     |     | 277 | 1863 | 7,836 | 345 | 666 | 622 |
| 1849 | 6,587 |     |     | 446 | 1864 | 8,022 | 329 | 622 | 619 |
| 1850 | 6,737 |     |     | 549 | 1865 | 8,151 | 296 | 621 | 695 |

Source: Minute Books, Jersey Merchant Seamen's Benefit Society, Société Jersiaise, St Helier.

# APPENDIX II.6

**Income and Expenditure, Jersey Merchant Seamen's Benefit Society,
1866-1898 (Pounds Sterling)**

| Year | Society Funds | Crew Lists In | Total Income From Lists | Total Expen. | Year | Society Funds | Crew Lists In | Total Income From Lists | Total Expen. |
|------|------|------|------|------|------|------|------|------|------|
| 1866 | 7,608 | 323 | 618 | 750 | 1883 | 7,375 | 98 | 211 | 520 |
| 1867 | 7,694 | 296 | 632 | 745 | 1884 | 7,369 | 105 | 235 | 477 |
| 1868 | 7,711 | 304 | 601 | 755 | 1885 | 7,312 | 102 | 219 | 500 |
| 1869 | 7,674 | 273 | 568 | 792 | 1886 | 7,212 | 84 | 161 | 501 |
| 1870 | 7,680 | 259 | 588 | 787 | 1887 | 7,061 | 82 | 167 | 525 |
| 1871 | 7,609 | 246 | 475 | 774 | 1888 | 6,907 | 68 | 142 | 494 |
| 1872 | 7,574 | 237 | 515 | 754 | 1889 | 6,763 | 65 | 115 | 457 |
| 1873 | 7,521 | 207 | 485 | 795 | 1890 | 6,667 | 57 | 120 | 452 |
| 1874 | 7,325 | 172 | 326 | 732 | 1891 | 6,575 | 57 | 123 | 414 |
| 1875 | 7,324 | 160 | 336 | 559 | 1892 | 6,417 | 51 | 84 | 421 |
| 1876 | 7,348 | 128 | 298 | 502 | 1893 | 6,374 | 50 | 84 | 403 |
| 1877 | 7,353 | 120 | 286 | 502 | 1894 | 6,117 | 52 | 99 | 423 |
| 1878 | 7,368 | 113 | 280 | 487 | 1895 | 7,010 | 48 | 82 | 629 |
| 1879 | 7,418 | 122 | 284 | 465 | 1896 | 7,432 | 31 | 42 | 593 |
| 1880 | 7,460 | 100 | 249 | 487 | 1897 | 7,050 | 8 | 8 | 526 |
| 1881 | 7,490 | 95 | 238 | 442 | 1898 | 6,691 | 0 | 0 | 519 |
| 1882 | 7,445 | 98 | 205 | 503 | | | | | |

Source: Minute Books, Jersey Merchant Seamen's Benefit Society, Société Jersiaise, St Helier

# Appendix II.7

**Pensions and Allowances Paid by the Jersey Merchant Seamen's Benefit Society, 1841-1880 (number of cases)**

| Year | Widows | Child. | Allow. | Superan. Seamen | Year | Widows | Child. | Allow. | Superan. Seamen |
|------|--------|--------|--------|------------------|------|--------|--------|--------|------------------|
| 1841 | 3 | 2 | 1 | | 1861 | 231 | 186 | 59 | 54 |
| 1842 | 5 | 10 | 3 | | 1862 | 236 | 197 | 66 | 64 |
| 1843 | 9 | 13 | 4 | | 1863 | 254 | 189 | 41 | 64 |
| 1844 | 19 | 29 | 10 | 1 | 1864 | 258 | 201 | 55 | 60 |
| 1845 | 23 | 41 | 17 | 1 | 1865 | 258 | 212 | 40 | 73 |
| 1846 | 29 | 41 | 9 | 7 | 1866 | 271 | 220 | 53 | 83 |
| 1847 | 43 | 61 | 15 | 8 | 1867 | 281 | 240 | 58 | 86 |
| 1848 | 58 | 95 | 18 | 8 | 1868 | 281 | 178 | 61 | 98 |
| 1849 | 82 | 122 | 29 | 20 | 1869 | 293 | 240 | 55 | 108 |
| 1850 | 99 | 142 | 40 | 19 | 1870 | 298 | 228 | 48 | 107 |
| 1851 | 114 | 158 | 29 | 26 | 1871 | 311 | 222 | 44 | 107 |
| 1852 | 120 | 161 | 47 | 39 | 1872 | 302 | 225 | 41 | 97 |
| 1853 | 134 | 159 | 56 | 42 | 1873 | 315 | 224 | 40 | 111 |
| 1854 | 153 | 180 | 35 | 42 | 1874 | 313 | 193 | 29 | 111 |
| 1855 | 165 | 181 | 48 | 47 | 1875 | 297 | 184 | 36 | 115 |
| 1856 | 174 | 173 | 42 | 43 | 1876 | 302 | 181 | 27 | 116 |
| 1857 | 195 | 178 | 48 | 47 | 1877 | 306 | 185 | 40 | 108 |
| 1858 | 196 | 182 | 49 | 42 | 1878 | 308 | 184 | 31 | 114 |
| 1859 | 210 | 174 | 47 | 42 | 1879 | 310 | 167 | 24 | 114 |
| 1860 | 222 | 193 | 47 | 47 | 1880 | 318 | 172 | 37 | 104 |

Source: Recapitulation of Pensions and Allowances, Jersey, Merchant Seamen's Benefit Society, Société Jersiaise, St Helier

# APPENDIX II.8

## The De La Court Fund of Guernsey—Cases Relieved, 1833-1889

| | | | | | | | | | | |
|---|---|---|---|---|---|---|---|---|---|---|
| 1833 | 29 cases | £127 | 5 | 0 | | 1867 | 48 cases | £218 | 10 | 0 |
| 1834 | 15 cases | £46 | 4 | 9 | | 1868 | 68 cases | £373 | 15 | 0 |
| 1835 | 22 cases | £68 | 0 | 0 | | 1869 | 77 cases | £423 | 12 | 2 |
| 1836 | 36 cases | £115 | 5 | 6 | | 1870 | 31 cases | £179 | 19 | 8 |
| 1837 | 17 cases | £78 | 10 | 0 | | 1871 | 44 cases | £295 | 10 | 1 |
| 1838 | 36 cases | £124 | 10 | 5 | | 1872 | 45 cases | £282 | 18 | 0 |
| 1839 | 14 cases | £27 | 0 | 0 | | 1873 | 89 cases | £454 | 17 | 6 |
| 1840 | 36 cases | £118 | 9 | 0 | | 1874 | 49 cases | £264 | 5 | 8 |
| 1841 | 23 cases | £119 | 7 | 10 | | 1875 | 65 cases | £321 | 18 | 11 |
| 1842 | 30 cases | £89 | 15 | 0 | | 1876 | 59 cases | £345 | 1 | 0 |
| 1843 | 27 cases | £141 | 0 | 0 | | 1877 | 45 cases | £297 | 0 | 0 |
| 1844 | 25 cases | £86 | 19 | 0 | | 1878 | 45 cases | £296 | 15 | 6 |
| 1845 | 33 cases | £80 | 1 | 0 | | 1879 | 66 cases | £404 | 8 | 0 |
| 1846 | 31 cases | £181 | 13 | 6 | | 1880 | 66 cases | £493 | 12 | 0 |
| 1847 | 25 cases | £154 | 14 | 0 | | 1881 | 73 cases | £486 | 6 | 6 |
| 1848 | 38 cases | £197 | 12 | 0 | | 1882 | 59 cases | £374 | 11 | 6 |
| 1849 | 75 cases | £186 | 9 | 0 | | 1883 | 49 cases | £356 | 15 | 6 |
| 1850 | 27 cases | £138 | 11 | 7 | | 1884 | 52 cases | £231 | 14 | 6 |
| 1851 | 16 cases | £93 | 2 | 0 | | 1885 | 54 cases | £269 | 7 | 0 |
| 1852 | 38 cases | £158 | 16 | 0 | | 1886 | 74 cases | £434 | 0 | 0 |
| 1853 | 36 cases | £230 | 7 | 0 | | 1887 | 67 cases | £306 | 15 | 0 |
| 1854 | 21 cases | £63 | 5 | 0 | | 1888 | 36 cases | £204 | 10 | 0 |
| 1855 | 39 cases | £168 | 9 | 0 | | 1889 | 41 cases | £187 | 19 | 6 |
| 1856 | 33 cases | £175 | 10 | 11 | | | | | | |
| 1857 | 19 cases | £85 | 5 | 0 | | | | | | |
| 1858 | 39 cases | £180 | 0 | 0 | | | | | | |
| 1859 | 37 cases | £318 | 8 | 9 | | | | | | |
| 1860 | 28 cases | £235 | 5 | 0 | | | | | | |
| 1861 | 36 cases | £345 | 17 | 0 | | | | | | |
| 1862 | 26 cases | £167 | 4 | 7 | | | | | | |
| 1863 | 27 cases | £129 | 0 | 0 | | | | | | |
| 1864 | 37 cases | £284 | 12 | 9 | | | | | | |
| 1865 | 29 cases | £133 | 3 | 7 | | | | | | |
| 1866 | 59 cases | £333 | 0 | 0 | | | | | | |

Source: *The Star Almanack* of Guernsey

The De La Court Fund was established by Jean De La Court, Jurat of the Royal Court, in 1588. 'The fund is administered by the Royal Court, who generally appoint one or two Jurats to investigate the cases brought before that body for relief. After which, a Full Court decides upon the merits of the several cases, and awards such relief as each case may seem to deserve.'

# Appendix II.9

**The Sir William Collings Fund of Guernsey—Cases Relieved, 1849-1889**

| Year | Cases | Amount |
|------|-------|--------|
| 1849 | 1 case | £3 0 0 |
| 1850 | 2 cases | £6 0 0 |
| 1851 | 8 cases | £34 0 0 |
| 1852 | 3 cases | £13 0 0 |
| 1853 | 17 cases | £59 0 0 |
| 1854 | 4 cases | £9 0 0 |
| 1855 | 8 cases | £26 0 0 |
| 1856 | 21 cases | £55 15 0 |
| 1857 | 12 cases | £32 10 0 |
| 1858 | 6 cases | £19 5 6 |
| 1859 | 8 cases | £23 0 0 |
| 1860 | 5 cases | £29 5 0 |
| 1861 | 9 cases | £32 0 0 |
| 1862 | 16 cases | £45 10 0 |
| 1863 | 4 cases | £11 10 0 |
| 1864 | 7 cases | £21 11 0 |
| 1865 | 5 cases | £19 0 0 |
| 1866 | 2 cases | £6 0 0 |
| 1867 | 4 cases | £14 0 0 |
| 1868 | 6 cases | £34 0 0 |
| 1869 | 17 cases | £69 10 0 |
| 1870 | 12 cases | £32 5 0 |
| 1871 | 11 cases | £42 0 0 |
| 1872 | 13 cases | £37 16 3 |
| 1873 | 4 cases | £15 6 10 |
| 1874 | 18 cases | £82 19 2 |
| 1875 | 2 cases | £8 0 0 |
| 1876 | 6 cases | £22 10 0 |
| 1877 | 5 cases | £20 5 0 |
| 1878 | 6 cases | £25 10 0 |
| 1879 | 5 cases | £26 0 0 |
| 1880 | 8 cases | £51 0 0 |
| 1881 | 16 cases | £66 18 1 |
| 1882 | 12 cases | £53 7 0 |
| 1883 | 17 cases | £104 14 0 |
| 1884 | 6 cases | £46 0 0 |
| 1885 | 7 cases | £34 0 0 |
| 1886 | 11 cases | £72 0 0 |
| 1887 | 13 cases | £62 0 0 |
| 1888 | 13 cases | £46 0 0 |
| 1889 | 6 cases | £44 10 0 |

Source: *The Star Almanack* of Guernsey

The Sir William Collings Fund was established in 1849 by Sir William Collings, Jurat of the Royal Court, 'for the benefit of necessitous poor natives of this island, or naturalized inhabitants, and also of strangers who shall have resided in this island for a period of seven years, who, through any accident whatsoever, or from any unforseen cause, may need relief'.

# APPENDIX III.1

## Distribution of Population—Guernsey, 1831-1881

| Parishes | 1831 | 1841 | 1851 | 1861 | 1871 | 1881 | 1891 |
|---|---|---|---|---|---|---|---|
| St Peter Port | 13,893 | 15,304 | 17,047 | 16,388 | 16,166 | 16,588 | 17,041* |
| St Sampson | | 1,567 | 2,006 | 2,781 | 3,038 | 3,624 | 4,493* |
| Vale | | 1,698 | 2,110 | 2,455 | 2,867 | 3,477* | 3,947* |
| Castel | | 2,038 | 2,181 | 2,071 | 2,173 | 2,207* | 2,426* |
| St Saviour | | 1,034 | 1,037 | 942 | 946 | 884 | 916 |
| Torteval | | 387 | 355 | 365 | 354 | 377 | 446 |
| St Peter | | 1,180 | 1,152 | 1,141 | 1,142 | 1,171 | 1,322* |
| Forest | | 696 | 673 | 612 | 622 | 599 | 665 |
| St Martin | | 1,825 | 1,968 | 2,000 | 2,158 | 2,311* | 2,659* |
| St Andrew | | 1,021 | 1,203 | 1,049 | 1,127 | 1,141 | 1,303* |

Sources: *Henry Brouard's Almanac* (1840, 1855), *Guerin's Almanack* (1890, 1895); *British Press Almanac* (1855); *British Press and Jersey Times Almanac* (1880, 1885).

Notes: *includes civil and military population:
1881 total military population: 814

| | |
|---|---|
| St Peter Port: | 654 |
| Vale: | 39 |
| Castel: | 86 |
| St Martin: | 35 |

1891 total military population: 721

| | |
|---|---|
| St Peter Port: | 574 |
| St Sampson: | 38 |
| Vale: | 16 |
| Castel: | 4 |
| St Peter: | 26 |
| St Martin: | 27 |
| St Andrew: | 36 |

# Appendix III.2

## Distribution of Population—Jersey, 1831-1881

| Parishes | 1831 | 1841 | 1851 | 1861 | 1871 | 1881 |
|---|---|---|---|---|---|---|
| St Helier | 16,037 | 23,988 | 29,741 | 29,528 | 30,756 | (a) 28,020 |
| St Saviour | 2,196 | 2,732 | 3,404 | 3,723 | 3,883 | 3,890 |
| St Martin | 1,956 | 2,711 | 4,270 | 3,558 | 3,135 | (b) 2,913 |
| Trinity | 2,098 | 2,491 | 2,610 | 2,273 | 2,149 | 2,002 |
| Grouville | 2,080 | 2,372 | 2,743 | 2,628 | 2,461 | 2,385 |
| St Peter | 2,150 | 2,280 | 2,497 | 2,671 | 2,524 | (c) 2,488 |
| St Ouen | 1,916 | 2,264 | 2,456 | 2,320 | 2,247 | 2,267 |
| St Lawrence | 2,043 | 2,170 | 2,306 | 2,255 | 2,472 | 2,343 |
| St Brelade | 2,069 | 2,170 | 2,468 | 2,354 | 2,777 | (d) 2,192 |
| St John | 1,855 | 1,846 | 2,021 | 1,815 | 1,699 | 1,643 |
| St Clement | 1,215 | 1,491 | 1,553 | 1,448 | 1,445 | 1,313 |
| St Mary | 977 | 1,041 | 1,086 | 1,040 | 1,079 | 989 |

Sources: *British Press Almanac* (1850); *British Press and Jersey Times Almanac* (1865, 1885).

Notes: (a) Includes troops, on board ships in harbour, general hospital, gaol and house of correction—a total of 853 males, 274 females.
 (b) Includes Royal Navy and Merchantmen in Harbour—37.
 (c) Includes troops in Barracks—200.
 (d) Includes troops and merchant seamen—10 males, 2 females.

# Appendix III.3

# The Swan River Settlement

The attention of all parties contemplating emigration is invited to the free British Colony of Western Australia. As a field for the investment of capital, it possesses advantages unknown in any of the other colonies. Its proximity to the Cape, Mauritius, India, China, the Islands of the Southern Ocean, Sydney, Van Dieman's Land, South Australia, and New Zealand, gives it the most commanding situation as the central emporium of Indian and Australasian commerce, and aided by its salubrious climate, will render it the sanatorium of India, and the seminary for her children; while its natural productions, consisting of forests of valuable naval timber, impervious to corruption, beds of china clay, strata of brick earth, quarries of lime and freestones, iron ore, etc., constitute the elements of a great and prosperous country. The bays are plentifully visited by whales; the climate and soil favour the growth of vines, olives, and all the fruits of the tropics, as well as all European fruits and vegetables; barilla, soda, and potash may be obtained for export; and a profitable trade in salt fish has already been commenced. The climate and pasture are favourable to the breed of horses for the Indian cavalry. Tobacco may be cultivated with profit and to a large extent, and numerous other articles can be produced for the neighbouring markets. Land of first quality may be purchased at 4s or 5s an acre; and some farms are to be had rent free for the first years. Sheep farming may be prosecuted under great advantages, and the soil produces wheat and barley, hay and green crops, of superior quality, and in large quantities. The roads are in an improving state; carts, wagons, and farming implements are manufactured in the colony; and every facility is offered to agriculturists, the natives not only being peaceably disposed, but rendering great assistance to the settlers for small portions of rice or flour. The wages of mechanics and labourers of all descriptions are very good, and provisions and living being economical, they have every opportunity of forming small properties of their own. Small farmers may take charge of the flocks of large sheep holders, on most excellent terms, whether for pecuniary payment, or for a share of the increase – by the latter means commencing the formation of flocks themselves. To half-pay officers, and small annuitants, the economy, comfort, and respectability of living, must prove attractive; while, to Indian valetudinarians, the renovating and invigorating effects of the climate will recommend this eligible colony. To all classes of emigrants, it must be gratifying to learn that the settlement which possesses these advantages has a population composed of a most respectable class of British yeomen, and is entirely freed

134

from the contamination of convict society, Western Australia not being a penal colony; whilst the climate is of the most genial and salubrious character, and especially favourable in all cases of consumption and pulmonary complaints, the atmosphere being free from fogs, drought being unknown, and ice rarely seen. The heat of the summer is temperate, and prevented from being oppressive by the regular land and sea breezes.

Printed in *The Star,* 27 February 1845

# APPENDIX III.4

**Country of Birth of Mariners on Board Ship on Census Night (31 March 1851)**

| | Total | England | Scotland | Ireland | C.I | Colony | Not Known |
|---|---|---|---|---|---|---|---|
| Total | 120,186 | 79,192 | 27,920 | 10,026 | 2,747 | 244 | 57 |
| In Vessels in British Ports on 31/3 | 24,750 | 16,755 | 4,769 | 2,473 | 537 | 174 | 42 |
| In Home-Trade Vessels Arriving in Port in April | 14,087 | 11,326 | 1,702 | 674 | 300 | 70 | 15 |
| In Foreign-Going Vessels Absent from U.K | 81,349 | 51,111 | 21,449 | 6,879 | 1,910 | - | - |

Source: PP 1852-3, Vol.LXXXVIII

# Appendix III.5

**Nationality of Mariners Serving Abroad in Foreign-Trading Merchant Vessels on Census Night, 3 April 1881**

| Capacities | Total All Ages | England and Wales | Scotland | Ireland | C.I & I of M | Other |
|---|---|---|---|---|---|---|
| Masters | 6,206 | 3,868 | 1,226 | 343 | 146 | 623 |
| Mates | 11,424 | 6,978 | 2,720 | 605 | 255 | 866 |
| Able/Ordinary Seamen | 52,715 | 19,720 | 5,260 | 3,572 | 970 | 23,193 |
| Apprentices | 4,816 | 3,398 | 997 | 175 | 50 | 196 |
| Boys | 1,455 | 1,008 | 151 | 104 | 23 | 169 |
| Engineers/ Firemen & Others | 44,033 | 23,712 | 10,224 | 3,619 | 685 | 5,793 |
| **Total** | **120,649** | **58,684** | **20,578** | **8,418** | **2,129** | **30,840** |

Source: PP 1883, Vol.LXXX

Note: Other consists of mariners from colonies (7,154), foreign parts (23,236), born at sea (106), not known (344)

# APPENDIX III.6

**Age Distribution of Jersey-born Sailors Serving on Jersey-Registered Vessels, 1850**

| Age Range | No. | % of Total |
|-----------|-----|------------|
| 10-14 | 22 | 1.46 |
| 15-19 | 272 | 18.07 |
| 20-29 | 666 | 44.25 |
| 30-39 | 337 | 22.39 |
| 40-49 | 140 | 9.30 |
| 50-59 | 54 | 3.59 |
| 60-69 | 6 | 0.40 |
| Over 70 | 1 | 0.07 |
| Not Known | 7 | 0.46 |
| **Total** | **1,505** | **100** |

Source: *Jersey Merchant Seamen's Benefit Society* (1 January–31 December 1850)

# Appendix III.7

**Age Distribution of Jersey-born Sailors Serving on Jersey-Registered Vessels, 1880-1**

| Age Range | No. | % of Total |
|-----------|-----|------------|
| 10-14 | 11 | 1.18 |
| 15-19 | 211 | 22.69 |
| 20-29 | 377 | 40.54 |
| 30-39 | 175 | 18.82 |
| 40-49 | 94 | 10.11 |
| 50-59 | 38 | 4.09 |
| 60-69 | 13 | 1.40 |
| Over 70 | - | - |
| Not Known | 11 | 1.18 |
| | | |
| **Total** | **930** | **100** |

Source: *Jersey Merchant Seamen's Benefit Society* (1 January 1880-31 December 1881)

# Notes

Introduction, pp.xi–xvii

1. Gregory Stevens Cox, *St Peter Port 1680-1830: The History of an International Entrepôt* (Boydell Press, 1999).
2. *Ibid.*, footnote 7, p.144.
3. 17 & 18 Vict., c.104. Masters were also required to record births and marriages at sea, wages due to seamen who died and the money raised from the sale of their personal effects, etc. The instructions to masters filled the first couple of pages of every official log book. Masters of coasting vessels, however, were not required to keep log books.
4. Official Log, *Geffard* (1856), PRO BT 98/4505
5. Official Log, *Atrevida* (1856), in *ibid.*
6. Official Log, *Laura* (1856), PRO BT 98/4484
7. Official Log, *Byzantium* (1856), PRO BT 98/4504.
8. John D. Kelleher, *The Triumph of the Country: The Rural Community in Nineteenth Century Jersey* (John Appleby Publishing, 1995), and G.C. Powell, 'The Part Played by Immigrants in Jersey's Economic Development over the Centuries', *ABSJ*, Vol.24 (1988).
9. Quoted in *ibid.*, p.537.
10. Kelleher, *The Triumph of the Country*, p.55.
11. *Jersey Times*, 25 February 1848.
12. Quoted in Kelleher, *The Triumph of the Country*, p.48.
13. *Jersey Times*, 11 January 1848.
14. See the correspondence exchanged between Bailiffs, 12 April and 19 April 1845, Royal Court Letter Book I (1843-46), St Peter Port.
15. Kelleher, *The Triumph of the Country*, p.48.
16. Stevens Cox, *St Peter Port*, pp.85-6.
17. 'Report of the Committee appointed by the Royal Court to inquire into the present state of Her Majesty's Prison in this Island', 26 November 1850, Royal Court Letter Book IV (1849-51), St Peter Port.
18. See, for example, the correspondence of Peter Stafford Cary, 10 December 1850, 23 December 1850, 10 June 1853, and 3 December 1853, Royal Court Letter Books IV (1849-51) and VI (1853-4).
19. See George Symes Hooper, *A Paper on the History and Statistics of Asian Cholera in Jersey* (Jersey, 1833), especially pp.9-11, 45. For a discussion of the effects of the epidemic in Guernsey, see S.K. Kellet-Smith, 'The Guernsey Cholera Epidemic of 1832', *R&TSG*, Vol.XX, pp.643-55.
20. Hooper, '*A Paper on … Asiatic Cholera …*', p.47.
21. Stevens Cox, *St Peter Port*, p.74.

The Channel Islands and Maritime Trade, 1815-1865, pp.1-20

1. John D. Kelleher, *The Triumph of the Country: The Rural Community in Nineteenth*

*Century Jersey* (John Appleby Publishing, 1995), p.67.

2.  Ferdinand B. Tupper, *The History of Guernsey and its Bailiwick, with occasional notices of Jersey* (2nd edition, 1876), p.505.

3.  People in work were said to be earning 40 sols a day—the cost of a pot of cider. Kelleher, *The Triumph of the Country*, p.67.

4.  Tupper, *History of Guernsey*, p.505.

5.  According to Gregory Stevens Cox, it was mainly the poor who emigrated—principally to America and Canada. Wealthy Islanders were protected against economic difficulties by their foreign investments, which were flourishing. See Gregory Stevens Cox, *St Peter Port 1680-1830: The History of an International Entrepôt* (Boydell Press, 1999), p.89. Emigrants left Guernsey in some numbers before 1815, however. See, for example, Alan Jamieson, 'The Channel Islands and Overseas Settlement, 1600-1900', in A.G. Jamieson, (ed.), *A People of the Sea: The Maritime History of the Channel Islands* (Methuen, 1986), p.281.

6.  Petition to Major General Bayly, 11 April 1817, Minute Books, Guernsey Chamber of Commerce (hereafter GCC). See also Eric W. Sharp, 'The Toll of the Sea; Guernsey Ships and their Fate', *R&TSG*, Vol.20 (1979), p.517. Sharp cites an 1819 advertisement for passages to the United States: 'The new brig *Union* of 117 tons D. Maillard, Master, excellently fitted for the comfortable accommodation of passengers and well found in every respect will be ready to sail from Guernsey on or about the 1st June 1819 for one of the above cities in the United States [i.e. Baltimore or Philadelphia] being a central situation from whence it is easy to go to the first cities in the States or to the best lands in the back settlements on and to the westward of the Ohio or to Canada by means of the steamboats which take only five or six days to go from Baltimore to Montreal.'

7.  Emigration from the Channel Islands certainly did not cease during these years: as Jamieson has shown, Islanders emigrated in some numbers during this period to the U.S., Canada and Australia. See Alan Jamieson, 'The Channel Islands and Australia: Maritime Links in the 1850s', *The Great Circle*, Vol.5, No.1 (1983), pp.40-7. See also Jean Le Pelley, 'Guernsey Pioneers in Australia, 1841-1862', *R&TSG*, Vol.18 (1966), pp.63-86. Many would no doubt have been attracted by advertisements such as that published in February 1845 in *The Star* of Guernsey designed to attract permanent settlers to Western Australia. For the text of the advertisement, see Appendix III.3.

8.  G.C. Powell, 'The Part Played by Immigrants in Jersey's Economic Development over the Centuries', *ABSJ*, Vol.24 (1988), p.536.

9.  Census Report, PP 1851, Vol.XLIII. See also the final part of this study.

10. This was not, of course, the Islands' first experience of immigration. From at least the 16th century both Jersey and Guernsey experienced frequent waves of immigration. Early in the 17th century, for example, several Jersey merchants petitioned the Crown to prohibit foreigners establishing shops on the Island, claiming that they enjoyed unfair advantages, in the sense that they benefited from equal privileges as natives but 'bear no burden in taxes or like public payments'. From the end of the 17th century to the end of the 18th, religious persecution in France drove first Huguenots and then Royalists and Catholics to the Islands. Although some Huguenot families settled permanently in the Channel Islands, for most refugees this was but a temporary asylum—a staging post on their way to England. Then, in the 18th century, many English artisans and retailers were actually encouraged to migrate to Guernsey, at least, and those migrants whose skills were in high demand—shipbuilders, coopers, and

sailmakers, for instance—were welcomed in the Island. By the 19th century, however, the attitudes of Islanders towards outsiders had clearly become more ambiguous. Whilst wealthy immigrants were welcomed, Islanders' attitudes towards poorer immigrants was far more negative. There is, for example, ample evidence of efforts being made by the Island authorities to prevent the arrival of the very poor. In many cases, moreover, efforts were also made to return poor families to their places of origin. In 1850, for example, the Royal Court of Guernsey ordered to be removed to Ireland six of the 11 children of one John McKenna. Four of the 11 children, orphaned after the death of their father, a Royal Artillery Pensioner, in November 1848, and then that of their mother, of cholera, in September 1849, were allowed to remain, as they were all in employment (three as servants and one as a sailor). But the six children who had been maintained in the workhouse since November 1848 were sent to Ormagh Union Workhouse in March 1850, from where the Royal Court believed their father to have originated. For details of the McKenna case, see William Stanley to Sir George Grey, Dublin, 28 May 1850, Royal Court Letter Book IV (1849-51), St Peter Port, Guernsey. For a further discussion of these issues, see Stevens Cox, *St Peter Port*, esp. chapter 5. See also Powell, 'The Part Played by Immigrants', pp.533-4, and Kelleher, *The Triumph of the Country*, pp.48 and 55.

11. Rosemary Ommer, 'A Peculiar and Immediate Dependence of the Crown': The Basis of the Jersey Merchant Triangle', *Business History*, Vol.26 (1984), p.107.

12. See Alec Podger, 'Shipbuilding in Jersey', *ABSJ* (1962), pp.229-35; Victor Coysh, 'The Guernsey Shipbuilding Industry', *R&TSG* (1952), pp.208-18; Eric W.Sharp, 'The Shipbuilders of Guernsey', *R&TSG* (1970), pp.478-502; and Jamieson, 'Shipbuilding in the Channel Islands', in Jamieson (ed.), *A People of the Sea*, pp.290-311. For details of the ships built by one prominent shipbuilding firm in Jersey—George Deslandes & Co.—see Appendix Table I.9.

13. Britain and, for Jersey, British North America, were the principal suppliers of vessels built outside the island. Between 1817 and 1890, British shipyards supplied 12.23% of all new built Guernsey tonnage, and 7.78% of Jersey tonnage. 14.69% of all new built tonnage registered in Jersey came from the shipyards of British North America. These figures are calculated from Jamieson (ed.), *A People of the Sea*, table 12.4, p.304.

14. For more detailed figures for the period 1812-50, see Appendix Tables I.1 and I.2.

15. Jamieson, 'Shipbuilding', in Jamieson (ed.), *A People of the Sea*, pp.290-1.

16. The move towards building larger vessels is evident throughout Britain during these years. David Williams' study of the trans-Atlantic trades from Liverpool, shows the rapid growth in the tonnage of vessels in the two decades between 1832 and 1853. In 1832, there were only 22 vessels over 600 tons employed on these routes, the largest measuring 723 tons. By 1853, the number of vessels over 600 tons totalled 822, of which 53 measured between 1,500 and 2,200 tons. See David Williams, 'Crew Size in Trans-Atlantic Trades in the Mid-Nineteenth Century', in Rosemary Ommer and Gerald Panting (eds.), *Working Men Who Got Wet* (Maritime History Group, Memorial University of Newfoundland, 1980), Table 1, p.111.

17. See also Appendix Tables I.3 and I.4.

18. Appendix Table I.1 shows, however, that the number and tonnage of vessels registered in Guernsey had fallen between 1812 and 1815—from 76 vessels (8,312 tons) to 61 (6,662 tons). In Jersey, the number and tonnage of vessels had increased between these years—from 54 (5,369 tons) to 69 (7,519 tons). For the sources of the figures presented in Table 1, see Appendix Tables I.1

and I.2, *British Press and Jersey Times Almanac* (1865), and *Barbet's Almanac* (1866). See also Footnote 3, Part II.

19.  Ommer, 'A Peculiar and Immediate Dependence ...', pp.107-8.
20.  As Ommer explains, cod provided the Island with 'the means for economic growth unrestrained by territorial limits and utilizing a prolific resource which was in high demand ...': Rosemary Ommer, 'The Cod Trade in the New World', in Jamieson (ed.), *A People of the Sea*, p.246.
21.  Quoted in Ommer, *From Outpost to Outport: A Structural Analysis of the Jersey-Gaspé Cod Fishery, 1767-1886* (McGill-Queen's University Press, Montreal, 1991), p.161.
22.  As Ommer explains, the term applies to the *structure* of the trade rather than the physical pattern, and if it incorporates three different foci—ownership, production, and marketing—the trade continues to be triangular even when the product is sold in two or more markets.
23.  'By 1820, when Jersey-built tonnage overtook tonnage built elsewhere, it was dominated by cod-trade merchants; from 1818 to 1821, tonnage owned by cod merchants was always more than 90% of all new Jersey-built vessels, and from 1822 to 1825 it was still more than 50%.' Ommer, *From Outpost to Outport*, p.154.
24.  Indeed, according to the late John Sarre, one Guernsey vessel engaged in the cod trade with Newfoundland was recorded in Poole as early as 1521. See John Sarre's forthcoming study, 'A History of the Development of Sailing Ships and Trade'. I am grateful to Mr Sarre for allowing me access to his manuscript and other data.
25.  *Ibid*. See also C.R. Fay, *The Channel Islands and Newfoundland* (Cambridge, 1961), p.36, and more generally Chapter 5.
26.  This partnership continued until the early 1820s. See also Sarre, *op.cit.*
27.  Quoted in Ommer, *From Outpost to Outport*, p.141.
28.  Quoted in Ommer, 'The Cod Trade', p.263.
29.  Minute Books, Jersey Chamber of Commerce (hereafter JCC), St Helier, 14 April 1853.
30.  Henry Inglis, *The Channel Islands* (London, 1835), p.84.
31.  Extracts from 'Commerce of Guernsey', published in *The Star*, 11 December 1837.
32.  Tupper, *History of Guernsey*, pp.508-10. As measured by the tonnage of vessels built for non-Island owners, F.C. Clarke was the most successful of Jersey's shipbuilders. Almost 14,000 tons of shipping (13,580) were built in Clarke's yards for non-Islanders, at least 7,762 tons of which was built for the two firms of Scrutton & Co. (of London) and Melhuish & Co. (of Liverpool) alone. See John Jean, *Jersey Sailing Ships* (Phillimore, 1982), Appendix 4, pp.168-9.
33.  Inglis, *The Channel Islands*, p.88.
34.  See Ommer, 'The Cod Trade', p.265.
35.  Although there appears to have been some confusion among masters of Channel Island vessels as to the application of the Act in the Islands, most, though by no means all, seem fully to have complied with the law. The Crew Lists record details of all vessels undertaking voyages in the foreign trade (name, tonnage, port and number of registration), of the voyages conducted (port of departure, final destination, and port to which the vessel returned in the United Kingdom), and of the crew, including the master and all apprentices (name, place of birth, capacity in which employed, previous vessel on which each seaman served, date and place of employment and discharge, and registration number). The Crew Agreements—literally the contract signed by the master and his crew—contain much the same information, but also include the agreed wages to be paid to each crew member and sometimes describe in greater detail the voyage to be undertaken. The Crew Agreements, which were retained by the master for the

duration of the voyage for the purpose of recording any changes in the manning of the vessel, were to be endorsed by the consular authorities at all ports at which the vessel called, and then returned to the Registrar of Shipping on completion of the voyage. Masters of coasting vessels, who were not required to return crew lists after every completed voyages, were nevertheless obliged to make returns at six monthly intervals, detailing all voyages made or the trade in which the vessel was employed (e.g. coal, stone), and of the men employed during each six month period. These were known as Coasting Articles. Vessels engaged in both foreign and domestic trades returned Crew Agreements and Coasting Articles, in accordance with the voyage completed.

36.  The Liverpool Bills have been used successfully to analyse, for example, cotton imports into the port of Liverpool during the 19th century, and man-ton ratios on vessels engaged in trans-Atlantic trades. For details of the Bills of Entry, see Edward Carson, 'Customs Bills of Entry', *Maritime History*, pp.176-89. For examples of the uses to which the Bills may be put, see David M. Williams, 'The Shipping of the North Atlantic Cotton Trade in the Mid-Nineteenth Century', in David Alexander and Rosemary Ommer (eds.), *Volumes Not Values: Canadian Sailing Ships and World Trade* (Maritime History Group, Memorial University of Newfoundland, 1979), pp.305-25. Guernsey's granite trade is discussed in greater detail later in this study.

37.  The figures have been calculated from the Shipping List published in *Barbet's Almanack* (1845), and do not correspond exactly to those published in Parliamentary Papers.

38.  The set includes all crew lists and agreements for voyages beginning between 1 January and 31 December 1845, even though some of these were not completed until 1846. The Crew Lists may be found in PRO BT 98/664, 98/937, 98/938. All those for vessels mentioned in the text may be found here.

39.  Calculated from the Shipping Lists published in *British Press Almanac* (1845).

40.  These comprise all voyages begun between 1 January and 31 December 1845, and include two voyages beginning in the fisheries. The relevant crew lists and agreements may be found in PRO BT 98/678, 98/956, 98/957, 98/958, 98/959. Crew lists for all vessels mentioned in the text may be found here.

41.  See, for example, the occasions on which problems like these occurred to Captain Philip de Gruchy, Letter/Log Book of Captain Philip de Gruchy, September 1868—July 1869, Société Jersiaise, St Helier.

42.  Captain Philip de Gruchy to Messrs Le Maistre & Co., Rio de Janeiro, 7 August 1869, *ibid*.

43.  For details of the sources upon which Tables 2 and 3 are based, see footnotes 38 (Guernsey) and 40 (Jersey) above.

44.  For details of sources, see Footnote 40.

45.  Captain Philip de Gruchy to Messrs Le Maistre & Co., New York, 30 November 1869, Letter/Log Book of Captain Philip de Gruchy.

46.  *London Customs Bills of Entry*, 1 January—31 December 1845.

47.  Ommer, *From Outpost to Outport*, p.150.

48.  See Footnote 40.

49.  The *London Customs Bills of Entry* show in considerable detail the cargoes carried in Channel Island vessels. See, for example, Appendix Tables I.5 and I.6 at the end of this study.

50.  Ommer, *From Outpost to Outport*, p.166.

51.  Sarah Palmer, *Politics, shipping, and the repeal of the Navigation Laws* (Manchester University Press, Manchester, 1990), p.4. An excellent example of the ways in which vessels 'danced to the tune of trade' was the discovery of guano on a

remote African island. See Robin Craig, 'The African Guano Trade', *Mariner's Mirror* (February 1969), pp.25-55.

52. Eric W. Sharp, 'The Harbours and Shipping of Guernsey at the turn of the 19th Century', *R&TSG*, Vol.16 (1959), p.477.

53. *The Star*, 30 October 1837.

54. Jamieson, 'Voyage Patterns and Trades of Channel Island Vessels, 1700-1900', in Jamieson (ed.), *A People of the Sea*, pp.387-8.

55. AGM, 25 January 1865, Minute Books, GCC.

56. A.G. Jamieson, 'Voyage Patterns and Trades', in Jamieson (ed.), *A People of the Sea*, pp.387-8.

57. While Jersey did have a small export trade in stone in did not compare in volume with that of Guernsey. Jersey's stone trade is discussed later in this study.

58. Figures are based on the sample of extant crew lists for 1845, which represent only a proportion of voyages conducted over the course of that year.

59. *London Customs Bills of Entry*, 1 January 1845—31 December 1845. See also Appendix Tables I.5 and I.6.

60. Kelleher, *The Triumph of the Country*, p.

61. Linda Clarke, *Building Capitalism: Historical change and the labour process in the production of the built environment* (Routledge, 1992), p.198. According to Inglis, writing in the 1830s, Guernsey granite was found to be of better quality than Aberdeen granite: 'a cubic foot of this stone weighs 2999 oz: while a cubic foot of Aberdeen, weighs 2690 oz.' See Inglis, *The Channel Islands*, p.88. Later in the century, Guernsey began to face competition from Belgian granite. See General Meeting, 14 October 1879, and AGM, 26 February 1883, Minute Books, GCC.

62. Ansted, *The Channel Islands* (London, 1893), p.415. See also Eric W.Sharp, 'The Harbours and Shipping of Guernsey at the turn of the 19th Century', *R&TSG* Vol.16 (1959), pp.469, 477.

63. *Almanac of Guernsey* (1830).

64. *The Star*, 6 July 1835. 'We are not surprised', the report continued, 'at the increasing demand for our excellent stone, which has been proved, by actual experiment, superior to any other. We recommend strangers, especially geologists and those interested in architecture, to visit the quarries, and we believe most will find the hardness and density of the stone greater than they expected.'

65. Jamieson, 'Voyage Patterns', in Jamieson (ed.), *A People of the Sea*, p.385. Jersey vessels carried five shipments.

66. These figures are drawn from the *Almanac of Guernsey* (1855), p.30.

### THE DECLINE OF CHANNEL ISLAND SHIPPING, 1865-1900

1. See, for example, Alan G. Jamieson, 'Voyage Patterns and Trades of Channel Island Vessels, 1700-1900', in A.G. Jamieson (ed.), *A People of the Sea: The Maritime History of the Channel Islands* (Methuen, 1986), pp.367-403.

2. Quoted in Rosemary Ommer, 'The Trade and Navigation of the Island', in David Alexander and Rosemary Ommer (eds.), *Volumes Not Values: Canadian Sailing Ships and World Trades* (Maritime History Group, Memorial University of Newfoundland, 1979), p.38.

3. See *Parliamentary Papers*, Vol.XI (1816), p.194; *British Press and Jersey Times Almanac* (1865); and *Barbet's Almanac* (Guernsey, 1866). An almost complete series of almanacs, published annually throughout the 19th century in Jersey and Guernsey, may be found at the Société Jersiaise (St Helier) and the Priaulx Library (St Peter Port).

4. The precise figure for Guernsey is 39,382 tons. See A.G. Jamieson, 'Shipbuilding in the Channel Islands', in Jamieson (ed.), *A People of the Sea*, Table 12.1, p.291.

5. Rosemary Ommer explains that the crash of 1886, which was caused by the mismanagement of funds in what was known as the States Bank by manager Philip Gosset, 'destroyed the financial basis of the two greatest cod-trade firms in Gaspé, CRC and Le Boutillier, as well as other smaller concerns'. In addition, because the bank acted as a credit bank, and because nearly all the most prominent families in the cod trade and associated businesses were among its shareholders, the effects of the crash were widespread. For details, see Rosemary Ommer, *From Outpost to Outport: A Structural Analysis of the Jersey-Gaspé Cod Fishery, 1767-1886* (McGill-Queen's University Press, Montreal, 1991), pp.145-8

6. *Ibid.*, 145-48, 165-7. For a shorter, more accessible analysis of Jersey's links with the fisheries, see Rosemary Ommer, 'The Cod Trade in the New World', in Jamieson (ed.), *A People of the Sea*. See also A.G. Jamieson, 'The Channel Islands and Overseas Settlement, 1600-1900', in *ibid.*, p.278.

7. The set includes all voyages begun between 1 January and 31 December 1845, and include two voyages beginning in the fisheries. The relevant crew lists and agreements may be found in PRO BT 98/678, 98/956, 98/957, 98/958, 98/959. Crew lists for all vessels mentioned in the text may be found here.

8. The set includes all crew lists and agreements for voyages beginning between 1 January and 31 December 1845, even though some of these were not completed until 1846. The Crew Lists may be found in PRO BT 98/664, 98/937, 98/938. All those for vessels mentioned in the text may be found here.

9. Ferdinand Brock Tupper, *The History of Guernsey and its Bailiwick, with occasional notices of Jersey* (2nd edition, 1876), p.444.

10. AGM, 25 January 1865, Minute Books, Guernsey Chamber of Commerce (hereafter GCC). See also John Sarre's introduction to his forthcoming study of Guernsey sailing ships, 'A History of the Development of Sailing Ships and Trade'.

11. Ommer, *From Outpost to Outport*, pp.181-3.

12. AGM, 26 March 1868, Minute Books, GCC.

13. AGM, 11 March 1868, Minute Books, Jersey Chamber of Commerce (hereafter JCC).

14. On this subject, see Rosemary Ommer, 'The decline of the eastern Canadian shipping industry, 1880-1895', *Journal of Transport History* (1984), pp.25-44. See also Stephanie Jones, 'Merchant Shipbuilding in the North East and South West of England, 1870-1913', in Stephen Fisher (ed.), *British Shipping and Seamen, 1630-1960* (Exeter Papers in Economic History, University of Exeter, 1984).

15. From 1892 to 1914, Britain alone produced between 60% and 79% of the world's mercantile tonnage. See Sidney Pollard, 'British and World Shipbuilding, 1890-1914: A Study in Comparative Costs', *Journal of Economic History*, Vol. XVII, No. 3 (1957), p.427

16. Steamers did make an appearance on the Baltic and Mediterranean in the 1850s, but their employment here at this time was a consequence of the high freight rates caused by the Crimean War. See P.L. Cottrell, 'The steamship on the Mersey, 1815-80: investment and ownership', in P.L. Cottrell and D.H. Aldcroft (eds.), *Shipping, Trade and Commerce: Essays in Memory of Ralph Davis* (Leicester University Press, Leicester, 1981), p.142. For an analysis of early experiments in steamship building between 1820 and 1850, see Sarah Palmer, 'Experience, Experiment and Economics: Factors in the Construction of Early Merchant Steamships', in Keith Matthews and Gerald Panting (eds.), *Ships and*

*Shipbuilding in the North Atlantic Region* (Maritime History Group, Memorial University of Newfoundland, 1978).

17. *Ibid.*

18. Ommer, *From Outpost to Outport*, p.181.

19. Cottrell, 'The steamships on the Mersey', Table 21, p.139 and pp.141-2.

20. *Ibid.*, pp.142-3.

21. *Ibid.*, p.141.

22. See Ommer, 'The decline of the eastern Canadian shipping industry', pp.25-9. See also Gerald S. Graham, 'The Ascendancy of the Sailing Ship, 1850-85', *Economic History Review*, Vol.IX (1956-7), pp.74-88.

23. Sidney Pollard and Paul Robertson, *The British Shipbuilding Industry, 1870-1914* (Harvard University Press, Cambridge, Massachusetts, 1979), p.13

24. *Ibid.*, pp.49, 51, 55-6. See also Pollard, 'British and World Shipbuilding', pp.433, 436, 441; and Alan Jamieson, 'Shipbuilding in the Channel Islands', in Jamieson (ed.), *A People of the Sea*, p.305.

25. Pollard and Robertson, *British Shipbuilding*, p.56. The decline of shipbuilding on the Thames, where iron, coal and labour were more expensive, had been anticipated as early as 1862. See the 17 October 1862 editorial from *The Engineer*, quoted in Cottrell, 'The steamships on the Mersey', footnote 3, p.189.

26. For the effects of these developments on the south-west of England, see Jones, 'Merchant Shipbuilding', in Fisher (ed.), *British Shipping and Seamen*, pp.68-85.

27. Alan Jamieson, 'The Channel Islands and Australia: Maritime Links in the 1850s', *The Great Circle*, Vol.5 (1983), No.1, p.40.

28. Tupper, *The History of Guernsey*. See the editor's note to the second edition, p.508.

29. AGM, 19 February 1880, Minute Books, GCC.

30. *Ibid.*

31. Tupper, *The History of Guernsey*, editor's note, p.508.

32. On this subject see also Ommer, *From Outpost to Outport*, pp.181-3.

33. See the Shipping Lists published in *Guernsey and Jersey Almanack* (1826), *British Press Almanac* (1845, 1855), *British Press and Jersey Times Almanac* (1865, 1875, 1885), and *Jersey Express Almanac* (1895). Where gross and net tonnages are given in the Shipping Lists, gross tonnage has been used to calculate the figures presented in this table.

34. AGM, 13 March 1885, Minute Books, JCC.

35. See the Minute Books of the Jersey Merchant Seamen's Benefit Society (hereafter JMSBS), Société Jersiaise, St Helier, Jersey. For details of the establishment of the Society, see also Philip Syvret, 'Société de Bienfaisance pour la Marine Marchand', *ABSJ*, Vol.19 (1965), pp.75-83.

36. Figures are calculated from *British Press and Jersey Times Almanac* (1880), and the ledgers of seamen's contributions of the JMSBS (1880).

37. This figure includes some 45 small craft, each measuring under 15 tons. These are included in the analysis because seamen on small boats were also entitled, indeed were encouraged, to become members of the Benefit Society.

38. Figures are calculated from *British Press Almanac* (1850) and the ledgers of seamen's contributions of the JMSBS (1850). In addition, masters of 12 vessels not listed in the 1850 Almanac returned crew lists and seamen's contributions. Some of these had come on to the register over the course of the year. See the ledgers of the JMSBS (1850, 1880). See also John Jean, *Jersey Sailing Ships* (Phillimore, 1982).

39. John Sarre, 'A History of the Development of Sailing Ships and Trade', forthcoming.

40. See, for example, AGM, 11 March 1880, Minute Books, JCC.

41. Ansted, *The Channel Islands*, p.414. Figures on imports and re-exports, published by the *British Press and Jersey Times Almanac*, confirm that the Island's links with the fisheries continued in the mid-1880s. In 1884, 31,488 cwt. of fish/cod were imported in Jersey, of which 23,531 were re-exported. See *British Press and Jersey Times Almanac* (1885).

42. According to *Staddon and Grigg's Almanack* of 1876, 'Other vessels have been purchased by Jersey owners and registered in Guernsey and elsewhere, owing to the local taxation on Shipping, and the Jersey Merchant Seamen's Fund, which both act towards making the expenses of Jersey heavier to its own ships than to those of other ports. This is slowly but surely decreasing the number of vessels registered here ... Of late whole shoals of vessels have been transferred to Guernsey. Hitherto Jersey vessels have borne a good name, soon there will be but few to bear it. About 40 vessels really belonging to Jersey owners are registered in Guernsey alone, and mostly large ones.'

43. Annual Report, 17 March 1875, Minute Books, JMSBS.

44. Annual Report, 16 March 1881, Minute Books, JMSBS.

45. Annual Report, 15 March 1893, Minute Books, JMSBS.

46. Annual Report, 17 March 1875, Minute Books, JMSBS.

47. Annual Report, 16 March 1881, Minute Books, JMSBS.

48. Annual Report, 19 March 1890, Minute Books, JMSBS.

49. Special General Meeting, 13 April 1894, Minute Books, JMSBS.

50. See the Shipping Lists published in *Barbet's Almanac* (1830, 1845, 1855, 1866); and *Guerin's Almanack* (1885, 1900). It should be noted that where old and new tonnage was given, new tonnage was used to calculate the figures given in this table.

51. See, for example, AGM, 3 March 1886, and AGM, 13 March 1888, Minute Books, GCC.

52. Jamieson, 'Shipbuilding', in Jamieson (ed.), *A People of the Sea*, Table 12.1, p.291.

53. *Ibid.*

54. Ommer, *From Outpost to Outport*, p.182.

55. Jamieson, 'Shipbuilding', in Jamieson (ed.), *A People of the Sea*, Table 12.1, p.291.

56. Extraordinary General Meeting, 20 April 1869, Minute Books, GCC.

57. AGM, 9 March 1870, Minute Books, JCC.

58. John Kelleher, *The Triumph of the Country: The Rural Community in Nineteenth Century Jersey* (John Appleby Publishing/Société Jersiaise, St Helier, 1994), p.195, and *British Press and Jersey Times Almanac* (1875). The figures for 1851 printed in the *Almanac* are slightly lower—57,020.

59. Jamieson, 'Shipbuilding', in Jamieson (ed.), *A People of the Sea*, pp.303-4.

60. *British Press and Jersey Times Alamanac* (1875, 1885), and Kelleher, *The Triumph of the Country*, pp.196, 199.

61. General Meeting, 28 December 1883, Minute Books, JCC.

62. AGM, 22 March 1892, Minute Books, JCC.

63. The following figures are based on the analysis of seamen's contributions entered in the ledgers of the Jersey Merchant Seamen's Benefit Society for the years 1850, 1880 and 1881.

64. See the *Almanacs* of Guernsey of 1840, 1855, 1890, 1895; and of Jersey, 1855.

65. General Meeting, 28 December 1883, Minute Books, JCC.

66. Census Report, PP 1883, VOL.LXXX, p.732. Figures for Guernsey include the other islands of the bailiwick.

67. Census Report, PP 1852-3, Vol.LXXXVIII.

68. Census Report, PP 1883, Vol.LXXX, p.732; and Census Report, PP 1852-3,

Vol.LXXXVIII.

69. Alan Jamieson, 'The Channel Islands and Overseas Settlement, 1600-1900', in Jamieson (ed.), *A People of the Sea*, pp.281-9; and Jamieson, 'The Channel Islands and Australia', pp.40-5.

70. A comparison of the development of the Island economies during the 19th century must await further research, in particular for Guernsey. For the development of Jersey agriculture during the 19th century, see Kelleher, *The Triumph of the Country*.

71. *Ibid.*, p.66.

72. AGM, 29 January 1866, Minute Books, GCC.

73. General Meeting, 22 December 1868, Minute Books, GCC.

74. AGM, 21 February 1867, Minute Books, GCC.

75. See Ommer, *From Outpost to Outport*, p.181.

76. AGM, 18 March 1869, Minute Books, GCC.

77. Further arguments were put forward at this meeting. One was that the proposals should be supported 'on the ground of justice to the shipowner'. Another argument was that 'it was still more strongly demanded on the ground of humanity to the working shipwright. At present the workmen employed on a ship's bottom had to lie on their backs in the mud and wet, and in a painful position, whereby they were soon worn out with rheumatism'. Extraordinary General Meeting, 20 April 1869, Minute Books, GCC.

78. The patent slips of St Peter Port and St Sampson were still in operation in 1895. See *Guerin's Almanack* (1895), p.85.

79. AGM, 26 February 1874, Minute Books, GCC.

80. AGM, 19 February 1880, Minute Books, GCC.

81. Jamieson, 'Shipbuilding', in Jamieson (ed.), *A People of the Sea*, p.309.

82. AGM, 15 March 1877, Minute Books, JCC.

83. AGM, 13 March 1879, Minute Books, JCC.

84. AGM, 10 March 1882, Minute Books, JCC.

85. AGM, 9 March 1883, Minute Books, JCC.

86. General Meeting, 28 December 1883, Minute Books, JCC. According to *Lloyds Register* (1884), there were by this time one floating wooden graving dock in St Helier (6-10 cranes); two patent slips at St Peter Port (10 cranes), and a further two patent slips at St Sampson (10 cranes). I am grateful to Robin Craig for providing me with this information.

87. This term applies to a dock which floats on the water, but which can be submerged to allow the entry of a ship, and then raised again to keep it dry.

88. AGM, 26 March 1895, Minute Books, JCC.

89. Ommer, 'The Cod Trade', in Jamieson (ed.), *A People of the Sea*, p.249.

90. Kelleher, *The Triumph of the Country*, pp.43, 72, 89, and 91-2.

91. AGM, 14 March 1884, Minute Books, JCC.

92. Agriculturists were under-represented in the Guernsey Chamber of Commerce. At the 1886 AGM it was reported that 'we have in this Chamber so few members of the agricultural portion of our community, as if it were otherwise, this Chamber might be made the means of forwarding and assisting their interests'. See AGM, 2 March 1886, Minute Books, GCC.

93. Monthly Meeting, 15 December 1882, Minute Books, JCC.

94. Kelleher, *The Triumph of the Country*, pp.86-7.

95. These figures are drawn from the reports presented to the AGMs of the Chamber of Commerce on the following dates: 14 March 1884; 13 March 1885; 13 March 1888; 13 March 1889; 12 March 1890; 10 March 1891; 17 March 1896; 4 March

1898; 24 March 1899; 16 March 1900. See Minute Books, JCC.

96.  See, for example, the minutes of the AGMs of 8 March 1881, 9 March 1883, and
     13 March 1885, Minute Books, GCC.

97.  AGM, 11 March 1875, Minute Books, JCC.

98.  AGM, 13 March 1885, Minute Books, JCC.

99.  Kelleher, *The Triumph of the Country*, pp.87-8.

100. *Ibid.*, p.85.

101. *Ibid.*, pp.76-7.

102. AGM, 13 March 1889, Minute Books, JCC.

103. Ansted, *The Channel Islands*, p.417.

104. See AGMs of 4 March 1898 and 24 March 1899, Minute Books, JCC.

105. AGM, 16 March 1900, Minute Books, JCC.

106. AGM, 18 March 1869, Minute Books, GCC. According to Ansted, writing in the
     mid-1890s, all the largest of the Channel Islands grew potatoes for the London
     market: since here they were ready for sale three weeks earlier even than those
     grown in Cornwall 'the quantity sent in the early part of the season is almost
     incredible'. See Ansted, *The Channel Islands*, p.416.

107. AGM, 3 March 1886, Minute Books, GCC.

108. All figures were given at the Annual General Meetings of the following dates:
     7 March 1890; 19 March 1891; 21 April 1892; 9 July 1895; and 3 May 1898.
     These meetings were reported in *The Star* on 8 March 1890; 21 March 1891;
     23 April 1892; 11 July 1895; and 5 May 1898. According to the minutes of
     the AGM of 2 March 1886 the total for the year 1885 was 220,000 packages.
     See Minute Books, GCC.

109. The figures for 1883 were: tomatoes, beans and radishes, 44,000 (31.8%); broccoli,
     19,048 (13.8%); flowers, 8,660 (6.3%); grapes, 40,300 (29.1%); and potatoes,
     26,500 (19.1%). The breakdown of exports for 1884 were: tomatoes, beans and
     radishes, 52,600 (28.5%); broccoli, 22,000 (11.9%); flowers, 11,200 (6.1%); grapes,
     51,000 (27.6%); and potatoes, 48,000 (26%). The corresponding figures for 1885
     were: tomatoes, beans and radishes, 68,000 (30.9%); broccoli, 22,000 (10%);
     flowers, 16,000 (7.3%); grapes, 60,000 (27.3%); and potatoes, 54,000 (24.5%).
     See AGM, 2 March 1886, Minute Books, GCC.

110. Quoted in Kelleher, *The Triumph of the Country*, p.87.

111. Guernsey Chamber of Commerce AGM, 7 March 1890, reported in *The Star*, 8
     March 1890.

112. For the text of the advertisement, see Gregory Stevens Cox (ed.), *The Guernsey
     Chamber of Commerce, 1808-1983* (published by The Chamber of Commerce,
     Guernsey, 1983).

113. AGM, 9 March 1870, Minute Books, JCC.

114. AGM, 13 March 1873, Minute Books, JCC.

115. AGM, 14 March 1884, Minute Books, JCC.

116. AGM, 24 March 1899, Minute Books, JCC.

117. Based on figures presented to the AGMs of the following dates: 9 March 1883, 14
     March 1884, 13 March 1885, 12 March 1890, 10 March 1891, 22 March 1892,
     24 March 1893, 26 March 1895, 17 March 1896. See Minute Books, JCC.

118. AGM, 19 March 1891, reported in *The Star*, 21 March 1891.

119. AGM, 26 February 1874, Minute Books, GCC.

120. A.G. Jamieson, 'Voyage Patterns and Trades of Channel Island Vessels', in Jamieson
     (ed.), *A People of the Sea*, p.385.

121. *London Customs Bills of Entry*, 'A' Bills, British Library, Colindale (1868, 1883, 1887).

122. AGM, 18 March 1869, Minute Books, GCC. Some potato cargoes were,

nevertheless, sent by sail. Writing in 1870, C.P.Le Cornu stated that during the 1868 potato season steamers had carried produce from Jersey to Southampton, Weymouth and Littlehampton, while sailing vessels had carried loose cargoes to Plymouth, Cardiff, Liverpool and Barbados. See Kelleher, *The Triumph of the Country*, p.87.

123. Monthly Meeting, 15 December 1882, Minute Books, JCC.

124. AGMs of 9 July 1895 and 3 May 1898, reported in *The Star*, 11 July 1895 and 5 May 1898.

125. AGM, 14 March 1884, Minute Books, JCC.

126. AGM, 13 March 1885, Minute Books, JCC.

127. AGM, 11 March 1887, Minute Books, JCC.

128. Ansted, *The Channel Islands*, p.416. See also Kelleher, *The Triumph of the Country*, p.52.

129. For figures on Jersey's stone exports in 1879 and 1883, and gravel exports in 1879 and 1884, see *British Press and Jersey Times Almanac*, 1880, p.191, and 1885, p.142. For figures on Guernsey's stone exports, see Table 16. For figures on exports from both Islands to the mainland, see the *London Customs Bills of Entry*, 1 January to 31 December 1887, British Library.

130. Ansted, *The Channel Islands*, p.415.

131. AGM, 26 February 1883, Minute Books, GCC. In October 1879 it was also reported at a meeting of the Chamber that the Island's export of granite had reached 230,000 tons per annum, 'which calculating it as part broken and part dressed, would yield a return of at least £100,000'. See the report of the General Meeting of 14 October 1879, in *ibid*. According to Ferdinand Brock Tupper, the price per ton, in 1854, 'for spalls or unbroken stone was 2s.4d., and for road metal or small broken stone 4s.9d., both on board; and the average freight to London for some years has been about 7s.6d. per ton'. Tupper, *The History of Guernsey*, pp.511-12.

132. These figures were reported at the AGM of 13 March 1888, and 1889 (no date), Minute Books, GCC.

133. See Table 12.

134. Robin Craig, 'Conference Summary', in Alexander and Ommer (eds.), *Volumes Not Values*, p.362.

135. Linda Clarke, *Building Capitalism: Historical change and the labour process in the production of the built environment* (Routledge, 1992), p.198. Later in the century, Guernsey began to face competition from Belgian granite. See General Meeting, 14 October 1879, and AGM, 26 February 1883, Minute Books, GCC.

136. *Almanac of Guernsey* (1830).

137. Jamieson, 'Voyage Patterns', in Jamieson (ed.), *A People of the Sea*, p.385. Jersey vessels carried five shipments.

138. Ansted, *The Channel Islands*, p.415.

139. AGM, 25 January 1865, Minute Books, GCC.

140. Tupper, *The History of Guernsey*, p.510. Some vessels were, however, newly-built for this trade. As we saw in Part I, *The Star* of Guernsey reported in 1837 that William Machon was then building a brig for R.W. Isemonger, and that it was 'no doubt destined for the coal and stone trade'.

141. AGM, 17 February 1870, Minute Books, GCC.

142. *Ibid*.

143. The Vale was another important area of quarrying. See *Guerin's Almanack* (1897).

144. Ansted, *The Channel Islands*, p.415.

145. *British Press Almanac* (Jersey, 1855), p.49, and *Guerin's Almanack* (Guernsey, 1895), p.249.

146. AGM, 29 January 1866, Minute Books, GCC.
147. For the figures for 1863-88, see the reports of the AGMs of the following dates: 25 January 1865, 21 February 1867, 26 March 1868, 17 February 1870, 20 February 1873, 25 February 1875, 15 February 1876, 25 February 1878, 14 February 1879, 19 February 1880, 25 February 1881, 21 February 1882, 26 February 1883, 26 February 1884, 10 March 1885, 3 March 1886, 13 March 1888, and 1889 (no date). All may be found in Minute Books, GCC. The figures for the years 1889-97 were also reported at the Chamber of Commerce's AGMs, but the Minute Books corresponding to these years have been lost. The Annual General Meetings were, however, coverered in the press, so the figures for the latter years may be found in *The Star* of 8 March 1890, 21 March 1891, 23 April 1892, 11 July 1895, and 5 May 1898.
148. AGM, 17 February 1870, Minute Books, GCC.
149. General Meeting, 14 October 1879, Minute Books, GCC.
150. Cottrell, 'The steamship on the Mersey', p.149.
151. AGM, 19 February 1880, and General Meeting, 14 October 1879, Minute Books, GCC.
152. AGM, 26 February 1883, Minute Books, GCC. In 1897 *Guerin's Almanack* stated that 'this branch of industry employs many hundred hands, the stone quarries lying in the immediate locality of St Sampson and the Vale'.
153. See Appendix Table II.2.
154. General Meeting, 14 October 1879, Minute Books, GCC.
155. *London Customs Bills of Entry*, 'A' Bills, 1 January to 31 December 1868.
156. *London Customs Bills of Entry*, 'A' Bills, 1 January to 31 December 1883.
157. AGM, 19 March 1891, reported in *The Star*, 21 March 1891.
158. This table and the analysis that follows are based on *London Customs Bills of Entry*, 'A' Bills, 1 January to 31 December 1868; and *Mercantile Navy List*, 1868 and 1869. I am grateful to Mr Robin Craig for his help and advice in preparing the information used in Tables 16 and 17, and in Appendix Tables II.1 and II.2.
159. See Table 15.
160. These figures are calculated from the *London Customs Bills of Entry*, 'A' Bills, (1868).
161. I am grateful to Mr. Robin Craig for drawing this to my attention.
162. Figures calculated from *London Customs Bills of Entry* 'A' Bills, 1845 and 1868, and Shipping Lists, *Barbet's Almanacs*, 1845 and 1870.
163. For details of the ownership of vessels employed in the stone trade in 1868, see Appendix Table II.1. This discussion is based on the details presented in the Appendix Table, and on the ownership details included in the Shipping List published in 1870 in *Barbet's Almanac*.
164. Julia Williams appears in the Shipping Lists published in the Almanacs under the name of Julia Silke.
165. AGM, 21 February 1882, Minute Books, GCC.
166. Based on *London Customs Bills of Entry*, 'A' Bills, 1 January to 31 December 1883; and *Mercantile Navy List*, 1883 and 1884; *Lloyd's Register*, 1884.
167. In 1890, the Chamber of Commerce reported that as a consequence of large-scale glasshouse building in the Island, imports of timber, glass and iron, used in construction, and of coal, used for the purpose of heating, had increased substantially. See, for example, the report of the Chamber of Commerce's AGM of 1890 in *The Star*, 8 March 1890.
168. Ansted, *The Channel Islands*, p.415.
169. *Ibid.* According to Ansted, steamers carried stone as ballast.
170. For Cheeswright's connections with the Channel Islands, see, for example,

Jamieson, 'The Coming of Steam: Cross-Channel Services and Island Steamers', in Jamieson (ed.), *A People of the Sea*, pp.450-2.

171.  *London Customs Bills of Entry* (1883); *Mercantile Navy List* (1883, 1884), *Guerin's Almanack* (1885).

172.  Chamber of Commerce AGM, 9 July 1895, reported in *The Star*, 11 July 1895.

173.  AGM, 26 February 1883, Minute Books, GCC.

174.  Quoted in Cottrell, 'The steamship on the Mersey', p.143.

175.  AGM, 10 March 1885, Minute Books, GCC.

176.  *Ibid.*

177.  *Ibid.*

178.  Cottrell, 'The steamship on the Mersey', p.144.

179.  AGM, 2 March 1886, Minute Books, GCC.

180.  *Ibid.*

181.  These figures are calculated from *London Customs Bills of Entry*, 'A' Bills, 1 January to 31 December 1887.

182.  See, for example, AGM, 22 March 1887, Minute Books, GCC.

183.  AGM, 13 March 1888, Minute Books, GCC.

## POPULATION, EMPLOYMENT AND MARITIME TRADE, 1821-1881, PP.65-99

1.  Census Report, PP 1851, Vol.XLIII. According to Robert Mudie, Jersey was experiencing high rates of growth before 1821. In 1839, Mudie commented that the Island's population had increased by 60% between 1806 and 1839, and that this 'was almost unprecedented except in single manufacturing towns under very extraordinary circumstances'. Quoted in G.C. Powell, 'The Part Played by Immigrants in Jersey's Economic Development Over the Centuries', *Bulletin Société Jersiaise*, Vol.24, No.4 (1988), pp.534-5. Figures published in the *British Press and Jersey Times Almanac* (1870) showing rates of population growth across England and Wales as a whole indicate that the growth of Jersey's population between 1821 and 1851 was exceptional: the population of England and Wales grew by 48% overall, compared with 99.4% in Jersey. Rosemary Ommer also commented on this phenomenon, showing that between 1824 and 1851, the annual growth rate in Jersey was 2.23%, compared with 1.6% in Guernsey, and 0.88% in the Isle of Man—islands of roughly comparable size. Growth rates in England and Wales were 1.28%, and in Scotland, 1.04%. Ommer properly cautions, however, against direct comparisons between the Islands on the one hand and Scotland, England and Wales on the other, given that there were very significant regional variations within the latter areas. See Rosemary Ommer, *From Outpost to Outport: A Structural Analysis of the Jersey-Gaspé Cod Fishery, 1767-1886* (McGill-Queen's University Press, Montreal, 1991), p.143, and footnote 16, p.226.

2.  The Census Reports do not distinguish between Guernsey and the other Islands of the Bailiwick. The figure for Guernsey's population in 1851 is therefore drawn from *Henry Broaurd's Almanac* (1855). The figure for 1821 is estimated. According to a report on the censuses published in the *British Press and Jersey Times Almanac*, no return was made for Alderney in 1821, which means that Alderney's population is not included in the figures for the Bailiwick in that year. The total of 20,227 is therefore based on the assumption that the population of Sark, Herm, and Jethou is not likely to have exceeded 600 at that time. See *British Press and Jersey Times Almanac* (1885). For estimates on population growth during the 18th century, see Gregory Stevens Cox, *St Peter Port 1680-1830: The History of an International Entrepôt* (Boydell Press, 1999), pp.64-70.

3. Census Report, PP 1851, Vol.XLIII.

4. Figures for Jersey, and for the Bailiwick of Guernsey are based on Census Report, PP 1851, Vol.XLIII; and Census Report, PP 1883, Vol.LXXX. The figures for Guernsey (excluding Alderney, Sark, Herm and Jethou) for the year 1800 are drawn from Stevens Cox, 'The Transformation of St Peter Port', pp.48-9; all others are drawn from *Henry Brouard's Almanac* (1840, 1855), *Guerin's Almanack* (1890, 1895), and *British Press and Jersey Times Almanac* (1875, 1880, 1885). Starred figures (**) are estimates. Figures for Jersey for 1891 are calculated on the basis of a loss of 2,073 between 1881 and 1891. See John Kelleher, *The Triumph of the Country: The Rural Community in Nineteenth Century Jersey* (John Appleby Publishing/Société Jersiaise, St Helier, 1994), p.196. Figures for the Bailiwick for 1891 are drawn from *Guerin's Almanack* (1895). It should also be noted that there are some minor discrepancies in the figures given in some of the almanacs; these discrepancies have not been recorded for the sake of consistency.

5. Kelleher, *The Triumph of the Country*, pp.195-6.

6. The extent to which we might attribute some of the immigration of these years to the construction of a new fortified harbour at Alderney—work on which was begun in 1847 and continued until the end of the 1860s—or the St Catherine's harbour project in Jersey—which was abandoned in the early 1850s—is unclear. On the debate surrounding the construction of fortifications in the Channel Islands, see A.G. Jamieson, 'The Channel Islands and British Maritime Strategy, 1689-1945', in A.G. Jamieson (ed.), *A People of the Sea: The Maritime History of the Channel Islands* (Methuen, 1986), pp.227-243. Jamieson provides a detailed background to the decision to begin work on the harbours and associated fortifications, especially in Alderney, and of the opposition to the projects throughout their duration.

7. Based on Census Report, PP 1851, Vol.XLIII.

8. Extraordinary General Meeting, 20 April 1869, Minute Books, Guernsey Chamber of Commerce (hereafter GCC).

9. AGM, 17 February 1870, Minute Books, GCC.

10. AGM, 9 March 1870, Minute Books, Jersey Chamber of Commerce (hereafter JCC). See also Part II of this study.

11. The 1840s had witnessed an economic crisis, however, and been a period of low wages, which caused the ship-carpenters riot of 1847. See Kelleher, *The Triumph of the Country*, p.195.

12. Alan Jamieson, 'The Channel Islands and Australia: Maritime Links in the 1850s', *The Great Circle*, Vol.5, No.1, pp.40-4.

13. Tupper noted that 85 emigrants, chiefly from Guernsey, left the Islands in 1842. See Ferdinand Brock Tupper, *The History of Guernsey and its Bailiwick, with occasional notices of Jersey* (2nd edition, 1876), footnote 2, p.505. See also Jamieson, 'The Channel Islands and Australia', p.40.

14. A.G. Jamieson, 'Shipbuilding in the Channel Islands', in Jamieson (ed.), *A People of the Sea*, pp.303-4.

15. *British Press and Jersey Times Almanac* (1875). In fact, the population of St Mary showed a very slight increase between 1861 and 1871—from 1,040 to 1,079. For figures on the distribution of the population in Jersey between 1831 and 1881, see Appendix Table III.2.

16. *British Press and Jersey Times Almanac* (1875, 1885), and Kelleher, *The Triumph of the Country*, pp.196, 199.

17. For figures on the distribution of the Island's population by parish, see Appendix

Table III.2.

18. General Meeting, 28 December 1883, Minute Books, JCC.

19. According to Jamieson, emigrants had left Jersey in larger numbers prior to 1800, but, after Guernsey's position as a base for smuggling was undermined by laws of 1805 and 1807, this Island came to dominate emigration. See A.G. Jamieson, 'The Channel Islands and Overseas Settlement, 1600-1900', in Jamieson (ed.), *A People of the Sea*, p.281.

20. For figures on the distribution of population by parish, see Appendix Table III.1.

21. See Appendix III.1. The 1891 figures for St Sampson and Vale include small military populations of 38 and 16, respectively. See *Guerin's Almanack* (1895), p.249.

22. General Meeting, 28 December 1883, Minute Books, GCC.

23. Census of Guernsey (1881), St Sampson, District No.2.

24. Based on Census Report, PP 1883, Vol.LXXX.

25. In Alderney completion of the harbour and associated fortifications had a marked impact on the size of the population. According to a report on the censuses of 1861 and 1871 published in the *British Press and Jersey Times Almanac* (1880), between 1861, when the works were still in progress, and 1871, by which time only some repairs remained to be completed, the Island's population fell by 45%, from 4,932 to 2,738. According to Kelleher, completion of work on the St Catherine harbour led to the dispersal of more than 350 labourers employed in its construction. See *The Triumph of the Country*, p.199, and footnote 7, p.302.

26. Census Report, PP 1883, Vol.LXXX.

27. Kelleher, *The Triumph of the Country*, pp.205-6. Kelleher gives the proportions of French immigrants in six parishes (St Saviour, St Clement, St Brelade, St John, Grouville and St Ouen), and compares these with the proportions of English immigrants in the total population. His figures show that in 1851, in these six parishes, the French constituted 4.3% of the total population (averaged); in 1881, 8.7%. The English, by contrast, constituted 11.3% of the total population in 1851, but only 7.8% by 1881. Some of these were in any case mainly rural parishes, and these tended to attract many more French than English. See *ibid.*, Figure 13, p.205.

28. According to Marie-Louise Backhurst, in the 1850s many French labourers came to the Island as seasonal workers. Her research suggests that because agriculture was in crisis in the early 1850s—following the potato blight—the number of seasonal French labourers in the Island at this time would have been lower than usual. This would not affect the census figures for 1851, however: because the census was carried out in March, it did not include seasonal labourers. Marie Louise Backhurst, "L'ile divin': A study of the French community in Jersey in 1851" (Unpublished manuscript), pp.5, 10.

29. The French in Guernsey did, however, constitute the majority of the foreign-born (86.79%). See Census Report, PP 1883, Vol.LXXX. According to the same Census Report, the number of French-born in Jersey totalled 3,972 (7.57% of the total).

30. The immigrant population in St Sampson in the early 1880s is discussed in greater detail later in this study.

31. According to Tupper, the wages of carpenters and seamen were 10% lower in Jersey, and the cost of building and equipping vessels was £2 less per ton. Tupper, *History of Guernsey*, pp.508-10.

32. Rosemary Ommer, 'The Cod Trade in the New World', in Jamieson (ed.), *A People of the Sea*, pp.265-6.

33. Quoted in *ibid.*, p.263.

34. Cited in *ibid*. See also A.G. Jamieson, 'The Channel Islands and Overseas Settlement, 1600-1900', in Jamieson (ed.), *A People of the Sea*, p.280.
35. The crew list of the *Farrago* may be found in PRO BT 98/957.
36. For the crew list of the *St Anne*, see PRO BT 98/678.
37. According to Rosemary Ommer, even before the peak of the Island's involvement in the cod fisheries, British North America was a major export market for Jersey manufactures—in 1835, these included cider, biscuit, flour and potatoes, as well as boots and shoes. The export trade to the fisheries resulted in part, Ommer explains, from the fact that by law Jersey could not manufacture goods from imported raw materials for free export to England, but could do so for export to the fisheries. See Ommer, 'The Cod Trade', p.263.
38. As De Quetteville pointed out, 'The trade gives employment to about 8000 tons of shipping exclusive of those vessels which carry fish to the Brazilian and other markets from this Island'. *Ibid.*, p.263.
39. Tupper, *History of Guernsey*, p.509; and Ommer, *From Outpost to Outport*.
40. In 1851, the census authorities, mindful of the need to analyse not just occupational but also industrial information, introduced for the first time a system of classification which divided the wide variety of occupations found in the manuscript returns into a series of orders and sub-orders, intended to serve as industrial categories and sub-categories. The usefulness to the historian of the classification scheme adopted in 1851 is undermined, however, by the fact that further changes and refinements were made at each of the following censuses, resulting in the movement of large groups of working people from one category to another, and making comparison from decade to decade extremely problematic. For details of the methodology adopted in this study, see W.A. Armstrong, 'The Use of Information About Occupation', in E.A. Wrigley (ed.), *Nineteenth Century Society: Essays in the use of quantitative methods for the study of social data* (Cambridge University Press, 1981), pp.226-310.
41. The districts were contiguous, encompassing households in the following streets: Esplanade, Patriotic St., Patriotic Place, Newgate St., Gloucester St., Parade Place, Seaton Place, Seale St., York St., Charing Cross, Payn St., Anley St., Sand St., Castle St., Broad St., Commercial Road, Conway St., Bond St., Cross St., Wharf St., Hope St., Pier Rd., Caledonia Rd. and Old Ordnance Yard.
42. The households in this sample were located along the following streets: Pollet St., Truchot, Canichers, Well Rd., Glategny, Bosq Lane, Amballes Rd., New Paris Rd., Paris St., George Esplanade, Salter St., Mt.Pleasant, Bruce Lane, Beauregard Lane, Doyle St., New Ground, Portland Pl. and York Pl.
43. George Symes Hooper, *A Paper on The History and Statistics of Asiatic Cholera in Jersey* (Jersey, 1833), p.39.
44. The survey of male migrants was ordered by the authorities in Guernsey because they were concerned that unrest in the south of England (the 'Swing Riots') would spill over to St Peter Port's migrant population. Stevens Cox, *St Peter Port*, p.89.
45. Although some certainly did: the shipbuilders Frederick C. Clarke and George Deslandes, of Deslandes & Sons, resided in St Helier's District No.7, for instance.
46. *British Press Almanac* (1850); *British Press and Jersey Times Almanac* (1865). See also Powell, 'The Part Played by Immigrants'. For figures on the distribution of the population by parish, see the Appendix Tables.
47. *Henry Brouard's Almanack of Guernsey* (1855).
48. See Appendix III.1. The 1891 figures for St Sampson and Vale include small military populations of 38 and 16, respectively. See *Guerin's Almanack* (1895), p.249.

49. Val Burton, 'A Floating Population: Vessel Enumeration Returns in the Censuses, 1851-1921', *Local Population Studies* (1987), pp.36-43.

50. PP 1852-3, Vol.LXXXVIII.

51. The consequences for the local historian of the enumeration of sailors on board vessels in home waters in each of the censuses between 1851 and 1921 is discussed by Burton, 'A Floating Population'. Burton shows that the population on board vessels in home waters or inland rivers and waterways were amalgamated with the household schedules for the enumeration districts closest to the location of the vessel, regardless of the place of origin of the crew.

52. *British Press Almanac* (1855).

53. Channel Island seamen had been paying contributions to the Greenwich Hospital Fund since 1731. See Ralph Davis, 'Seamen's Sixpences: An Index of Commercial Activity, 1627-1828', *Economica* (November, 1956), pp.328-9. For details of the establishment of the Society, see Minute Books, Jersey Merchant Seamen's Benefit Society (hereafter JMSBS), and Philip Syvret, 'Société de Bienfaisance pour la Marine Marchand', *Bulletin Société Jersiaise*, Vol.19 (1965), pp.75-6.

54. Work is, however, currently being undertaken at the Société Jersiaise, in St Helier, to put the information contained in the ledgers of the Society onto a large database.

55. Upon receipt of the contributions collected by masters, the officers of the Society recorded all payments made by individual seamen in each of its two ledgers. In the first ledger, the name of the vessel was entered, along with the names of the crew, their ages and places of birth (in the case of the Jersey-born, the parish of birth in most cases), the period of employment specified in months and days, the total sum paid by each sailor, and also the name of the previous vessel on which he had served. The same information was then posted in a second ledger, the pages of which were divided up into separate accounts, corresponding to individual sailors. This ledger thus contains each man's record of employment: all vessels in which he served were listed in chronological order, together with the sums paid to the Society. All surviving ledgers are to be found at the Société Jersiaise, St Helier.

56. Sarah Palmer, *Politics, Shipping, and the Repeal of the Navigation Laws* (Manchester University Press, 1990), pp.10-11.

57. Census of Jersey (1851), St Helier, District No.7.

58. *British Press Almanac* (1855), p.53.

59. Stevens Cox, *St Peter Port*, p.85.

60. Palmer, *Politics, shipping*, pp.10-11.

61. PRO BT 107/396.

62. AGM, 19 February 1880, Minute Books, GCC.

63. Table 21 is based on figures drawn from Census Report, PP 1852-3, Vol.LXXXVIII, Part 1. For a detailed description of the methodology applied, see Armstrong, 'The Use of Information About Occupation', in Wrigley (ed.), *Nineteenth Century Society*, pp.226-310.

64. *British Press and Jersey Times Almanac* (1880).

65. In his *Making Sense of the Census: The Manuscript Returns of England and Wales, 1801-1901* (London, HMSO, 1989), p.80, Edward Higgs also found that it was common in fishing communities, for example, to alternate between work on land and work on sea; that combinations of complementary jobs such as butcher and grazier, are commonly found in the census returns; and that calculating numbers employed in retailing is complicated by the fact that the separation between making and selling (shoes and bread, for instance) was far less clear during the 19th century.

66. Examples selected from St Helier, Census of Jersey (1851).

67. Census of Guernsey (1851), Districts 3, 4, 5 and 7. Thirty-two Irishmen described as pensioners were identified in the districts selected from the 1851 census of St Helier, of whom eight claimed also to be employed: one was described as a labourer, three as porters, two as tailor journeymen, one as a hotel keeper, and one as a publican. See Census of Jersey (1851), St Helier, Districts 1, 2, 3 and 7.

68. Instructions to householders stipulated from 1851 onwards that occupations 'may' be inserted in order of importance; this became 'must' by 1861. Higgs points out, however, that given that many people were vague even about single occupations, there has to be some doubt regarding the recording of multiple occupations. See Higgs, *Making Sense of the Census*, p.80.

69. The figures shown for the manufacturing sector are slightly over-estimated, and this has to do with the inclusion, in manufacturing, of small numbers of dealers in particular materials—wool, silk, leather, hemp, paper. As Edward Higgs pointed out, this has to do with the fact that the distinction between making and selling goods was less clear in the 19th century than it later became. See Armstrong, 'The Use of Information About Occupation', in Wrigley (ed.), *Nineteenth Century Society*, p.231, and Higgs, *Making Sense of the Census*, p.80.

70. The Industrial Services sector was composed principally of labourers, a workforce which could be employed in varied industries—the proportion in each being impossible to calculate because of the absence of specific information about the nature of the work they did. The requirement to indicate the nature of the business of the employer was not introduced until this century. See Higgs, *Making Sense of the Census*, p.78.

71. The Public Service and Professional sector seems somewhat inflated in both Jersey and Guernsey, accounting for a high of 11.8% and 10.6% of adult males in 1851. This can be accounted for by the large numbers of army and navy personnel included in the figures, representing nearly 65% of the total for the sector in Jersey (1,111 of 1,732) and 60% in Guernsey and the smaller Islands (562 of 940). The figures for Jersey include 498 soldiers, 88 army officers, 15 Royal Navy seamen, and 44 naval officers. In addition, 41% of the 1,111 men (a total of 454) were retired or half-pay officers. The figures for Guernsey include 288 soldiers, 46 army officers, 1 Royal Navy seaman, and 17 naval officers. In this Island, 36% of the 562 army and navy personnel enumerated (a total of 203), were retired or half-pay officers. Figures drawn from Census Report, 1852-3, Vol.LXXXVIII, Part 1. As we have seen, however, the inclusion of retired personnel in this sector conceals the fact that many pensioners were also engaged in a variety of occupations.

72. Rosemary Ommer showed that even before the peak of the Island's involvement in the cod fisheries, British North America was a major market for Jersey manufactures—this included not just boots and shoes, but also cider, biscuit, flour and potatoes. The importance of the fisheries as a market for Jersey derived partly from the fact that by law Jersey could not manufacture goods from imported raw materials for free importation into England, but could do so into the fisheries. See Ommer, 'The Cod Trade', p.263.

73. Ansted, *The Channel Islands* (London, 1893), p.416.

74. AGM, 25 January 1865, Minute Books, GCC.

75. Kelleher, *The Triumph of the Country*, pp.209-10.

76. Stevens Cox, *St Peter Port*, p.80.

77. *Ibid.*, pp.80-1.

78. Stevens Cox explained that rural 'push' factors combined with urban 'pull' factors—the latter including the development of a tertiary sector in St Peter Port to serve the needs of a growing wealthy population, and the expansion of trade, which created new employment opportunities. *Ibid.*, p.82-5.

79. It should be noted, however, that this may well have been at the root of the higher incidence of emigration from the smaller Island which Jamieson found in the years after 1800. See Jamieson, 'Overseas Settlement of Islanders', p.281.

80. Census of Jersey (1851).

81. Census of Guernsey (1851).

82. According to Stevens Cox, work currently in progress on Guernsey's church registers indicates that similar patterns of migration applied in the 18th century: 'between 1727 and 1800 there was a steady outmigration from the countryside. At the same time, the sex ratios at birth and death in St Peter Port differed; the 'skew' suggests that the town was gaining females as immigrants. It is highly probable that there was a significant movement of girls and young women into St Peter Port where they found employment as domestics and widened their marriage horizons.' Stevens Cox, *St Peter Port*, p.82.

83. 1851 Census of Jersey, St Helier, Districts 1, 2, 3 and 7. The occupational breakdown of the 145 adult men in the sample who gave places other than St Helier as their place of birth is as follows: agent (general), 1; architect, 1; bakers, 2; blacksmith, 7; blockmaker, 1; brickmaker, 1; house builder master, 1; butcher, 1; carpenters, 15; carters, 5; clerk, 1; draper, 1; ironmonger, 1; joiners, 2; magistrate (Royal Court), 1; mariners, 25; masons, 4; merchants (various), 12; merchant shipowner, 1; miller, 1; notary, 1; plasterer, 1; proprietors (land/houses), 3; publicans, 5; retired (cooper, shipcarpenter, wine merchant), 3; sawyer, 1; servants, 3; shipbuilder, 2; shipcarpenter, 1; shipcaulker, 1; shipowner, 1; shiprigger, 2; shipwright, 14; shoemakers, 8; stone cutter, 1; storekeeper, 1; tailor, 8; tobacco manufacturers, 2; watchmaker, 2; waterman, 1. These figures do not differentiate between masters, journeymen, etc.

84. Palmer, *Politics, shipping*, p.10.

85. In the census returns, Matthew J. Valpy was described as a shipbuilder employing 40 men; Frederick C. Clarke, as a shipbuilder employing 203 men; and George Deslandes, as a shipbuilder employing 200 men. Census of Jersey (1851): St Helier, District No.7.

86. Palmer, *Politics, Shipping*, Table 4, p.11.

87. PP 1852-3, Vol.LXXXVIII.

88. Many mariners were at home, however: 109 were identified in the St Helier sample, 31 in the St Peter Port sample.

89. In addition, four of the 45 women were described as wives of shipowners, shipbuilders or ship carpenters, and another as the wife of a boatman. Of the remaining women whose husband's occupations were specified, two were described as wives of carpenters, one as a house-builder's wife, one an artillery pensioner's, seven as soldiers' wives, one as a stone mason's, one as a waiter's, and one as a writing clerk's wife. Census of Jersey (1851): St Helier, Districts 1, 2, 3 and 7.

90. Census of Guernsey (1851): St Peter Port, Districts 3, 4, 5 and 7.

91. Based on all surviving crew lists and agreements corresponding to voyages begun in 1845. See PRO BT 98/678, 98/956, 98/957, 98/958, 98/959.

92. Of the 109 seamen identified in the St Helier sample, 51 were Jersey-born, 43 were English-born, and 3 were Irish-born. Of 31 sailors identified in the St Peter Port sample, 14 were Guernsey-born; 14 were English-born.

93. Finance Accounts, PP XXXI (1851), p.134. The Shipping List published in *Henry*

*Broaurd's Almanack* of 1850 shows a total tonnage for Guernsey of 16,894 at the end of 1849 (excluding vessels being lengthened; old tonnage where available).

94. AGM, 25 January 1865, Minute Books, GCC.

95. On the factors influencing crew size on vessels leaving Liverpool on trans-Atlantic voyages, for example, see David Williams, 'Crew Size in Trans-Atlantic Trades in the Mid-Nineteenth Century', in Rosemary Ommer and Gerald Panting (eds.), *Working Men Who Got Wet* (Maritime History Group, Memorial University of Newfoundland, 1980).

96. Finance Accounts, PP Vol.XXXI (1851). The Shipping List published in *British Press Almanac* (1850) shows a total registered tonnage of 32,823.

97. This includes 45 small craft, each measuring under 15 tons, which were included in this analysis because the crews of these vessels paid contributions to the Society in 1850. According to returns of the Registrar of Shipping, there were registered at Jersey on 31 December 1849, 340 vessels totalling 32,056 tons. See PP Vol.XXXIII (1850).

98. The ledgers only records the name of the vessel, and not its tonnage. Details of tonnage are drawn from the shipping lists published in the Almanacs.

99. Entries for the *Mary Ann* (41 tons), *Bagatelle* (21 tons), *Betsy and Jane* (103 tons), and *Brador* (85 tons), correspond to voyages begun after February 1850. John Jean shows that these were bought by Islanders during that year. The *John Booth* also appears after February 1850, but is not included in Jean's list of 19th century Jersey-owned vessels, and nor does the steamer *Polka*. The remaining vessels—*St Brelade* (120 tons), *Fruiterer* (59 tons), *Intrepid* (69 tons), *Rowena* (84 tons), *Fairfax* (270 tons), and *Zig Zag* (53 tons)—are included in Jean's list, but not in the 1850 Shipping List. See John Jean, *Jersey Sailing Ships* (Phillimore, 1982).

100. The process of extracting all multiple entries from the database of sailors based on the 1850 ledgers was complicated by the fact that the same surnames and Christian names came up again and again. There were, for example, 11 entries in the 1850 ledger under the name of Philip Syvret (corresponding to five different people), and 11 entries under the name of John Blampied (corresponding to eight different people). Decisions about whether repeated entries under the same name referred to one or more men were made on the basis of all the details included in the ledger: age, place of origin, the vessels on which each had previously served, including period of employment, and, the most crucial detail, the page number which cross-references the entry in the first ledger with each sailor's separate account in the second. Sometimes, there are several entries when all the details coincide; in those cases where they didn't, however, a consistent method of analysis had to be adopted: the two pieces of information which were found most likely to be consistent, upon close examination of some 400 entries in both ledgers, were the seaman's name, and the number which links the entry in the first ledger with his individual account in the second.

101. All figures are based on the analysis of all contributions paid to the Benefit Society between 1 January and 31 December 1850.

102. Other interesting cases also emerge from time to time, such as the German-born sailor William Lyon who was probably also a Jersey resident, since he served repeatedly on Island-registered vessels—the *Ellen*, the *Jeffery*, the *William* (twice), and the *United*. See the ledgers of the JMSBS (1880-81), ff.3700, 3702, 3733.

103. AGM, 3 March 1886, Minute Books, GCC.

104. See, for example, AGM, 13 March 1885, Minute Books, JCC.

105. Based on Census Report, PP 1852-3, Vol.LXXXVIII, and Census Report, PP 1883, Vol.LXXX.

106.  Additionally, three vessels not included in the Shipping List appeared in the ledgers.
      Figures are calculated from *British Press and Jersey Times Almanac* (1880), and the
      ledgers of the Jersey Merchant Seamen's Benefit Society (1880-81).
107.  Based on the analysis of all seamen's contributions posted in the ledgers of the
      Jersey Merchant Seamen's Benefit Society (1 January 1880 to 31 December 1881).
108.  Based on Census Report, PP 1852-3, Vol.LXXXVIII, and Census Report, PP
      1883, Vol.LXXX.
109.  Because Guernsey, much like Jersey, had a large immigrant population throughout
      these decades, it is impossible to estimate how many of the English and Irish-born
      in the St Sampson sample were immigrants to this parish rather than migrants from
      St Peter Port, having arrived there and then moved on to St Sampson as the
      quarries developed and other economic sectors went into decline.
110.  Census of Guernsey (1881).
111.  Tupper, *History of Guernsey*, pp.512-14.
112.  Indeed, Hamley claimed that he alone employed 105 sailors on his fleet of vessels.
      See, for example, AGM, 19 February 1880, Minute Books, GCC.

# BIBLIOGRAPHY

Alexander, David and Ommer, Rosemary (eds.), *Volumes Not Values: Canadian Sailing Ships and World Trade* (Maritime History Group, Memorial University of Newfoundland, 1979).

Ansted, D. and Latham, R., *The Channel Islands* (London, 1893).

Armstrong, W.A., 'The Use of Information About Occupation', in E.A.Wrigley (ed.), *Nineteenth Century Society: Essays in the use of quantitative methods for the study of social data* (Cambridge University Press, 1981).

Backhurst, Marie Louise, "L'ile divin": A study of the French community in Jersey in 1851' (Unpublished Manuscript).

Burton, Val, 'A Floating Population: Vessel Enumeration Returns in the Censuses, 1851-1921', *Local Population Studies* (1987), pp.36-43.

Carson, Edward, 'Customs Bills of Entry', *Maritime History*, Vol.I, No.2 (1971), pp.176-89.

Clarke, Linda, *Building Capitalism: Historical change and the labour process in the production of the built environment* (Routledge, London, 1992).

Cottrell, P.L., 'The steamship on the Mersey, 1815-1880: investment and ownership', in P.L. Cottrell and D.H. Aldcroft (eds.), *Shipping, Trade and Commerce: Essays in Memory of Ralph Davis* (Leicester University Press, Leicester, 1981).

Cottrell, P.L. and Aldcroft, D.H. (eds.), *Shipping, Trade and Commerce: Essays in Memory of Ralph Davis* (Leicester University Press, Leicester, 1981).

Cox, Gregory Stevens (ed.), *The Guernsey Chamber of Commerce, 1808-1983* (The Chamber of Commerce, Guernsey, 1983).

Cox, Gregory Stevens, *St Peter Port 1680-1830: The History of an International Entrepôt* (Boydell Press, 1999).

Cox, Nicholas, 'The Records of the Registrar-General of Shipping and Seamen', *Maritime History*, Vol.II, No.2 (1972), pp.168-88.

Coysh, Victor, 'The Guernsey Shipbuilding Industry', *Transactions Société Guernsiaise*, Vol.XV (1952), pp.208-18.

Craig, Robin, 'The African Guano Trade', *Mariner's Mirror* (February, 1969), pp.25-55.

Craig, Robin, 'Conference Summary', in David Alexander and Rosemary Ommer (eds.), *Volumes Not Values: Canadian Sailing Ships and World Trade* (Maritime History Group, Memorial University of Newfoundland, 1979).

Craig, Robin, 'William Gray & Company: a West Hartlepool shipbuilding enterprise, 1864-1913', in P.L. Cottrell and D.H. Aldcroft (eds.), *Shipping,*

*Trade and Commerce: Essays in Memory of Ralph Davis* (Leicester University Press, Leicester, 1981).

Craig, Robin, 'Carmarthenshire Shipping in the Eighteen Forties', *The Carmarthenshire Antiquary*, Vol.XXI (1985), pp.49-57.

Davis, Ralph, 'Seamen's Sixpences: An Index of Commercial Activity, 1627-1828', *Economica* (November, 1956), pp.328-43.

Fay, C.R., *The Channel Islands and Newfoundland* (Cambridge, 1961).

Fisher, Stephen (ed.), *British Shipping and Seamen, 1630-1960* (Exeter Papers in Economic History, University of Exeter, 1984).

Graham, Gerald S., 'The Ascendancy of the Sailing Ship, 1850-85', *Economic History Review*, Vol.IX (1956-7), pp.74-88.

Higgs, Edward, *Making Sense of the Census: The Manuscript Returns of England and Wales, 1801-1901* (London, HMSO, 1989).

Hooper, George S., *A Paper on the History and Statistics of Asian Cholera in Jersey* (Jersey, 1833).

Inglis, Henry, *The Channel Islands* (London, 1835).

Jamieson, A.G., 'The Channel Islands and Australia: Maritime Links in the 1850s', *The Great Circle*, Vol.5 (1983), pp.40-47.

Jamieson, A.G. (ed.), *A People of the Sea: The Maritime History of the Channel Islands* (Methuen, 1986).

Jean, John, *Jersey Sailing Ships* (Phillimore, 1982).

Jones, Stephanie, 'Merchant Shipbuilding in the North East and South West of England, 1870-1913', in Stephen Fisher (ed.), *British Shipping and Seamen, 1630-1960* (Exeter Papers in Economic History, University of Exeter, 1984).

Kelleher, John, *The Triumph of the Country: The Rural Community in Nineteenth Century Jersey* (John Appleby Publishing, 1995).

Kellet-Smith, 'The Guernsey Cholera Epidemic of 1832', *Transactions Société Guernsiaise*, Vol.20 (1980), pp.643-55.

Le Pelley, Jean, 'Guernsey Pioneers in Australia, 1841-1862', *Transactions Société Guernsiaise*, Vol.18 (1966), pp.63-86.

Matthews, Keith and Panting, Gerald (eds.), *Ships and Shipbuilding in the North Atlantic Region* (Maritime History Group, Memorial University of Newfoundland, 1978).

Ommer, Rosemary, 'The Trade and Navigation of the Island', in David Alexander and Rosemary Ommer (eds.), *Volumes Not Values: Canadian Sailing Ships and World Trade* (Maritime History Group, Memorial University of Newfoundland, 1979).

Ommer, Rosemary and Panting, Gerald (eds.), *Working Men Who Got Wet* (Maritime History Group, Memorial University of Newfoundland, 1980).

Ommer, Rosemary, 'The decline of the eastern Canadian shipping industry, 1880-1895', *Journal of Transport History* (1984), pp.25-44.

Ommer, Rosemary, 'The Cod Trade in the New World', in A.G. Jamieson (ed.), *A People of the Sea: The Maritime History of the Channel Islands* (Methuen, 1986).

Ommer, Rosemary, *From Outpost to Outport: A Structural Analysis of the Jersey-*

*Gaspé Cod Fishery, 1767-1886* (McGill-Queen's University Press, Montreal, 1991).

Ommer, Rosemary, 'A Peculiar and Immediate Dependence of the Crown: The Basis of the Jersey Merchant Triangle, *Business History*, Vol.26 (1984), pp.107-24.

Palmer, Sarah, 'Experience, Experiment and Economics: Factors in the Construction of Early Merchant Steamships', in Keith Matthews and Gerald Panting (eds.), *Ships and Shipbuilding in the North Atlantic Region* (Maritime History Group, Memorial University of Newfoundland, 1978).

Palmer, Sarah and Williams, Glyndwr (eds.), *Charted and Uncharted Waters* (National Maritime Museum/Queen Mary College London, 1981).

Palmer, Sarah, *Politics, shipping, and the repeal of the Navigation Laws* (Manchester University Press, 1990).

Podger, Alec, 'Shipbuilding in Jersey', *Bulletin Société Jersiaise*, Vol.18 (1962), pp.229-35.

Pollard, Sidney, 'British and World Shipbuilding, 1890-1914: A Study in Comparative Costs', *Journal of Economic History*, Vol.XVII, No.3 (1957), pp.426-44.

Pollard, Sidney and Robertson, Paul (eds.), *The British Shipbuilding Industry, 1870-1914* (Harvard University Press, Cambridge, Massachusetts, 1979).

Powell, G.C., 'The Part Played by Immigrants in Jersey's Economic Development Over the Centuries', *Bulletin Société Jersiaise*, Vol.24 (1988), pp.531-42.

Sarre, John and Forbrigger, Lorena, 'Some Guernsey Connections with Cape Breton Island', *Transactions Société Guernsiaise* (1991), pp.173-81.

Sarre, John, 'A History of the Development of Sailing Ships and Trade in Guernsey' (Unpublished Manuscript).

Sharp, Eric W., 'The Harbours and Shipping of Guernsey at the turn of the 19th Century', *Transactions Société Guernsiaise*, Vol.16 (1959), pp.469-83.

Sharp, Eric W., 'The Shipbuilders of Guernsey', *Transactions Société Guernsiaise*, Vol.23 (1970), pp.478-502.

Sharp, Eric W., 'The Toll of the Sea; Guernsey Ships and their Fate', *Transactions Société Guernsiaise*, Vol.20 (1979), pp.515-49.

Syvret, Philip, 'Société de Bienfaisance pour la Marine Marchand', *Bulletin Société Jersiaise*, Vol.19 (1965), pp.75-83.

Tupper, Ferdinand B., *The History of Guernsey and its Bailiwick, with occasional notices of Jersey* (2nd edition, 1876).

Williams, David, 'The Shipping of the North Atlantic Cotton Trade in the Mid-Nineteenth Century', in David Alexander and Rosemary Ommer (eds.), *Volumes Not Values: Canadian Sailing Ships and World Trade* (Maritime History Group, Memorial University of Newfoundland, 1979).

Williams, David, 'Crew Size in Trans-Atlantic Trades in the Mid-Nineteenth century', in Rosemary Ommer and Gerald Panting (eds.), *Working men Who Got Wet* (Maritime History Group, Memorial University of Newfoundland, 1980).

Wrigley, E.A. (ed.), *Nineteenth Century Society: Essays in the use of quantitative methods for the study of social data* (Cambridge University Press, 1981).

# INDEX

References which relate to illustrations only are given in **bold**.